She Knows You Know!

Jean Fergusson

She Knows You Know!

The remarkable story of Hylda Baker

The Breedon Books
Publishing Company
Derby

First published in Great Britain by
The Breedon Books Publishing Company Limited
Breedon House, 44 Friar Gate, Derby, DE1 1DA.
1997

To my best friend Spoon

ISBN 1 85983 101 X

Printed and bound by Butler & Tanner Ltd., Selwood Printing Works, Caxton Road, Frome, Somerset.

Colour separations by RPS Ltd, Leicester.

Jackets by Lawrence-Allen Colour Printers, Weston-super-Mare, Avon.

Contents

FOREWORD

The Start Of It All

IT WAS Christmas 1990 and little did I realise then that I was about to embark upon a long, hard, exciting, frustrating, life-shortening, but above all, fascinating journey tracing a life story that has gripped me ever since, the remarkable life story of Hylda Baker.

Some say it is she who is holding on to me with the same fierce determination with which she lived her colourful life, and I have come to accept that this may be true, particularly in the light of the rather strange and unexplained things that have happened to me along the way! But more of this in a later chapter. I know now that it really all started way back in the 1950s when Hylda Baker became a household name and I used to watch her on television in *The Good Old Days*, broadcast from the famous City Varieties Theatre in Leeds. I thought her act was the most hysterical thing I had ever seen, and I was not alone, for it appeared the rest of the viewing public thought so too. Indeed, even today, if you mention her name to those people who remember her innovative and zany stand-up comedy act, they will come out with her famous catchphrases such as: "Oh, I must get a little hand put on this watch," "That's rickidoodleous," "Be sooon, I said, be soooooon!!" and, of course, "She knows you know!"

As I watched her, I used to sit with pen and paper copying down her jokes, and then learn them off by heart. How I wish I had kept those pieces of paper! I would 'do' my Hylda Baker act at the drop of a hat, in the school playground, in the classroom, in the street, in fact anywhere I could get an audience. Ironically, my parents used to beg me to come into the sitting room and do my routine for their guests, but I was really only prepared to do it when I wanted to.

Unbeknown to me at that young age was the fact that eventually she was to almost take over my life. When I was ten years old, I had no idea that one day, by researching and writing a book about her, I would be responsible for telling the story of a pioneer and a genius who was ahead of her time, a 'one-off' with a comedic talent that was timeless, spanning 65 years through the First and Second World Wars, and showing an insight into a piece of important social history. How strange that history was never a subject that interested me even slightly when I was at school, but perhaps the older we get the more nostalgic and curious we are as to the 'reason for it all', and how and why our society has changed.

My own interest in theatre began in 1960 when I joined an amateur dramatic society who were looking for new members, particularly girls, to be in a production of Arthur Miller's *The Crucible*. Luck plays a very large and frustrating role in the life of an actor and it was certainly on my side all those years ago. The leading juvenile role of Abigail suddenly became available and I was given the part. From that moment on there was no stopping me, although prior to this I had never played anything other than Mr Collins in a school production of *Pride And Prejudice* — much against my will. Oh, the trials of having a deep voice! I was so embarrassed about the latter that I wanted no one to see the play and in fact was mortified when my mother sneaked in without telling me. There is in existence a photograph of me lurking furtively around some curtains at the back of the stage with an extremely bad tempered look upon my face, desperately trying not to be in the 'production photograph'. Sadly, there are no photographs of my role in *The Crucible*, which is probably just as well, considering I thought I looked rather wonderful, and I fear that if one were to come to light today it would cause me equal embarrassment. I've done it now, haven't I? Someone from my past will no doubt rake one up and send it to me, so let's just hope that person (and only that person!) doesn't read this book.

Having become 'hooked' on acting, it was then necessary to persuade very reluctant parents that I had decided what I wanted as my career, and that drama school was the next course of action. I will not bore the reader with THIS little piece of social history, but suffice it to say that a drama school accepted me, a two-year acting course was completed, and I entered into a world which everyone knows is filled with broken dreams, hard work, frustration, horrendous 'lows', often empty cupboards and even emptier pockets, but, oh joy of joys, now and again, terrific excitement and wonderful 'highs'. I regret not one moment of the last 30 years and would not have missed it for the world. I have learnt so much, met, worked with, and made some wonderful friends. However, I say to the young reader to think very carefully should you be wishing to follow the same path; you must be sure that what you are searching for is not fame and fortune, glamour and glitz, for many fall by the wayside who think this is what showbusiness is about. Hylda Baker was 50 when she became a household name, and up until then her life and career had by no means been easy, but what drove her on was a passion and an inner knowledge, a striving for perfection and an obsession with one day becoming a star. As we trace her life in detail, it will become all too apparent that the price she had to pay for this was a dear one.

Without going into too great a detail about my own career, I feel it important to mention certain milestones which have finally led me to this book. Luck, as I have said, or maybe it's fate, who knows, has played a part in most people's careers and I can honestly say that it's not only been hard work but definitely one or two instances of lucky coincidence (is luck really only coincidence I wonder?) that have shaped mine. Many years of repertory in the provinces, interspersed with out-of-work periods when you feel that you'll never get another theatre job, are normal for all actors. In fact, some of the varied in-between jobs are perhaps worth a mention here. This book is supposed to be about the world of comedy after all!

While 'resting' I have one or two interesting tales to tell, the first of which, at the time, did not seem at all amusing to me, but in retrospect has helped to give me an insight into human behaviour, which is so vital for an actor. There was a time when, to earn a couple of pounds a morning, I went house cleaning (I will impress upon the reader here that this was in the early 1970s!) for the wealthier London households, and to this day cannot understand how anyone could expect you to vacuum the whole house, dust and polish all the furniture, (often three-storied houses), scrub the kitchen and clean the bathrooms and loos, and sometimes keep an eye on the children at the same time, in just three hours! They were not all like this, of course, although, sad to say, the considerate ones were more often than not in the minority.

In one pleasant household I never saw the lady of the house, just the nanny who I liked a great deal, and I arrived one morning in great glee as I had just heard that I had got a theatre job and was to start the following week. The lady of the house happened to be there that day and insisted that I stay and have lunch as a sort of celebration. The nanny went off to the park with the children and we were left alone. She offered me a drink and I declined. She had one herself, a rather large one, drank it, refilled her glass once more, drank it, and asked me again what I would like. I declined once more, but this time she became somewhat insistent to say the least. As I had always been taught to be polite, but was also concerned as I had not yet been paid for my morning's work, I said I would have a small sherry, whereupon she poured me at least a quarter of a pint. She then decided that she didn't like my make up, and insisted that she should give me a 'make over'. I declined, she once more insisted, and the next minute my face (and most of my hair) was covered in cleansing cream and she set to work! I have to say at this juncture that I was actually quite shy of strangers at that time, in case anyone is wondering why I didn't just say no, and there was, of course, the worry about when and if I would get my meagre wage. The result of this beauty treatment was bright green eye shadow right up to my brows, an eyeline which was about a quarter of an inch above my lashes, false eyelashes stuck about half-way up my lids, round red circles on my cheeks, and lipstick which was about a quarter of an inch outside my own lip-line (Chipperfield's circus would most certainly have been happy to employ me!). Surrounding all this the hair was still matted with cleanser. I couldn't wait to make a speedy exit and asked if I could use the loo before I departed, and "Could I remind you I haven't been paid yet?"

She replied that I could have my money as I left but that under NO circumstances was I to wash off the make up in the loo (which, of course, had been my intention). While in there I stuffed handfuls of tissues into my coat pockets, came out, she gave me the money and I had to walk out into the busy London street, get on the Underground and make quite a long journey home. As I walked I kept my arms up to shield my face, and at the same time used the tissues to try to remove the stuff. Needless to say, I did not succeed and in fact ended up looking worse than ever. People say that no one notices anything in London, and that most people go around accepting and ignoring the bizarre — I have most definitely experienced proof to the contrary!

The second occurrence was when I was asked to 'house sit' a luxury flat for two weeks, for a wealthy American. It was bliss! He left me a fridge and deep freeze bursting with food, with orders to eat it all before he returned. There was the most enormous colour TV (at that time not many people could afford colour) and it was Wimbledon fortnight. I only had to sit and watch the tennis and eat myself stupid to earn money. At the end of the second week, the doorbell rang and two friends of his from the States informed me they had come to stay. I knew nothing about this and it transpired that he had forgotten to tell me they might turn up. These ladies were wonderful and insisted that I show them London and that they would pay for everything. Taxis were ordered, and meals booked in the best restaurants. Once or twice I had to go out cleaning for 'regulars', and when I got back to the flat they ran my bath, mixed exotic cocktails and ordered the taxi for our next outing!

One day they said they'd like to go on the river and would I organise a trip? I replied that the only thing I knew about were the river trips from Westminster pier, and they said that would be fine. We arranged to meet there at lunchtime, and when I arrived they were carrying a Fortnum's hamper packed with goodies like smoked salmon and cream cakes. There we sat, as if it were a private launch at our disposal, which I sincerely hope was not what they had envisaged. If it was, they were far too generous and polite to mention it. On one occasion I even made them go on the Underground when they were determined to get a taxi for a short journey, and once, when I was asked to go and clean up someone's kitchen that had had a fire, I told the ladies I would not be able to go out with them that night as it would take ages to get sorted. They grabbed rubber gloves and pinafores and insisted that they come and help me so that I would be able to finish in time. Much later, I discovered that one of them was rather friendly with a member of the royal family!

One of the final 'resting' jobs was more closely connected with the theatre, and proved to be interesting in more ways than one. A friend of mine was 'dressing' on the controversial show *Oh! Calcutta!*, at the Duchess Theatre, and to anyone who asks, "What could there be to do in the way of dressing on that show as they were all nude?", I will say now that it was the hardest work on that front in the whole of the West End. The reason was that there were many short sketches, a cast of about nine, and in each sketch they started off fully clothed, but eventually took them all off. Many a search had to be made for items that had been caught up in the scenery, thrown into the 'flies', got wheeled over by trucks etc, all of which had then to be taken up the endless stairs (we were not allowed to use the lift during performance) to the wardrobe. I can assure the reader that not only were there some very fit backstage workers in that show, but they got fed up of people thinking it was an easy job and would have given anything to be working on a normal show, with a bit of dry cleaning each week and a few shirts and dresses to launder. Perhaps I am more adamant about this because I ended up being the wardrobe mistress as well.

They were looking for a short-term replacement and I was asked if I would consider it. As there was no acting work on the horizon I agreed, with the understanding that if I got a job I could leave at a moment's notice. Imagine trying to find something as old-fashioned as paper knickers, which had really been all the rage in the 1960s, and here we were in the mid 1970s. Having searched the whole of the West End, for some reason I went into a tiny branch of Boots, which used to be halfway down the Strand, and asked if they had any of these knickers. Would you believe, I felt I had struck gold because this wonderful little lady said she had some 'out the back', and not just one box, but six. The show needed one pair per performance, and this find amounted to 300 pairs or so. I was so excited I said, "I'll take the lot!", paid for them and rushed back to the theatre. Goodness knows what that lady thought as I never explained why I wanted them.

It was quite strange, though, on my very first day working as a dresser, as I had said to my friend Viv, who had got me the job, that if people were naked I would be somewhat embarrassed and wouldn't know where to look. She assured me that nobody took the slightest notice, they were so used to it, but I wasn't convinced. I started on the Monday, and we all went to a matinee in Town on the Wednesday. That night during the interval I was having a discussion on the stairs with three of the male members of the cast, about the show we'd seen. It lasted about ten minutes before I went up to the dressing rooms and it was some time later that I realised they hadn't had a stitch on.

One evening, I was in the 'quick change' room at the side of the stage when one of the actresses came off and fell, injuring her knee. She was on the floor in great pain and it was obvious that she couldn't go on. The music played for the opening of the next scene, it kept playing, and playing, the understudy was called over the Tannoy but no one could find her. They turned to me and said, "You'll have to go on and do it, you know all the words, you've heard them every night." I would like to point out at this juncture that I was dressed in very scruffy jeans, a very ancient Laura Ashley smock with pins stuck into every available bit of the yoke, an old pair of down-at-heel plimsolls, and last but not least a pair of black-rimmed square glasses with one leg (I had not graduated to contact lenses).

I said that if I went on, I would not be taking my clothes off under any circumstances. I would have played the scene just as I was, although the part called for an extremely glamorous French maid. This happened within a very short space of time and just as I was about to reluctantly go into the wings and on to the stage for my very first West End appearance, the understudy appeared and the audience (not to mention what we called the 'mackintosh brigade') were saved from a very odd experience. The whole cast were so wonderful on that show and we all had a great time. It was a very happy period in my life and I still meet up with many of them and wouldn't have missed it for the world.

Ironically, my very next job after this was a tour of *Winnie The Pooh*, dressed from head to toe in an animal skin, playing Kanga, who I have to admit clanked a bit as she hopped, the pouch being very useful for storing dressing room keys, cigarettes, and the not-to-be-forgotten one-legged glasses.

One day a couple of years later, I was telephoned at 4pm and asked to rush down to Bournemouth that evening to take over the next night in a tour of the play *A Bedfull Of Foreigners*, as one of the cast had been taken ill. It was a chance not to be missed as I knew the company consisted of Terry Scott, June Whitfield, Linda Baron, Slim Ramsden and Colin Jeavons. I arrived on Bournemouth station, having been told to hold the script — which I had collected from the office in London on the way — in front of me as identification. There was no one to meet me, so after half an hour and as it was by now nearly 10pm, I decided to go to the hotel next to the theatre, as that would no doubt be where Terry Scott was staying. On arrival I was told that he, too, was ill and had gone back home to London, but two of the cast were rehearsing upstairs. When I got up to the room, there was

Linda Baron rehearsing the author of the play, the lovely Dave Freeman, who is not an actor, through Terry's lines! I then quickly discovered that we had a 20-minute dialogue to play at the start of the show, and panic set in. The whole night was spent learning, but it was difficult stuff, and when the time came to do the show the next evening it really was the blind leading the blind. Linda and Slim hid in the wardrobe behind the louvred doors on one side of the stage whispering instructions, with the stage manager on the other, and me pulling the well over 6ft tall Dave around the stage like a demented lunatic. The amazing thing was that the audience laughed, but perhaps it was because as we were supposed to be in a state of panic within the situation, what they didn't realise was what they were actually getting was real!

The late 1970s and early 1980s found me still leaping about the country, touring, repertory and some quite nice parts on televsion: *Crossroads*, *All Creatures Great And Small*, a wonderful scene with John Duttine in *A Woman Of Substance*, and so on, but it was by a strange quirk of fate that the sending of a 'get well soon' card created the turning point in my career.

I had worked a good deal in a repertory company in the north of England and the director, Colin McIntyre, became a great friend as well as employer. We even acted together on occasions and got rather mirthful at times, most especially when we shouldn't, for example, in the middle of a thriller! Time went on, I came back to London and some years later I heard that Colin had been ill. I had not really kept in touch, such is the nature of our business when you go to pastures new, but I knew he was working for a producer in London. I sent the card to the business address, hoping they would forward it. Two days later, the telephone rang and it was another producer, Mark Furness, who I had never worked for, asking me if I would go the next day for an audition to play a blousy blonde in the stage version of *Last Of The Summer Wine*, which was going to Eastbourne for the summer season.

I went for the interview, only to find that they had already started rehearsals and there before me were Peter Sallis, Bill Owen and Jane Freeman, who went off for a coffee break while I read the script for the director. I must add here that *Last Of The Summer Wine* was always one of my favourite programmes, so you can imagine my feelings. I got the part and was immediately whisked around to the company's office to ring my agent and 'do the deal'.

It was quite some time later before I discovered that the day my 'get well' card had been received, Colin happened to get a telephone call from the producer of the *Summer Wine* play, asking if he knew of anyone who could play the part, and as I was in his mind he suggested me. If the card had been sent a day or two later, well, I won't dwell on THAT!

The show was a great success in Eastbourne, and I have so many happy memories of that hot summer, with a wonderful company. The following year we went to Bournemouth with the show, met with the same success and even more happy memories. Roy Clarke came to Bournemouth and said he was thinking of putting the three new characters in the play — Howard, Marina and Pearl — into the television series. I don't think we ever believed it would happen, but it did! That was 14 years ago. We haven't looked back since and it has been the most wonderful experience being involved with that marvellous team of people.

Now, back to that memorable Christmas of 1990 where the next important chapter of my life was to begin. I was appearing in pantomime as Fairy Marina, with the eyelashes, bicycle and mini skirt, when, after the show one night, Michael Vine, the manager of one of the cast said, "Do you know, this is going to sound strange, but on stage when you're working with the audience, you remind me of Hylda Baker." I thought this somewhat strange as Hylda was tiny and dark haired ...very far removed from Marina.

However, he then went on to say that someone should research her life as she was a certain genius and also the forerunner of our stand-up comediennes today, and that she had in fact died only four years previously, in 1986, in relative obscurity. I began my research with the objective of writing a short play about her life, particularly as the press like to ask the question, "And what are you working on at the moment?" and if you are out of work (or 'resting' is the parlance they love to quote, although what's restful about wondering when the bills are going to be paid, I've never been able to fathom!) you're certainly not going to say so. Thus I would say, "Well at present I am extremely busy researching and writing a play about the life of Hylda Baker, and I would be grateful if any of your readers has any recollections of her, or perhaps knew her, then I would love to hear from them." To be honest, I never really expected to get very far, but I really was intrigued by the idea. The very first person I heard from, wrote to me only a few days after the first newspaper article had appeared in the paper, and this led me to a wonderful lady in Stourport, called Hilda Darby, with whom Hylda Baker had stayed on occasions. She gave me some newspaper cuttings, some stories and some wonderful quotes. The snowball began to roll that was to eventually become an avalanche.

Sadly Hilda Darby died very recently, but my greatest joy is that she saw the play about Hylda's life, both when it was on tour and also on the memorable night when I did one performance at the Fortune Theatre in London, in 1995, and she was full of fun when we talked after the show. Thanks must go here to John and Ann Stirling, who arranged that evening as a charity event for The Michael Elliott Trust in Derbyshire, and who work so very hard. It was a most exciting evening, coupled with the fact that we knew the proceeds were to go to all the donkeys that they have rescued and have in their dedicated care.

As my early research continued, I discovered it was sometimes not going to be too easy to get people to talk to me, especially as many were worried that I was planning to bring out the bad side and do what they call a 'hatchet job'. This, to me, said a great deal about Hylda as she could be incredibly difficult to work with due to her fierce professionalism and her constant and untiring search for perfection. In my opinion the latter can never be achieved, because how can you know when you're there?

The next job after the birth of the idea of writing the play saw me playing the part of Mrs Malaprop in *The Rivals* at the West Yorkshire Playhouse, and this was to be the beginning of the many strange coincidences that were to become such a part of my life. Hylda had been nicknamed a latter-day Mrs Malaprop because of her wonderful inventiveness with the mispronunciation of words. Some of her famous ones included, "That's rickidoodleous," "He was insaturated with her," and "Menthol? I'm not suffering from illuminations!" One of Mrs Malaprop's famous lines from *The Rivals* is, "Oh, she's like an allegory on the banks of the Nile," and, "I would have her learn geometry, that she might know something of the contagious countries." However, in *The Stage* newspaper (September 1970) it was said that these 'pale into insignificance when set against some of Hylda's more exuberant efforts'. What a compliment!

During the run of *The Rivals* I once more managed to get a newspaper to mention that I was searching for information about Hylda's life, and once again I received only one reply, but what a valuable one! It was from a local music-hall historian called Geoff Mellor, who gave me a great deal of important information. This served to encourage me greatly because where could I start? My main problem had been that there was no single book about Hylda and, indeed, very little about her in general reference books? The next thing was to talk to her agent, Bill Roberton, who gave me more important information and some very funny stories. He also recommended various people that I should talk to and one vital contact was Hylda's niece, Ann.

Time went on and after interviewing many people who had been a part of Hylda's colourful life, the clear picture of the play began to emerge. I had never written anything before, apart from the odd Christmas concert when I was in junior school, and honestly didn't believe that I could! (I now hear the reader saying, "Alright, so how does she think she can write a book then?" Well, we'll see!)

Then came the task of piecing together this huge jigsaw of facts which, by this time, had taken three years to collect. I really didn't have any confidence about writing the whole thing myself, so I asked a great friend of mine, John Gleeson, if he would consider co-writing with me. He and his wife Carol had been with me for one memorable summer season in Guernsey in 1971, we had been good friends ever since and I knew that he had become a well-respected writer. We got together to discuss the way forward and one day, when we had just begun to work on the dialogue, I kept saying, "No, she wouldn't say it like that, she'd say it like this." Eventually John said, "Fergie," (for that is my nickname and I lay claim to the fact that I was bearing it long before a certain member of the royal family), "You've got to write this yourself, nobody else can." At that point I started to write, the pen fairly flew across the page, and John says to this day that he felt it rather 'spooky', as if someone else had taken over.

It was a great surprise to me because I found myself really beginning to enjoy it. I remember, clearly, sitting at my desk one evening at 9pm and, before I knew it, it was 5am and I was distracted through the window by a bird doggedly pulling a worm out of the ground, a rather brave (or perhaps stupid) bird, as he was certainly so intent on getting breakfast that he had no thought of the danger from local cats. At this point I will gloss over the number of hours spent rewriting and fiddling with the text, but suffice it to say that it took a considerable time to reach anywhere near the perfect version. The next task was to get it on a stage somewhere, and luckily a small production company offered their services. We were off!

A few 'try out' dates followed and the play was very well received, after which I decided to do some re-writes, and finally it seemed a good idea to try to produce the show myself. What a learning process that turned out to be, and no doubt the reader will note that this is just another example of how much certain aspects of my endeavours to 'set the record straight' on Hylda Baker's life meant that very often I was following in her footsteps in more ways than one!

My 'other half', Paul, who I must say is most tolerant of all my exploits, had been nagging me over a period of three years, prior to doing the 'try outs' saying, "Oh, she'll never get it off the ground. I've told her to get on and write it before it's too late . . . I'll believe that play when I see it!" Now, after all the trials of touring the show, latterly being my own production company, publicist, secretary, wardrobe mistress, writer, on occasions driver, manager and, last but by no means least, actress, he finds that not only do I rarely see him but the mere mention of the Hylda Baker play can bring him near to apoplexy. He did, however, design the set, (cleverly scaling the door etc to be larger in order to make me appear small) organise transport (often driving at unearthly hours), wield the angle grinder to cut the innards out of a piano, paint and varnish furniture and often help with all the fit-ups and get-outs at theatres (*ie* getting the whole lot into a theatre in three hours and then two hours later, after the show, getting it all out again!). Mention must be made here of the day he had neatly laid all the piano keys out on the drive, ready to put back in order into the piano, when I blindly stepped out of the door and tripped over them. It put me in mind of a play I did once called *The Keys To Murder*! Needless to say, though, considering the fact that he is an architect and, until he met me, not involved in the working side of the theatre, except in a professional designing and refurbishing capacity, he gets top marks for stamina.

On one memorable occasion Paul and I had just arrived back from a performance at about 2am and had to unload everything off the van and get all the set put away under cover in order to be able to return the van to the garage first thing in the morning. The problem was that there were only the two of us to do it, the rest of the team having gone home straight from the venue. It really is amazing how, when the need is great, superhuman efforts can come into play. It normally took at least three (usually four) people to manoeuvre the piano and the hospital bed on and off, as there was no hydraulic tail lift, and again at least three to lift and carry the scenery. Paul and I found strength we didn't know we possessed. Luckily, this did not happen frequently and once when we got back late again, there was much sound of jollity coming from next door. They were having a party, to which we had been invited but obviously couldn't attend, and when they heard us return we ended up with more help from mirthful partygoers than we needed.

Running out of diesel on the M4 on the way to do just one performance at the Grand Theatre, Swansea, was another incident which is only amusing in retrospect. It was a very cold February night and we were chugging along with only a few miles between us and hot meal, looking forward to the end of the long journey with no idea that the fuel gauge was faulty. The van just coasted to a halt. Being aware that it is not advisable to sit in the vehicle should anything hit you from behind, we got out and the others went off in search of the emergency telephone to find out exactly where we were (it was difficult to give the AA an exact location from our mobile phone). While I was waiting, it got even colder and it seemed like a good idea to make use of my Hylda Baker stage costume from the back of the van — the AA man who arrived some time later never said a word!

I am sure that the majority of people in Paul's village considered us to be totally mad, especially when we were seen wheeling and carrying various strange items back and forth across the road to the garage where a lot of the stuff was kept. How often does one see an authentic 1960s hospital bed in a country lane, with a theatre dressing table and mirror piled on top of it? Once, when the piano was being trundled across, there came trotting around the corner a horse and rider. Quite understandably the horse took exception to this and shied, whereupon the rider spoke sharply to it.

I apologised profusely but the rider's only reply was, "Well, he'll have to get used to things like that!" How often would any self-respecting horse be asked to ignore a piano in the road?

Here, too, I will mention the wonderful stage management team who stuck by me through thick and thin. Jo Longworth (and Joyce, her mother, who twice came with us to help, and has also made the odd 'prop'), Tracy Haddock (also known as Tracy Fish!), who managed to escape and get a 'proper' job at the theatre in Ipswich, Andy Grogan who managed to find impossible props like monkey outfits and a *This Is Your Life* book, Anita Graham who has drummed up support and seen the play more times than anyone, Carlene Pence who reproduced Hylda's stage costume brilliantly, and latterly the wonderful Mark Simons who seems to manage to carry the whole set with one finger, and last but by no means least, Jo's friend Liz Griffiths who, like my partner, is not in the theatre but who helped out at most venues for no pay and sometimes, when in great back pain, was seen — and much chastised — for carrying large items of furniture to and fro! On one occasion when we were short-staffed, she even worked the sound desk! In fact she and Jo even arrived at my dressing room door just before curtain up that evening with reams and reams of loose tape hanging from their fingers, wearing very believable crestfallen expressions. Needless to say, it didn't take long for me to realise it was a 'wind up'! The most important thing is that we have all managed to stay great friends in the face of it all. Mention must also go to my MD, Paul Davis (not to be confused with 'my' Paul) and his wife, actress Jacquie Toye, who also stuck by us and they, too, loaded and unloaded the set and the furniture, once Paul almost lacerating his hands on splinters — and hands to a pianist are his livelihood! Also John Garritt, from down the road, who offered his services on many an occasion, was taken up on it every time, who came to see the show at least three times and never asked for a free ticket! Bernard Mottram, too, has done his fair share of loading the van, although we had actually trapped him in the drive so he couldn't get his car out. We knew how to get those helping hands! I hope the reader will have borne with me on what sounds rather like an acceptance speech at an Oscar ceremony . . . "without whom it would have not been possible etc" . . . but without them it wouldn't!

Now to the very first performance of the play. I can say in all honesty that never before or since could one imagine the terrible attack of nerves when you know, as the curtain-up music begins, that the only performer for the next two hours is YOU! No one is going to come on and talk to you, no one is going to help you keep the pace going if it flags, no one is going to 'save' you if you forget a line. And most of all there are people out there who remember Hylda Baker and you have had the audacity to think you can equal her genius in getting laughs out of HOW she said things as well as WHAT she said. Actors, generally speaking, never have the chance to do 'stand-up' comedy, talking directly to a live audience and telling gags. The point is that in a play you have a character and situations to hide behind, but when doing stand-up, that is literally what you are doing — standing up in front of the jaws of the crocodile. If your act isn't good enough, you can't be saved from being chewed up and spat out!

Even when I was doing the play the second time around, when I produced it myself, if anything the nerves were worse, although this was possibly something to do with the added responsibility. My hands were shaking so much that I just couldn't get my false eyelashes on and my Paul had to hold my hand steady and guide it in the right direction!

Recently the play was performed at the Edinburgh Festival in what they call a 'stand-up' venue, and lo and behold I had the most exciting time because when it got to the part in the play where I perform her act, I found I could break off, talk to the audience (as Hylda!), improvise, get laughs, and then get back to the script. This was something I never ever envisaged being able to do in a month of Sundays, Mondays, Tuesdays or any other day of the week!

There was also the fact that Hylda was a wonderful singer and, of course, this would have to be a part of the play. Many years ago, when in repertory, I was told by one particular director that I couldn't sing. This was mainly due to the fact that because of my deep voice I couldn't get to the high notes except if I sang the tenor part with the men. Consequently, I had a complex about it, but have since learnt that there is such a thing as transposing into the key that suits you! Now, as Hylda, I sing big belting numbers in the show, thoroughly enjoy it, and hopefully without sounding too boastful, the audiences appear to enjoy it too. There is a lesson to be learnt here for everyone who is told they can't do something ...yes, you very often can, it's others who put you down.

Contrary to popular belief, actors are often extremely insecure. Hence the fact that they crave the love of an audience and will brave the fear of failure in order to get this accolade. Thus, imagine when one has only ever been involved in acting, and not thought a great deal about what goes into the other side of getting a production on the road, finding oneself 'cold calling' theatre managers and trying to sell the show, writing and sorting out artwork for programmes, designing and costing posters (until then I had no idea what a 'double crown' poster was) and sending 15,000 flyers to just one theatre for one night's performance. How on earth do you pack those up to send them, they weigh a ton? Then there was the small task of liaising with each theatre, sending out technical requirements and lighting plots etc. The latter had never occurred to me because, when on stage, you do your job and leave those very complicated aspects to others who are trained for it.

There is also the added fear as you sign a contract with a theatre as early as September for a booking the following March, and there are clauses which state that if you fail to appear you will owe them £1,000. There can be no understudy in a show like this and what if you're ill, get laryngitis, or some such disaster befalls? All of these things are enough to make you wish you'd never started this in the first place, but then the adrenalin starts to flow and you know you must see it through.

One of the very first performances in the provinces was at The City Varieties Theatre in Leeds, from where, as I have mentioned before, the TV show *The Good Old Days* was broadcast. It was certainly an emotional time but there were a few problems. It was a freezing cold day, a blizzard had caused the M62 to be practically closed, and my scenery and furniture were somewhere on that motorway in a van, well and truly stuck. Luckily the costumes were with me in my car so I knew, if the worst came to the worst, I could at least do the show with a few curtains and a table. The van did make it and all was well. At the end of the show, at the finale, I heard seats going up and, feeling rather deflated, thought, "Hello, they're all rushing off to catch their buses." What was actually happening was that people were standing up to applaud. A standing ovation! I was close to tears, it's something we all dream of but in this case it was particularly emotional for me as it was in that very theatre that Hylda became nationally famous through the power of television, and I recalled that it was on that very stage and in that programme that I had watched, laughed at and copied her all those years ago.

One of the most exciting outcomes of all of this is meeting, working with, and in many instances becoming friends with so many people I would probably never have had the opportunity to meet in my career as an actress. The twain do meet on occasion at functions etc, but I have now had the pleasure of working with many people from the world of variety, and learning a good deal along the way. As I have said before, it seems as if destiny has led me in this direction, but one of the oddest things is that I have sort of done it in reverse. Hylda's great desire was to be a serious actress, and by golly she could have been. She created this hysterically funny act, the public loved it, but she had created her own kind of monster. The audiences really only wanted to see the comedy genius, and producers and managers knew this. Even Nellie Pledge, her character in Granada TV's *Nearest And Dearest* was an extension of her character on stage. The garrulous little woman, getting her words mixed up, and constantly trying to take charge when things are going wrong.

The reason that things seem to have been in reverse for me is that, after 30 years of serious acting (well, how 'serious' is probably debatable), I suddenly found myself being asked to do her act, first of all for charity shows and benefits, then a proper variety tour, doing a 15-minute 'spot'. I replied, "I am not an impressionist. I am doing a play." How very glad am I that I was finally persuaded to accept the tour. It turned out to be such a wonderful time, with some great artists, and luckily it also proved that Hylda's comedy is timeless and today still has them rolling in the aisles. In the world of variety, actors are called 'lardies', and entertainers are 'turns'. A joyful day for me was when one of the company said, "Well, you're a real turn now!" I had been accepted.

Since the early version of the play, more information came to light, more people contacted me to tell me their stories, and the final play is in fact the eighth draft. Of course, you do eventually get to the point where you have to stop and say, "This is it," but the wonderful thing about it all is that, by writing this book, so many of the fascinating stories, the insight into her laughter and her tears, and all the anecdotes which would have made the play as long as the complete works of William Shakespeare, can now be told. It is a great luxury for me because many a time during rehearsals the pencil has been scored across something which I considered to be so valuable, but which had to be cut as it was impossible to stage.

What a complex lady Hylda was. Full of insecurities and fears, generous to a fault when you earned her trust, but the effort to earn this trust was such hard work that many who worked with her just gave up. She alienated herself from many who could have been her friends, by her fierceness and her determination and her refusal to ask for help when she was suffering inside. She had to fight all her life, and perhaps she felt it was a sign of weakness to show any signs of vulnerability. Needless to say, then, that I am sure Hylda would not wish me to stint on the humorous side of her life, or on her amazing ability to bounce back in the face of adversity. She has been such a big part of my life for six years now, and she still refuses to let me off the hook. Well, here goes Miss Baker! I hope I will do you proud.

CHAPTER ONE

In Through the Front Door

"I WAS born dead, will be the start of my book," said Hylda. So be it then, as this is her book. She was born on 14 February 1905, at 23 Ashworth Street, Farnworth, her grandmother's house, near Bolton, Lancashire. At this point I must apologise to her for putting the correct year. All her life she never revealed her true age, always making out that she was younger, and one of her favourite retorts when asked was, "My age is my own affair!" She was very tiny and when she reached adulthood would be no more than 4ft 10½ins tall and would be dubbed in later life as being 'Fifty-nine inches of fast talking fireball', along with 'Little Miss Sure Shot' and 'The Little Napoleon'.

She was born under the sign of Aquarius. It is written that when the world enters the sign of Aquarius there will be a great awakening to a new light and a new awareness of a brighter dawn. It is the day of the feast of St Brigid, the midwife in Jesus's nativity, the saint of healing and childbirth. St Brigid was also the very first woman to start a convent, the importance of this being that it was very much a male-dominated world, and we will see that this, too, is what Hylda was to experience. It is also the feast of St Blaise, the patron saint of throats. There is a ceremony in Ireland of 'blessing the throat' on this day. Hylda was to have many problems with hers. In Japan they scatter beans on this day in order to banish evil spirits.

Aquarians can be extremely rebellious, cranky, tactless or outspoken, especially if they have discovered something important or revolutionary. They are individualistic and quite happy to work on their own, but they always want to improve things. I am sure that many of the people who worked with Hylda during her stormy career will confirm that she was very typical of her birth sign, and as we see her life unfold it will be all too apparent that more often than not she took it to extremes.

Hylda was born with what is known as a caul, or cawl, which is a membrane of skin that covers the face, is somewhat rare and is the cause of much superstition. In olden days cauls were highly prized and often sold by midwives as they were regarded as an infallible preservative against drowning and were believed to prevent shipwreck, and thus were much in demand by seamen. In 1919 one was advertised in a shop for three guineas, but only a couple of years earlier the price of a cawl was one shilling and sixpence. When asked about this, the astute shopkeeper replied, "Yes, that was before the war. The submarine has made life at sea so dangerous now!" In 1691 it was documented, 'Some would persuade us that one born with a cawl is not so subject to the miseries and calamities of humanity as other persons.'" In 1708 one lady wrote, 'I have ever been told that being born with a cawl was a token of good luck, hitherto I have seen none, I am 22 and see no husband come, no not one wooer.' In 1897 it was written that if the parents did not take care of the cawl, the child would grow up a wanderer, and as recently as 1953 it was recorded that whatever happened to the cawl would happen to the child. It was also called a Hallihoo or Fortune Hood.

It is perhaps understandable that throughout her life Hylda was renowned for her extreme superstitions. Her grandmother kept the cawl, but it is not clear what happened to it later. No doubt it got mislaid. Throughout her life, Hylda suffered from nightmares, usually about dying or suffocating, and in particular she would dream that she had died and was up on the ceiling looking down at her dead body. In fact, it transpired that she did indeed suffer more than her fair share of bad luck, miseries and calamities, and did grow up to be a wanderer, so perhaps there is something in the superstition after all.

Hylda's own description of her birth was very dramatic, showing her great skill in embroidering a story for comedy license. She said that the midwife who delivered her thought she was dead, so they wrapped her in a blanket and cast her aside. They put the blanket into a corner and forgot about it, then after a while it moved, they revived her, and that was that!

She was the oldest of seven children. Ethel came along a year later, then two years later, Harold, another two years and there was Mildred, a year and a half and Brenda was born, four years later there was Eric, and finally three years later came Sydney. Her mother, Margaret, and father, Harold, had married when they were very young and her father was only 21 when she was born, so in fact he was only 35 when the final baby came along. It is not difficult to imagine what it must have been like bringing up seven children, particularly in those days when 'labour saving' devices were unheard of. They did, however, have a washing machine, which was something not many households could boast, except for the very wealthy. It was called a Magee Marshall and was made of wood. When it wasn't in use, it made a table, having a top which was removable. The boiler was in the kitchen, the machine would be filled from this and there were rollers that came up at the side to use as a mangle. Hylda's youngest sister, Brenda, clearly remembers that she and Mildred used to have a bath in it. Her father was a well-known and much respected comedian and by the time Hylda was ten years old he was running his own shows and doing very well. He was affectionately known as Chukky Baker. Indeed, Bob Monkhouse used his nickname when talking about Hylda. I must add at this point that Bob didn't actually work with him, considering Chukky gave up his career in 1924 when Bob was not yet even a twinkle in anyone's eye.

In the early days of Hylda's life, when he was away on tour, the children would get all dressed up in their best outfits and go to meet him at the station when he came home. Margaret Baker was a brilliant seamstress, who made all their clothes, and they were beautifully dressed, a sight to behold. She also made all her husband's stage clothes, luxurious silk shirts and even his overcoats. The household was firmly ruled by her, too. When it was time for him to go away again, he would line everyone up, make them hold out their hands and give each one a half-crown piece, which was a lot of money in 1915. But as soon as his taxi had rounded the corner and gone out of sight, Margaret lined them all up and collected the money back again! Every time father came home he gave each of his children a half-crown, and every time he went away the same thing happened — mother confiscated them all. No doubt this had a lasting effect on those little personalities. Certainly, once Hylda became a big star she had filing cabinet and one drawer had 'M' for money on it where she kept a good deal of cash. She never had much faith in banks, so perhaps it stemmed from all those years ago. Her mother is not to be blamed, though, because she must have had a hard time trying to make ends meet at times, and very early on in her own life money had never been plentiful. She had been 'the one that got away'. Her own parents had been rather poor. They were staunch Catholics, lived in a small cottage, and her father was known a religious 'hell raiser'. An aunt of Margaret's had a big dress shop and took classes in dressmaking, which is where her niece learnt the skill. In the early days of Margaret's married life, when times were hard, an aunt used to give her money from her 'bank'. This was actually in her petticoats which were well weighted down as she had sewn all her money into the hem.

There was many a problem, too, for the young couple because Margaret's family were unhappy that she had married outside the Catholic church, and the church weren't too full of understanding either. Hylda was taken to St Gregory's in Farnworth to be christened, a church for whom Margaret, before she was married, had given up her free time to run dressmaking classes for its benefit. She had done a great deal for them in the past. The priest asked, "Aren't you Margaret Halliwell that was? I don't remember you getting married." Margaret replied that she had been married in the register office, New Hall in Newport Street, by special licence. Angrily, the priest said, "Have you slipped out of the back door? You will be damned for that. I should never have taken your money." Margaret, who had just paid over a half-crown, retorted, "You are no angel of God — I will never come here again." Baby Hylda was quickly bundled up and taken home.

However, once Harold became a success there was many a perk, particularly on Bonfire Night when there was always great excitement for the Baker children as their father would arrive home laden with boxes and they always had the best fireworks in the street. On one occasion he came home with the most beautiful diamond ring for his wife, to which she said, "He must have had a heck of a good win!" He was something of a gambler and loved nothing better than a good game of cards. He taught Hylda to play and she loved it too. Indeed, some of this rubbed off on her in later life as she continued to enjoy playing cards and apparently loved a gamble — if there were two flies crawling up a wall, she'd have a bet. In 1969 she is quoted as saying, "I don't like bridge at all, it's far too heavy for me. All my friends know, however, that if there's a game of solo or poker going, they won't have to ask me twice!"

From an early age Harold Baker had been intrigued and fascinated by the skills of dancing, although none of his family were that way inclined. He was very much the odd man out. He learnt to dance, perfecting the soft-shoe shuffle and what they call the buck and wing, which is an extremely difficult step. Not only that, he was a champion clog dancer as well. He also danced on 'flaps' which again is so hard to perfect. They are shoes with long flaps at the front rather like flippers, and which formed part of his comedy act along with parodies of popular tunes of the day. One of these was a skit on *Claire de Lune* for which he 'blacked up' and sang as *Chlora de Lime*. It was a great success and, indeed, when Hylda later included it in her act, once again it proved very popular, but apparently Tessie O'Shea complained because she was also performing it, so Hylda cut it. It is possible that when

Hylda's father gave up the business, the man who had sold him the song later sold it to Tessie, which of course he probably should not have done. Harold Baker was a natural who had in fact come from a classical music background. His father had been a talented musician, playing the church organ, and he was a considerably wealthy man, but he had died young, aged only 45. No doubt this background of musical ability was something which was handed down to Hylda, as she really was very gifted musically.

An example of the kind of show in which Harold toured and of how successful he was can be gauged from the bill at the Hamilton Hippodrome in September 1923: 'William Revill presents Jack Cranston (The Real Light Comedian) and Harold Baker (The Little Bundle Of Fun) in his latest and most successful musical revue London To New York.' These two names were above the title; below it were Charlie Russell, Seymour Scott, Jack Teeney, Peggy Hall, Zillah Carmena, Six Parisienne Maids, Stan Daniels, Winnie Buchanan. The scenes were somewhat adventurous and impressive: 'Vestibule of the Celestial Hotel, London; Liverpool Landing Stage; Deck of the Dancania; Eight Avenue, New York; Roof Gardens of the Eight Avenue Hotel.' The price of the tickets is also worthy of mention. Boxes to seat five cost 12s 6d, Stalls 1s 6d, Pit 9d, Gallery 5d, but all prices were increased by a few pence on Saturdays and holidays.

Hylda's mother was stage struck, she loved it and encouraged all her children. She adored the theatre and would work hard whatever the task. She made all Hylda's stage costumes, in particular some beautiful dresses, and although it has always seemed that Harold was the one who wanted to push the children into the entertainment profession, there are so many instances where it was Margaret who was in the driving seat. Once 'Little Hilda Baker, Lancashire's Premier Juvenile Comedienne and a Dancer' (which is how she was billed) became a success, her mother was always there with her wherever she went. At first, though, Harold billed himself and Hylda thus: 'A Real New Original Act. Harold Baker and a Baby with and without a piano in Burlesques and Impressions.'

Margaret absolutely adored her daughter and would do anything for her. She was not a performer herself but one wonders whether she would have liked to have been. Once, when asked if she had been on the stage, she said, "Oh yes, yes, I used to be on the stage." In fact the only time she had was one Christmas time in what is called the 'ghost gag', when she ran around the stage as a ghost, dressed from head to toe in a huge white sheet. To be fair to her, though, she did live in the theatre more than many people who considered themselves to be in show business.

The weekend 'train calls' on a Sunday were a real test of stamina. They had large skips with tarpaulin flaps to carry the props and costumes, everyone met at the station and the baggage men would put the trunks and skips on the train. The journeys could be very tedious, sometimes taking all day. One such trip is documented on 4 November 1916, when Hylda was 11 years old. On that Sunday they travelled from the Empire Theatre, York, to the Palace Theatre, Aberdeen. With today's trains it is a long enough journey, but these were the days of the steam train, so one can imagine what it was like. Prior to their arrival in each town or city, Margaret had to write to obtain a license for Hylda to appear, which had to be granted by the local chief constable's office as she was under age. It also meant that she had to be ready to leave the theatre by 9.30pm, having changed and taken off her make up. As there were always two houses, the first at 6.30pm and the second at about 8.40pm, Hylda was usually put second on the bill so she could get out in time.

Some of the audiences were very rough and must have been pretty frightening for a child. In one theatre in Glasgow there was a cage built over the orchestra pit to protect the band because the audience was infamous for throwing missiles at the performers. Perhaps the management were far seeing enough to realise that if the band were kept safe at least they could carry on playing and keep the show going. Before Hylda went on at this theatre she was terrified, which is hardly surprising, and once out there on stage there was complete silence all through her act. When she had finished there was still silence, and then somebody at the back of the theatre blew an enormous raspberry. That, in fact, was the very best thing that could have happened, as the rest of the audience were so angry with the raspberry blower they applauded her like mad!

It is therefore obvious that both Hylda's parents had such a love of the theatre that their one desire would have been to run a family show. But it was Hylda alone who was to hit the big time, certainly because it was she who wanted so much to be a star that she would sacrifice everything to that end, but also for another reason. The truth of it is that she so craved for love and attention that it was this that really drove her on. She was, in truth, a very shy little girl, as is recalled by a lady called Mary Vale Irwin, who became friendly with Hylda when she was about 13 or 14 and whose mother ran a theatrical guest house in Stockport. Hylda and her parents stayed with them for two weeks, there was a lovely park next to the house and every afternoon the two little girls would go there for a long walk. Mary said, "She was such a very quiet, shy girl and really not very happy at all. I remember one Saturday, at the end of the show, she attended a party at the theatre and came home blind drunk, poor girl. She did NOT want drink at all, but I suppose she felt she had to be sociable. My mother sat up with her all night getting her to drink coffee and sober up. When they left Stockport, they went on to Liverpool and I went to spend a few days with them there. We had a lovely time and she was so very sad when she said goodbye at the railway station. Yes, I have so many memories of our dear Hylda, and now at the age of 90, I can remember her so well, and may I say with great affection. She was a really gifted girl, but sadly, a very unhappy one."

Such was his total obsession with life in front of the footlights, that Harold Baker was determined that all his children would learn to dance and to perform; so he taught them all himself. In their home, there were tap dancing mats everywhere. They could be found in the hall, in front of the fire, under all the rugs, ready to be brought out for practice at a moment's notice, and there was even one right in the kitchen doorway, so that every time anyone stepped on to the mat they had to do their own number. Presumably, those who didn't feel up to it on a particular day, did everything they could to avoid going into the kitchen.

Father used to put them through their paces and there they were, tapping up and down the hall while he sat watching them through the sitting room door. What a picture that conjures up. Ethel, Harold and Mildred loved it, but little Hylda was truly in her element. She said in a radio interview in 1969, "When I was three I could do the six Lancashire steps and a shuffle — wearing clogs! At this age I had my first pair of dancing clogs, and I would sing the songs of the day, making up a little act of my own and finishing up with my clog dancing. The Lancashire steps are accepted as the fundamental part of all dancing and in these six steps it includes all the rolls and cross rolls, which are beats with the feet without much movement from the body. Irish cross-rolling is the same, all buck and wing and tap."

It became obvious from an early age that Hylda had a great talent, although it has to be said that the others were also very accomplished. Her brother Harold was a truly wonderful dancer and he also played the violin. However, one day when he was working as a decorator he fell and smashed his wrist and that, sadly, was the end of the violin, although undaunted by this he decided to take up the banjo, mandolin and guitar. He played classical music on the banjo, which was most innovative, and for this he won many prizes. He also formed his own dance band, calling it 'The Supreme Syncopators', which were extremely popular because young Harold's music was really something and by golly he could sing too. He had a beautiful singing voice, and used to sing 'scat' with the band, which is a kind of jazz singing by improvising with all kinds of vowel sounds instead of words, and not easy to do well. He also had mastered the 'buck and wing' dance step when he was a boy and was so enormously thrilled when he found himself able to accomplish it that he did it at every available opportunity. Alas, one day he did it too much and damaged his knee — and anyone who has seen the Irish cross-rolling in today's *River Dance* can certainly understand how.

Hylda's sister Mildred was very talented, loved acrobatics and was a brilliant adagio dancer. Together with her partner, Harry Wilkinson, they did a very successful act and in fact Ethel toured with Hylda in later years and also understudied her. A member of the family remembers that Ethel would be there practising against the wall, her leg 'going up and down, up and down', and she says that Mildred lapped it up, bending herself this way and that (in fact she could still do the splits when she was over 70). Her young brother, Syd, appeared in Hylda's own shows after the Second World War — in his case it is that he is 'last but not least' — but more of this when we come to that chapter of Hylda's life; suffice it to say here that in one review he stole the show from her!

What was it like to live in Farnworth and Bolton leading up to 1915, and what was life like when the country was first embroiled in that awful time, the First World War? Little Hylda first trod the boards of the professional stage at the age of ten, when the war had already been raging for a year. What was it like in that little pocket of Lancashire for the first ten years of her life? Deep down she would never really forget her roots, they would be with her for always. Latterly, she only went back when work dictated it, but in her heart of hearts she had never really left.

Farnworth was really like a small village, known for its mining and cotton mills. There were pigeons, whippets and rag and bone men, and Market Street reputedly had more pubs than any other street in the north of England. The 'mucky' River Irwell ran past the factories and mills and if the locals felt like fishing in it, it would be almost impossible to spot the fish among all the rubbish. At least two other famous people hail from Farnworth: the actor Frank Finlay and the former England footballer, Alan Ball. Frank Finlay's first venture into amateur dramatics was at St Gregory The Great in the town and in a *TV Times* article in February 1975 he recalled that his most exciting childhood memory was when a horse bolted, a man ran after it and caught it, but in the process choked to death on his false teeth and thereby became a posthumous hero to all the kids. In the same article Alan Ball remembered that the Whit Walks were the high spot of the year. On one occasion he was a page to the Rose Queen and another time he carried the tasselled banner and was 'well chuffed'. He played his football in the street because it was considered cissy to play in the park! He says Farnworth people are the greatest in the world. What follows are some of Hylda's own descriptions of what life was like when she was about five years old. Precious few people today remember exactly what it was like in 1910, so it is invaluable that some of her memories are contained in the same article.

"I was always known as the lass from the chippie. The reason for this was that my grandmother ran a fish and chip shop in Plodder Lane. [It had been owned by Margaret's eldest sister, Rose, and Hylda's grandmother moved into the shop on a

Hylda's mother, Margaret, pictured in the 1890s.

Five of the Baker children pictured at the beginning of the First World War. From left to right of the back row are Hylda (aged 9½), Harold junior and Ethel. Front are Brenda and Mildred.

"Look at this pretty dress I've got. I'm going to a party." Hylda at the age of ten.

Miss Hilda Baker is selling her photographs for the benefit of the brave men at-the-Front

The money received is devoted to sending 1/- parcels (really 3/6 worth) of tobacco and cigarettes through "The Performer" Tobacco Fund.

And one of these photographs is enclosed in each parcel to liven up a Dug-out.

Will you help to make the men happy?

The more photographs you buy the more cigarettes will be sent, and the more men you will make happy. As nearly all the leading artistes are selling their photographs through "The Performer" Tobacco Fund, **you can make a souvenir collection** by sending your remittance direct to :—

Hon. Treasurer,
"The Performer" Tobacco Fund,
18 Charing Cross Road,
London, W.C. 2

5/- will buy a collection of **20** artistes
every one different and post free

10/- will buy a collection of **40** artistes
every one different, and post free

21/- will buy a collection of **100** artistes
every one different, and post free

£5 will buy a collection of **500** artistes
every one different, and post free

"The Performer" Tobacco Fund is a branch of the News papers Patriotic Tobacco Fund, which is approved by the War Office and licensed by the War Charities Act, 1916.

For 1/- we send 'Smokes' that would cost you 3/6 if you bought them in a shop at home

A special arrangement has been made with Martins Ltd., 210, Piccadilly, London, W., to pack and despatch these 1/- parcels duty free from in bond, thereby enabling "The Performer" Patriotic Tobacco Fund to send for 1/- what would cost 3/6 if bought in a shop at home. And the Military Authorities (*through the Director General of Voluntary Organisations—Sir Edward Ward*) have kindly undertaken to collect and deliver the parcels to the men at the-Front free of charge

P 448

Young Hylda did her bit for the War Effort by selling her photograph in aid of 'The Performer Tobacco Fund'. One of her pictures was included in each parcel of tobacco 'to liven up a Dug-out'.

Hylda (left) aged 12, with her sister Ethel.

Hylda, the pretty 12-year-old.

Hylda's father, Harold, in review as principal comedian. He is wearing 'flaps', shoes with which he perfected a difficult dance routine.

Harold and Margaret Baker pictured during the First World War.

At 14, in review with her father.

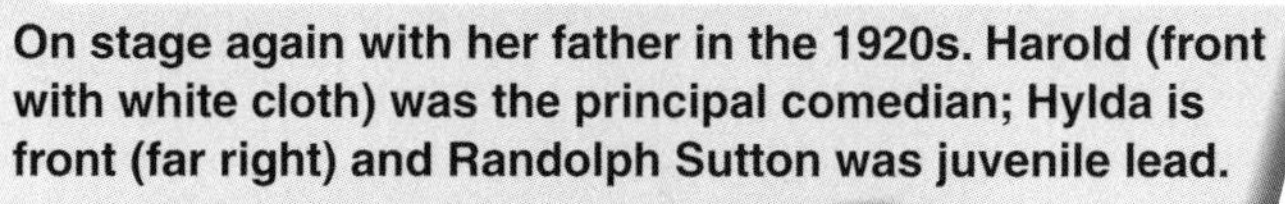

On stage again with her father in the 1920s. Harold (front with white cloth) was the principal comedian; Hylda is front (far right) and Randolph Sutton was juvenile lead.

Still 15, this time with an "almost anaesthetic look on her face!"

Publicity picture of the 15-year-old Hylda Baker.

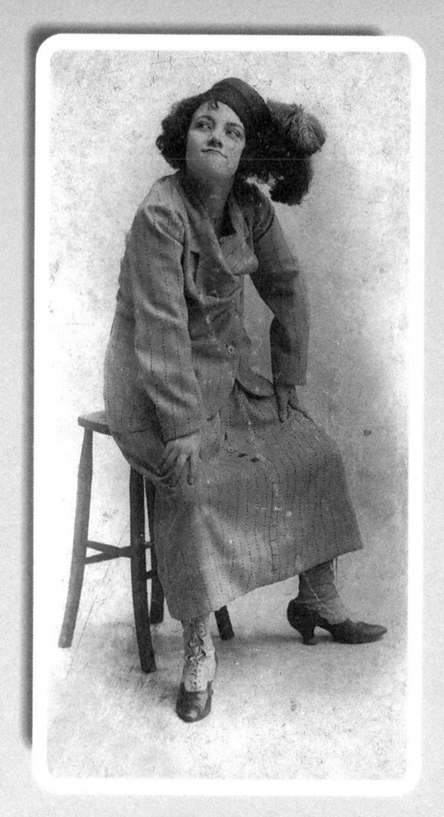

From the show *Jingles*. When Hylda first appeared in it she was 14 – but told the producer she was 18.

Blacked up and singing *Chlora-de-Lime*, which Hylda copied from her father's act. Tessie O'Shea complained!

Publicity photograph from around 1930.

1929, aged 24, with Harold Walden in the review *Lucky in Love*.

The sophisticated '30s look.

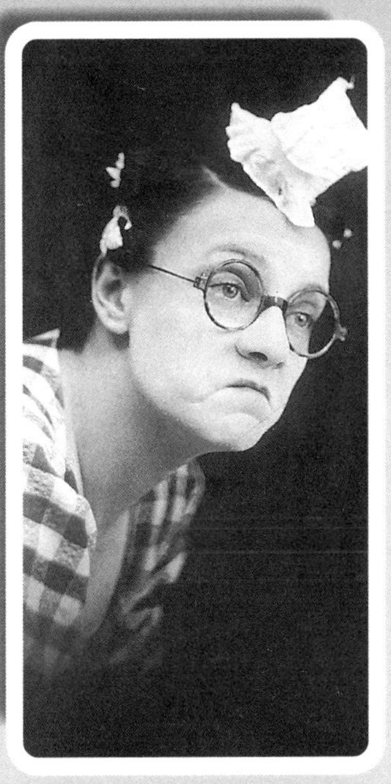

Playing Arabella, one of the Ugly Sisters in *Cinderella* at the Grand Theatre, Bolton, in 1933.

Pictured in Variety around 1937.

As Trixie the maid in *Sleeping Beauty* at Nottingham's Theatre Royal in 1936, pictured here with Billy Danvers.

The elegant Miss Baker in *Variety Show Boat*, 1938, sporting those soon to be famous false eyelashes!

'pay you later' basis. She used to get up at 4am to walk the three miles to Bolton to buy the fish, which she always skinned, so there was no black skin on it.] I was so small that Plodder Lane seemed five miles long and it was all farms and green fields. I had a very best friend called Molly, she had four legs and was the most beautiful cow. I'd know her anywhere and could pick her out from all the others. One day me and my uncle Joe, who was only about six and not much older than me, decided we'd try to milk Molly into an old humbug tin. The milk tasted terrible! We ran all the way home afterwards, absolutely terrified we'd be put in prison if we were caught. One of our favourite pastimes was to go fishing for tiddlers in what was called the 'mucky river' [the Irwell], using the same humbug tin and a jam jar with a long string handle. We needed bait for fishing, so my uncle used to make me dig out maggots from underneath the cow pats. That is something I will never forget. Ugh! All our family lived in the village, and we had a two-up, two-down stone cottage, no bathroom, just an outside lavatory, a water closet. The workmen used to come along to empty the closets at night and we nicknamed them the 'midnight mechanics'. My grandmother had ten children in Farnworth, and when I think about it I can still taste the sausages she used to cook over the open fire. One of my other uncles was what they called a 'knocker-up' for the pits — no one had any excuse for sleeping in in those days! He'd go round at five o'clock in the morning, knocking on the windows, and I'd wake up to the sound of clogs tramping as the men trooped by outside my window. It sounded for all the world just as if they were going to work on horseback."

Hylda's sister, Brenda, remembers the outside toilet well. It was called a 'tippler' and was made of a sort of brown stone with a wooden seat. Apparently, when you sat on it, it seemed to have a life of it's own, and 'tippled' when it wanted to. It was flushed with the water from the kitchen sink and was a big step up from the 'middies', which presumably was a name derived from the midnight emptying ritual.

There were stables next to the Co-op and for anyone who lived nearby, one of the well-known sounds of Farnworth was the clip clop of the hooves on the cobbles. They made clogs at the Co-op, they lasted for ever and nearly everyone wore them — indeed, if you were a man, you were a cissy if you didn't — so that was another sound that echoed all through the day, and as darkness fell the lamplighter would make his way round the streets lighting the gas street lamps.

There are some jottings of Hylda's which are reproduced here exactly as she wrote them, and they are so very evocative, almost poetic. They were found with the heading, 'Amusing incidents to be included in my autobiography'. Sadly, she never wrote more than a few.

"'Grandma making the tripe with tea gravy — I've tried to make it but it tastes dreadful! Grandfather sitting with a mug of tea and him drinking, and Auntie Agnes putting the cure herbs in it. Jenny going dancing with me along ...dancing with the man, with silk blouse and low bra, and me wondering what men must think. Grandfather said it was sinful, and I must say, my thoughts, that he was right there! Going with the little girl to see the dead body — 'cos she said we'd get some tea and a piece of cake! My thoughts when I saw the body ...and the body of my brother Eric. The only two dead people I had seen. Mother coming to Plodder Lane with a big hat on ...Playing cards with father ...The family with the fancy names. Mrs Indiana and her coconut-headed kids in the pub ...wondering how she got to the washtub with her stomach that was always big, 'cos she couldn't tell she was having a baby. She was nine months pregnant and she thought she'd got a worm. Horses, piano lessons, French meals. April, May, June, being baptised. The concerts, where I played the part of the hunchback! Carrying the princess in, the prop breaking, and the boys laughing at us. My brother Harold being spanked with my skipping rope! ...Kindergarten ...dancing on the blackboard, Algebra, my reactions.'

The story about 'Mrs Indiana' was that Hylda's mother had a washer woman (for younger readers this was someone you employed to do all your washing, rather like a human washing machine!) and this lady was very fat but a good worker. One day she'd been down the street working for an Indian lady who had married an officer in the army, and this lady had apparently practically shaved the heads of her two children as a precaution against them getting 'nits' in their hair. The washer woman was quite a character, but she had become somewhat fed up with the amount of work that this woman had expected her to do, and after doing the washing out in the scullery for Margaret Baker she came into the kitchen for a cup of tea. She was very het up, almost palpitating. "Oh Mrs Baker, Oh Mrs Baker, that woman, she had me doing the biggest lot of washing and she hasn't the facilities. Crocheted bedspreads and all sorts she expected me to do, so I turned round and said to her, 'You get back to India and sit under the palm trees with your coconut headed kids!'." The Baker children loved her, though, because although the cleaning woman, who their mother also employed, made sure they had food when she was away, this lady brought them delicious currant bread. They all had great difficulty in keeping straight faces when she told them stories about her life, in particular the one about her wedding day. She'd say, "Oh there was me in me blue alpaca and him in his purple suit." It certainly conjured up quite a picture.

Farnworth was known for McManus's meat pies, Scalper Jack the barber, and the smog from the factory chimneys that meant the locals couldn't see across the valley and which was sometimes so thick people used to get lost just crossing Plodder Lane to the chippie. There was Togs's ice-cream parlour and dancing at the Moor Hall, all brown paint and condensation. A regular treat was to listen to the brass band playing in New Park. In those days the front doors were always open and the children played their games in the street — marbles, hoops, tops, hop-scotch and 'piggy'. The latter was played with a cylindrical piece of wood shaped like a pig's snout. The object was to hit the piggy with a small plank of wood, first hitting down on the pointed end and, as it rose, hitting the piggy as far as possible up the street. There were two teams and the opposing team had to guess how many strides it would take to get to the piggy. If they did it within the number, they would win. Imagine trying to play that game in any street today, even a village street. Just one car passing every minute would cause the game to be a shambles.

In the early days Margaret Baker, who had a very strong personality, travelled with her husband on tour, so the children were sent to stay with various relatives and she paid for their keep. When she was at home she always employed a cleaning woman as well, who made sure they were fed if she wasn't there. Eventually Harold senior was doing so well that Hylda, Ethel, Harold junior and Mildred were sent to a boarding school, St Hillary's in Eastbourne. It was a big house set in its own grounds, and Harold apparently spent a great deal of time climbing the trees. Hylda was sent there when she was six years old and stayed there for three years. Margaret was pregnant with Brenda at the time and was touring with her husband. In fact, the baby was born in Altrincham, where Harold was appearing at the time, and toured the country with them.

Margaret loved the life, and during the day she and her husband would like nothing better than to play golf. She had all her skirts specially made for 'driving', and when they weren't playing golf Harold painted. He was a very accomplished artist, particularly in water colours, and Margaret did 'crewel' embroidery, a very intricate skill. Their life together was a very happy one, but Margaret was always very much in charge, was the strength of the family, and if there was any problem they could count on it that she would be there. She was also a very clever business woman. Harold was a very loving father and so important in all their lives in those early days, even though he was away so much.

Meanwhile, down at St Hillary's, Hylda found that as the eldest, it fell upon her to look after the rest of the family. Poor Mildred, who was, of course, only two or three years old was so young that her mother had to provide rubber sheets for her bed at the school. Harold had sent his children there for the beneficial air and in the hope that refined Southern accents would overtake their basic Lancashire (and how ironic it is that fame came to Hylda only by using her Lancashire roots and accent!). There was a great contrast between term time at St Hillary's — compulsory straw hats worn for walks along the promenade, and playing croquet on the lawns — and holidays back up north. Hylda learnt piano there, and being a very quick learner became very good at speaking French. Elocution lessons, too, were a most important part of their schooling.

Hylda laughingly said later, "Here's me, a little Lancashire lass. I'm at school with my sister and she's disappeared. 'Where's our Ethel?' I'm shouting. 'Our Ethel,' says the headmistress. 'Why OUR Ethel? Nobody's going to steal her from you.' I just got round to talking as they wanted and what happened? Three years later we all go back to Lancashire and the other children took the mickey out of me because they thought I was putting it on ... 'Ooh 'ark at 'er. Don't she talk la-di-dah!' I had to try and stop talking 'posh' because I didn't want to be out of it with the other kids. All the same, I began to notice the differences and was observing, even then."

On the way home on the train she must have had an inkling of what was to come as the guard said to them with a very strong accent, "Eh, don't you talk fine and affected?" She did not keep up this charade forever, though, and once away from home again always spoke very correctly. In fact later on, at the height of her fame, few of her public would realise this because she constantly played the garrulous little Northerner. She was also an excellent mimic, was brilliant at different accents, and at the boarding school she also appeared in and helped to stage most of the end-of-term concerts.

When Hylda returned to Bolton, in approximately 1914, even at that early age she also became aware of the difference, not only in the accents, but in the characteristics and mannerisms of people from the north compared to those in the south. With her great talent for comedy, and her love of dancing and singing she started appearing in local charity shows and concerts. She was still only nine and a half years old, but she began building up quite a reputation. It was becoming most apparent that she had a gift for entertaining and she was soon appearing in charity concerts to raise money for wounded soldiers during the First World War. One of the songs she sang was:

'Send him a cheerful letter,
'Tell him it's all OK
'Say that you ne'er felt better,
'Although it's all the other way.
'Don't send a page of sorrow,
'Send him a page of joy,
'And don't let the teardrops fall among the kisses
'When you write to your soldier boy.'

She also had a photograph which was sold to help provide the shilling parcels of tobacco for the soldiers at the front, in order to 'liven up a Dug-out'. The concerts where she sang and danced were very often for officers and she was given many presents, including a bracelet with a beautiful golden hand with a pearl set in it, which is indicative of how much they thought of her.

It was in 1915, when she was ten years old, that Hylda's father sent for her, telling her that she was to get all dressed up as there was a chance for her in the show he was in at the time. A child prodigy is what he called her. He convinced the management, they paid her £6 a week (a lot of money then, as full board and lodging in digs was only 12s a week) and she had yet to celebrate her 11th birthday. From that moment she toured with her father and that memorable first performance was during Easter week, at the Opera House, Tunbridge Wells. The building still stands today, although bingo was the only activity there until recently. However, it has been taken over by a brewery and although it is to be a pub and the stage to be a drinking area, apparently they have lovingly refurbished it, keeping the original boxes etc, which is to be applauded in these days when our history is sometimes removed in the name of progress.

Of that very first professional performance, Hylda said later, "I started off by singing *Hello, How Are You? How Are You?* I did two verses and two choruses, and what they call a buck and wing dance, then I went off, took my coat off, changed my boots into shoes and came back on and sang *In My Dear Old Home Town*. It was pure schmaltz and topped off with a song my father bought for me, called *Money In The Bank*, and which I made 'my' song in the true music hall tradition. Then I finished with comic impersonations of famous names of the day, like Charlie Chaplin, all while I was dancing. I was the first 'turn' on Monday night and was moved to third 'turn' for the second performance. Within a few months I was topping the bill!"

While touring with her father, she learnt to grow up very quickly, in fact too quickly, learning lessons that some of us don't ever have to deal with until adulthood, or indeed ever have to deal with at all. The vaudeville and variety theatres of the day were often extremely seedy places, the humour could be very suggestive, there was much competition and some of the individual acts would not take too kindly to a child not only coming on and making people laugh, but also being moved further up the bill than them. Often she would arrive early at the theatre with her band parts and music, put them on the piano, and everyone pushed in front of her, so very often she was the last one to rehearse her songs. She was a child in a man's world and in their eyes counted for little. This pattern of life, which continued for some time, was to shape her character and her attitude to her working life in later years, making her sometimes aggressive, hard and domineering, and therefore much misunderstood.

While on tour, it was the law that she had to appear in front of the magistrate in each new town every Monday morning so they could see that she was well nourished. She went to school during the day and performed in the evening. The main thought that springs to mind here is how very confusing it must have been to go to so many different schools. No time to make friends, or to feel part of the surroundings, and no continuity with lessons or teachers. In her own words, her schooling on tour is described in a radio interview from 1969.

"Some people ask if it was tough being a child performer. I didn't think so. It's very exciting really, that sort of thing is very exciting. To go to a different school every Monday, and to meet different children. Sometimes it was very nice and the teachers were very nice, but other times it wasn't quite so good. I think the other children thought I was something from another world nine times out of ten because that's the way they used to treat me, and of course I was always on show, and I suppose children like that!"

On one occasion the headmistress went to her parents and said, "She's very bright you know, and very clever. Do you realise what she could earn as a professional person?" Her father replied, "Do YOU realise how much she's earning now, and what she could earn as a star?"

On tour it was not all rosy. Sometimes the digs were awful, with soot-blackened lace curtains in cold and often gaslit houses, bare boards, no water other than a tap at a grimy kitchen sink, and sanitation either non existent or tucked away in a small shed at the bottom of the back yard. Often, the way to assess the quality of the establishment was to see what sort of fire they had going in the grate!

There are, however, one or two anecdotes which are certainly full of humour, although I doubt if Hylda thought it at the time. In 1919, in Bacup, Lancashire, they were touring in *Whirls And Girls*, her father's own show, and at this particular venue the first half was their show, and the second half was to be the showing of a silent film. One can assume that the theatre manager was a pretty sharp businessman, as it transpired that somewhere in the contract it said that the touring musical director had to play the piano for the film as well. He flatly refused, so immediately Harold told Hylda to do it. They did their half, and straight after the interval there she was sitting in the vast orchestra pit, desperately trying to crane her neck to see the cinema screen, as she was very tiny, and constantly jumping up and down, up and down, trying to see when she had to change from 'hurry' music for the chase scenes to 'hearts and flowers' for the love scenes.

Another time, again in a touring revue with her father, she was doing her usual comedy spot when one night it was discovered that the leading lady, a beautiful French dancer, had run off with a stage hand. Hylda's father once again told her to deputise. When she showed reluctance he pushed her on to the stage. She had to leap around banging two cymbals together, but the first thing she did was to gash her hand on one of them. Her hand was pouring with blood, she made a complete mess of the dance, burst into tears, and her father was shouting from the wings, "Kick those ruddy legs!" Naturally, the audience howled with laughter, and from then on, Hylda Baker was very much in the comedy business.

When she was still very much a juvenile, and appearing at the Grand Theatre in Bolton, her grandmother came to see the show and afterwards came backstage enthusing about Hylda. She said, "Your facial expressions are perfect. Why don't you let the film people have you?" Hylda said, "Granny thought that I only had to let them know I was available and they would come rushing! I very soon became aware, though, that all the glamorous film stars were usually to be found gracefully draping themselves over mantelpieces and the like, and at four feet ten and a half I'd have great difficulty in that department!"

She had no difficulty, though, when it came to showmanship. There is a story she told that once, when she was young and between theatre bookings, she got a job in the music department of F. W. Woolworth. She was employed to play the sheet music that was on display for the customers, for they actually used to have a piano in the department in those days. She played all the popular hits of the day and very soon got completely carried away, singing the songs as well and turning it into an act. Then she decided that the public in the store should know when she was going to begin, so she got a drum and banged on it to signal the start. Woolworths was packed out and people would queue up saying, "When's the next show starting?" In the end people couldn't always get in and they had 'House Full' signs on the pavement ...outside Woolworths!

Hylda learnt to have a great respect and fear of superstitions, especially those of a theatrical nature, and although we will hear of many instances later where perhaps her instincts were proven to be well-founded, one incident that her youngest sister, Brenda, encountered is well worth mentioning here, as it happened around this period.

While touring in revue, in 1921, Hylda had a 'spot' where she sang soprano, sitting at a table in a garden. She would wistfully fondle her jewellery while singing the jewel song from *Faust*. Nine-year-old Brenda was allowed to watch this from the wings and got rather carried away by it all, and being rather impressed, at the end of the scene she went off down the corridor humming the tune to herself. She went to her sister's dressing room, by which time she had begun to whistle the tune. At that point there was an almighty scream from Hylda, her dresser grabbed Brenda, shook her and pushed her straight to the stage door and out into the street, whereupon she was made to turn around and around many times. Poor bewildered Brenda was totally shocked and could not understand why she had been punished, while back in the dressing room, Hylda had gone quite hysterical and was being placated by Margaret. Brenda did, of course, learn much later that to whistle in the dressing room is one of the worst crimes you can commit in a theatre, as it reputedly conjures up every kind of bad luck imaginable.

Before Hylda's father ran his own show, he had one period where he went bankrupt. He had signed a contract to go back to perform at one particular venue a couple of years later, but when the time came he had begun to do very well indeed and was becoming well known. It was not convenient for him to appear, so he broke his contract not thinking for a moment that the management of the theatre would react as heavily as they did. The manager decided to sue him and as a result poor Harold went bankrupt. All they had was what was in Margaret's name. How sad that this happened just as he had begun to get the recognition he so rightly deserved. Times were hard but they struggled on and eventually Harold got back on his feet. His advice to his children was that you have to fight to get on in this world and must hit out (metaphorically speaking, of course) before they hit you first! It was carrying this advice with her, coupled with the fact that she had such a hard time before she eventually achieved the stardom she craved, which earned Hylda a reputation for being 'difficult'. When asked what they thought about one particular incident when Hylda was being stubborn, a friend of hers once said, "She's been pushed around so much in the past, now she's getting her own back."

"Entertaining is something that's in the blood," Hylda said in an interview in 1968, "It's like blue eyes or a Roman nose — you're born with it. When I was a kid in variety — with digs at 16s a week, seven shillings more with a piano! — I used to impersonate everybody's act. 'Don't do that,' my father said. 'Why not?' said I. 'I'm as good as that Florence Desmond any day.' 'That's not the point,' he said. 'Don't you impersonate other people, find your own act. Let someone impersonate YOU!' I thought that was a laugh, because who on earth would want to impersonate me? Yet my father insisted and said I had a lot to give, but it must be myself. I thought, 'Oh no, I can't.' I knew I was good at impersonations, but had not at that time thought of projecting Hylda Baker. I started to think about what would suit me and my personality, and used to do what they call 'point' numbers. They were usually about boys, and moon, June and swoon, and I never thought about them as sexy songs. To me they were love songs. I never forgot my father's advice."

He was right, too, because even 80 years later, in 1997, people still imitate her! One impersonation that she herself was proud of was Harry Weldon, and she did it on a *Sounds Familiar* radio programme in 1973:

"Back home in Tennessee, just try and picture me,

"Right on my mother's knee, she thinks the world of me.

"All I can think of tonight, as all the world seems bright,

"The roses round the door make me love mother more.

"Mother More? I knew Mother More before she was Mother More. I knew Mother More when her name was Lizzy Slackcabbage [the audience applaud at this stage, she quickly stops them by saying, "I haven't finished!"] And I know Old More too. I could tell Old More a few things about Lizzie I could, and I will tell him when I get back, when I get back to my home in Tennessee!" (*Rapturous applause*).

Nor did she ever forget the verse her father sent her when she opened in revue. Throughout her life she kept it in her dressing room.

'If you think you're outclassed you are.

'You've got to think high to rise.

'You've got to be sure of yourself

'Before you can win the prize.'

She also said, "I think my early life did make me a bit aggressive. It was not in my nature, you see, but something I had to learn in order to survive in that environment. After all, I was only a kid — and a very innocent one at that. My parents were very strict and my mother brought me up to believe that good women went to heaven, or got married, and bad ones went to hell. I soon began to notice, though, that many of the women my mother wouldn't have approved of were faring very well. They didn't go to hell at all. They went straight into the aristocracy and I saw their photos in *The Tatler* – married with three kids. When I was 14 I got the job as leading lady in a review called *Jingles* — and earning £25 a week — by telling the producer I was 18 because I most certainly wouldn't have got it otherwise. It wasn't easy being 14, having to pretend you were 18. At that time I hadn't really learned a single fact about life. As a child prodigy I had been pampered, dressed and undressed, laid down to rest, my hair was put up and put down, and I had been shielded by a chaperone. Now I was in a show and expected to take care of myself. When the cast told dirty stories, I didn't understand them, but howled my head off with laughter to show them that I did. To convince them, I laughed louder than anybody else and they all thought I must have the dirtiest mind in the business. Imagine them giving you your 21st birthday party on the stage when, in fact, you were really only 17. Try and work that lot out! I tried to tell them on my 21st — which was my 17th — that I was four years younger, and they all said, 'Come off it, you're having us on!' I had to pretend I knew it all and I didn't know a thing."

Poor Hylda, she had a lost childhood because she had to grow up too soon, and there is no doubt that this really did have a very strong bearing on her behaviour in later life. She was only 14 when she made the transition from child artist to leading lady, going on tour with her father as principal comedian. When she came skipping in at the front door of the family home with her frilly skirts right up to her bottom and little ankle strap shoes and socks, she was Hilda (with an 'i') Baker, the child wonder, dancing and singing her way through life. And she went out of the back door (now Hylda with a 'y'), as a glamourous leading lady with skirts down to her ankles. Her mother said at the time, "Going through the house, from the front door to the back door, she changed from a child into a woman." From that day forward she was a show lady, but this time she was on her own. In only four years she had gone from singing the innocent numbers, to songs like the following, entitled *I'm Going To Do It!* — and she was still but a child:

'I'm gonna do it if I like it.
'And I like it!
'I'm going to hold hands if I like it.
'And I like it!
'I hate to make mother and dad so terribly sad.
'But there are times when it's good to be bad!
'I'm going to snuggle if I like it.
'And I like it!
'A little squeezing is so pleasing when you're blue.
'And since the boy next door first realised
'I'd let him kiss me — well!
'You'd be surprised!
'I'm gonna do it if I like it,
'And I DO!'

Her career and her life in showbusiness were mapped out and the long hard struggle to the top had begun. The innocent young girl of 15, full of enthusiasm and bursting with talent was on her way.

CHAPTER TWO

Out Through the Back Door

LIFE went on for the Baker family, Ethel (now 14), Harold junior (12), Mildred (ten), Brenda (eight), Eric (four), and Sydney (2). They were now living in Eagle Street in Bolton, Hylda was away on tour a good deal of the time, and Harold senior too, the other children being 'farmed out' at times with various relatives. In the late 1920s they moved into a bigger house, in a much 'posher' area, 45 Bromwich Street, Bolton. It had no garden, the front door just opened on to the street, but it had a big sitting room and three bedrooms, and Margaret kept insisting that they were not going to stay there, it was just temporary. A block of flats now stands on the site.

All the children were required to help around the house, although their mother still employed the cleaning lady and the washer-woman. Margaret never did any housework herself, but the youngsters had to do their share. The girls were always given a room to 'bottom', as it was called, because although it was always understood that the cleaner would make the beds under Margaret's supervision and do the vegetables etc, she would only be called upon to 'bottom' on rare occasions. The beds alone were quite a task as they were all flock mattresses and feather which had to be 'turned' regularly. Margaret supervised the children in these tasks and the girls were also taught to become excellent cooks. Hylda, though, was usually unaware of the work going on at home and saw little of the efforts of the others, because she was away on tour and everything would be made shipshape for her return. Her mother would then see to it that she personally washed all Hylda's clothes by hand and did her own form of dry cleaning by using petrol.

Hylda used to send money home when she was working, as times were quite hard, but when she came home she made good use of her time and in fact learnt to drive in 1921, when she was still only 16. It was around 1922 that her father insisted that the girls learn a trade and have something to fall back on. And saving for the future was of the greatest importance. In case the entertainment profession proved to be a failure as a career, Hylda decided to learn tailoring, left the stage and went to work in a Bolton clothes factory which made 'off the peg' dresses. She said, "They gave me the job of picking up pins dropped on the floor by the tailors. I stood it for just 15 minutes, and then went to see the manager and demanded to be given a proper job. I was then put on the buttonhole machine!" So you see, she knew her own mind even then, and was certainly not afraid to speak out.

It was in this factory that she learnt to 'mouth' words, and emphasise them in a form of lip reading because the noise from the machines was so intense that the girls overcame the problem of carrying on a conversation by learning to do this. It was Hylda's observation of this strange form of communication, one which she found so amusing, which was to become the foundation of her act on stage in later years, when trying to communicate with her 'friend', the tall, gangly, and very silent Cynthia.

Her experience of the rag trade, however, was short-lived and she had gone from earning £25 a week on stage, to just 25s a week. She stayed for only six months. The lure of the footlights was too great. Every time she passed a poster for a show at a local theatre, she just knew she had to return to show business. She yearned for it and it was what she really wanted to do. Learning a trade was sensible, but the stage was her life, she just had to go back into it, and so 'off on the road' she went once more.

Life for Hylda, aged 17 now, was hard work but being away on tour was exhilarating and at times she could be quite adventurous. She once rode the Wall of Death at a fun fair in Newcastle because she wanted to experience the thrill and excitement of speed. She said afterwards, "The sensation was tremendous. I felt as though I had been decapitated!"

In those days of the big variety theatres, popular artists found themselves booked far in advance. The first time she played Manchester she was booked at the end of the week to appear there again the following year, and while still in her early teens she was often booked up 12 months ahead! Her first appearance in London was at the Hippodrome, Poplar, in 1923.

When she wasn't working she would come home to Bolton and live the relatively normal life of any teenager just after the First World War. She had not a few admirers, too, the very first one, important one, when she was 17, was Joe Atkinson, a tall, very handsome young man. Margaret Baker thought he was wonderful and she gave him every encouragement. He would call at the house when Hylda was home, and they used to play and sing together at the piano, for although he was an engineer, he really was a very good pianist. When Hylda was away he used to come round to the house and entertain Margaret and the children. In fact Mildred, who was now 12, and Brenda who was ten, thought he was absolutely wonderful and fell in love with him too. He eventually asked Hylda to marry him, she agreed and he bought her the most beautiful diamond ring. Sadly, on one train journey, she took it off to wash her hands, left it on the wash basin, and went back to her carriage. When she realised and went back to look for it, it had gone. This is but a small example of the problems she would have with her memory in later years. We can all be forgetful but unfortunately in poor Hylda's case it was to manifest itself in such a way as to cause great distress to her and to those around her.

The work situation was not too good for Joe, so he decided to emigrate to America, and in fact did very well out there. Not surprisingly, Hylda met someone else while he was away, a tall handsome violinist called Theo Goldstein. She fell for him in a big way and wrote to Joe telling him it was all over between them. He dropped everything and was soon on a steamer en route for England to see what had happened. When she told him, he was so upset he cried on Margaret's shoulders, but eventually, when he saw there was no hope, he went back to America. Hylda is really not to be blamed for this, as she was still only a teenager and, after all, what could Joe expect when he decided to go so far away. Theo, meanwhile, being an Orthodox Jew and very religious, made it clear to Hylda that marriage would be out of the question, so finally this romance petered out too. The next object of her affections was a handsome Frenchman called Tony Guzzi. All of this was to pale into insignificance, however, as just around the corner, the Baker family were to experience a disaster that was to change their lives — and was to haunt Hylda for ever.

In 1924, father was touring and one of the scenes was the 'get the ghost', where large sandbags are dropped from above the stage and the joke is that every time they drop they just miss hitting the person underneath. The idiotic management had put iron stage weights in these, to make them heavier and stop them swaying about as they were wont to do. During one performance, one of the bags dropped too far and Harold was directly underneath. His head was split open, there was blood pouring everywhere, panic set in and some extraordinarily stupid person decided that to stop the flow it would be a good idea to use liquid plaster, which was spread all over the wound and deep into the cut. Not surprisingly, Harold senior became seriously ill with blood poisoning, but the blow had also caused his mind to be affected and he never worked again. Compensation was unheard of in those days and there was no recompense for negligence by an employer.

Hylda's father began to suffer terrible headaches and eventually his personality would suddenly change. He would be so very charming and then, without warning, a little thing would turn him. On one occasion someone mentioned Three Castles cigarettes and he said venomously, "Oh yes. I should have three castles, I should have more than three castles, but I've been done out of it. It was the will you know, it was the will". When he was 21, he had been due to receive some money which had been left in trust from his father's estate, but it wasn't as much as he had expected, and through the years that disappointment had magnified within him.

On another occasion he said, "Craven A cigarettes? Don't talk to me about that. It means that I am craven, I'm a coward. I don't like Craven A. Don't bring them near me!" One day he even turned on Margaret, having convinced himself, although there was absolutely no foundation in it, that she had been unfaithful. He became very unpredictable and finally he was admitted to Whittingham Hospital at Goosnargh, near Preston. This was the man who was such a caring and loving person before the accident. What a tragedy for him and for those he loved, and who also loved him dearly.

Harold Baker spent the rest of his life in this hospital. He came out occasionally, but not often, as he was diagnosed as having 'acute melancholia', the dictionary definition of this being 'a mental state characterised by depression and irrational fears'; the medical definition, though, is schizophrenia, which is a progressive deterioration of the personality, a withdrawal from reality, and the sufferer experiences hallucinations and emotional instability. Nowadays there is help for this condition, but in 1924 they merely put you into a mental institution, called an asylum, which, sadly, is what happened to poor Harold. The family were devastated, and what was worse was that in those days there was a great stigma attached to those institutions, which nowadays are classed as psychotherapy units.

Margaret would visit him once a month and it really was quite a journey for her because she had to go from Bolton to Preston, Preston to Goosnargh, and then a very long walk from the bus up to the reception area. Mildred's daughter Ann remembers clearly that for a long time she didn't even know she had a grandfather because everyone kept it very quiet. It was not until the early 1950s, when he had been there for about 26 years, that Ann discovered the truth and insisted that she wanted to go and see him. She met her grandmother in Preston. There follows her own description of her impressions of that place:

"I remember going up the drive with these enormous buildings, bars against the windows and Magwitch-like characters peering out. This was quite frightening for a child. We went to the reception area where we queued to give his number (they gave the inmates numbers instead of their names), and then we went to the big hall, which had tables and chairs all around it, with the keepers selling teas at one end. Nanny had brought a picnic, we sat at this table and they brought the men up in bunches, several at a time. They all had very short hair, almost, but not quite, shaved, and were all wearing a sort of uniform of overalls and a jacket.

"I can remember seeing this particular group of men coming up, and there was this little man with a big nose and big ears. I stood up and said, 'That's my grandad!' I had only ever seen one photograph of him, playing an ugly sister in the hospital pantomime with one of the wardens playing the other, but I knew it was him. I used to go quite often with Nanny after that and when I was older I started going on my own. I would get boyfriends to take me. Once he was ill in bed, so instead of going into the hall we were taken down this massive corridor, through several doors, each one being locked after us until we got to this huge ward with a great number of beds. He was lying in bed in one corner and he was writing, so I said, 'What are you writing Grandad?' He said he was writing a pantomime, *Little Miss Muffet*, so I said, 'Who's going to be in it?' and he said, 'Well, our Hylda of course.' I asked who was to play Little Miss Muffet, to which he replied once again, 'Our Hylda.' I asked, 'Well, can I be in it?' He looked at me and said, 'You can be Little Miss Muffet's friend.' Then my boyfriend said, 'What about me?' Grandad looked at him, thought about it and said, 'Mmmm, well you can be the back of the donkey!'" Harold Baker was still a comedian, he hadn't lost his touch.

Harold actually escaped once, when he'd been in there for 30 odd years. He was on parole, just walked out and was missing for quite some time until he was finally found — outside Buckingham Palace! How he got there goodness knows but it was quite something to make his way there from Preston. On her next visit, Margaret was most amused when he said to her, "Eeh, Mag, it were different!"

However, back in 1924, at the time of his accident, Hylda was touring in a revue called *Frills And Flounces*, as a soubrette. There is little documentation of this except that it was produced by a man named Charlie Beanland. She continued to work as much as she could because she had to send money home to help support the family, there being little state welfare available in those days. In 1926, she starred in a very long-running show called *The Golden West*, when she was joined by her sister Ethel who understudied her. They toured together all over the country and it was quite a spectacular show with a Wild West theme. The children in the audience were given replica guns to take home. What an outcry there would be today!

Back home, the youngest child, Syd, was still very young and Margaret would not be able to go out to work, so Hylda tried to get as many bookings as she could, especially those that paid well. She said, "My father had always told me of the value of advertising, so I used to advertise in the theatrical newspaper *The Stage* every week, and I did get jobs through it." This was also a turning point for her because she decided that she must turn more to 'low' comedy as it was called then, as that was where the money was, and she concentrated less on the glamorous type of work. One disappointment for her, though, came when she was offered the lead in a show at the London Hippodrome, which she had to turn down as she was under contract to someone else. "But I knew stardom would happen ONE day," she said, "That was always my aim. What is the point of being in a business if you don't go for the top?"

One fact that certainly must not be ignored is that all of the Baker children who were old enough to work did so, it wasn't just Hylda who contributed. In fact every week they had to give up all their wages, every penny, and only young Harold was allowed to keep something — just £1 out of the money he earned with his dance band. Mildred earned a man's wage in a shirt-making factory. In fact she was an amazing worker and whenever the factory was on piece work she always earned the most, so much so that her fellow workers sometimes threatened to go on strike because of it!

In 1927 Hylda met the man she would eventually marry. It was during *The Golden West* tour and Ethel was celebrating her 21st birthday. Ethel had an admirer who was very much in love with her and who bought her a car, had a birthday cake made by the same confectioner who made them for Princess Mary, and arranged a huge party for her. They were appearing in Bury and he paid for the Floral Hall to be kept open after the show, with a free bar for everyone which he also paid for. It was quite a do! Mildred and young Harold were told to get all the local boys who were good dancers to come, as it was felt that the chorus girls would need good dancing partners. I doubt if anyone did much dancing, though, as the local lads got blind drunk, there were bodies everywhere and much revelry.

One of the locals (who went on to be a mayor of Bolton!) had some artificial teeth and for some reason this one chorus girl, who had taken a fancy to him, was walking about, her arms wrapped around him, clutching his teeth in her handkerchief. A young chap called Ben Pearson was in charge of the bar and was there because he was very good friends with Ethel's admirer. He came from Doncaster and his father was a licensed victualler. Ben took one look at Hylda and thought, "That's the girl for me!" They began to see each other regularly, but

Margaret was none too happy; she didn't like Ben at all and made it quite clear. In the light of what happened later, her instincts were proved correct. Normally Hylda could do no wrong in her mother's eyes, she worshipped her, but in this instance she was very much against her.

Two years later, in 1929, when Hylda was approaching her 24th birthday, she was on tour and appeared in Ben's home town of Doncaster, so he arranged that they would get married by special licence in the register office. He was only 27 but had already been married once and divorced. It was Saturday 12 January, a very cold, snowy day, and after the short ceremony Hylda had to go straight to the theatre to do two shows. The curtain came down at the end of the evening and the management kept Hylda waiting for some time while they sorted out her pay packet. Ben soon got fed up of waiting for his new wife and decided to return to their digs, leaving poor Hylda to walk home alone, late at night through the snow. What a wedding night! She had always said that if she ever married, she would never take her wedding ring off, but that very night she did — she threw it at him! The family were not told of their plans to get married and the first they knew of it — indeed, the only message they got — was a telegram from Hylda to her mother saying, 'I can't send you as much money now because I'm married.' That obviously upset her mother a good deal.

She toured throughout 1929, in a musical comedy revue called *Lucky In Love*, which title was rather ironic to say the least! Harold Walden (catchphrase, "But only me knows why!") was top of the bill with Hylda fourth. One particular date for this was 24 December 1929 at the Sunderland Empire.

Hylda's married life became very difficult and bad luck would strike again. She was keen to have children and no doubt felt that this would help the marriage to survive as well, but it was not to be, for she suffered a miscarriage. She was at her mother's house, 45 Bromwich Street, and everybody was out except Brenda, who was the youngest. The baby really was not much more than a few inches long but perfectly formed and Hylda insisted that it be put on one side in case the doctor wanted to see it. Poor Brenda was so shocked that she was physically sick and it took her a long time to get over it. Eventually Mildred came home and took charge, and then their mother arrived and everything was sorted out. Fifty years later, when relating the incident to a friend, Hylda described her baby as, "A thing, it was an awful thing." With this knowledge, one can truly understand how much it meant to Hylda in later life when she was so desperate to adopt a child.

Once she had recovered she went back on stage, working very hard to earn money, but disaster struck once more when she suffered her first ectopic pregnancy, which is the abnormal development of a fertilised egg, usually within a Fallopian tube. It came to light when she suddenly dropped unconscious on stage in the middle of her act. The management immediately asked if there was 'a doctor in the house', one was found and he came to see Hylda backstage in her dressing room. As she regained consciousness she was bleeding very badly, he was bending over her and she suddenly said, "Go away you. Get away from me. You've been drinking, you're drunk!" That poor man, he was out for the evening, off duty and enjoying himself!

Hylda was taken to hospital in Leeds where they operated. In those days it was a very dangerous thing to have an ectopic pregnancy. Ben was very thoughtful at that time, bringing her masses of chocolates and flowers. He also bought chocolates for the nurses and whisky for the doctors, indeed he could not have been more attentive. But when Hylda came to look in her handbag, where she kept a considerable amount of cash, it was empty. It was her money he had been spending. Ben had no work, so there was nothing for it but for Hylda to stay in work to keep them solvent. She was still only 25 years old and the chief breadwinner.

In the summer of 1930 she was in a show called *La Reve Parisienne*, playing theatres such as The Hippodrome, Birkenhead (4 August 1930) in which, at that time, she played the full glamour girl. The show was full of beautiful costumes, jewels and scenery to match, with a grand staircase sweeping down, and one imagines they were trying to emulate the Busby Barclay films of the time. Hylda did eventually decide, however, that she would give up the theatre and try every effort to make the marriage work. She decided to start up an advertising agency, selling advertising space for businesses, but Ben did not do so well at it and it was Hylda (again) who went out doing the selling and she finished up making the business work by herself. She was doing quite well at it but realised that she could earn more if she went back to the theatre. They had also moved back to Bolton, off Chorley New Road, which was very much the upmarket, residential part of the town, when much later it happened again, the final blow, another ectopic pregnancy!

She was in the kitchen of the house doing the vegetables when she passed out and fell on to the floor. When she came to, she realised she was in the kitchen and needed to get help, so she crawled to the back door and out into the garden, calling for help as best she could. Luckily the next-door neighbour was there and called an ambulance, and she was taken to Townley's Hospital in Farnworth. It is amazing, after all she had been through, and considering her huge sense of loss, that she was the life and soul of the ward, cracking jokes all the time, especially when the family visited her. She told exaggerated stories of the goings on in the hospital and had them all in fits, even though she really was very ill and had also been told that now she would never be able to have children.

This again is a very clear example of how Hylda hid her inner feelings from everyone, and how she would suffer in silence for what she felt most deeply about, always joking about the things that were hurting most. Those in later life who accused her of not being silent when things went wrong would never understand that on a professional level it was a different story, for work was another matter and was nothing to do with the private feelings deep in her soul. Margaret Baker, who as we are aware was no admirer of her son-in-law, was quite scathing about Ben at this time, but not lacking in humour. She said, "It's him. She shouldn't be married to him. It's his fault she can't have children. He can't do it straight so he must have a twisted thing!"

In 1932, Hylda and Ben went to live in Wallasey, near Harrison Drive beach, choosing this location because Ben was a keen swimmer. One day her sister Brenda came to visit and they had a picnic on the beach. It was quite a rough day and the wind was whipping its way across the sands. Ben wanted to go for a swim and tried to get Hylda to go too, but she refused, saying it was too cold. He was very annoyed and went off into the water on his own, but the crowning point of the whole day was that sand had got into the sandwiches. Of course, it could not have been avoided but he lost his temper completely which indicates his unreasonable nature.

At one time Hylda actually 'bought' Ben a show because he was always thinking that it was something he could do, as so many people over the decades have thought, although it is easier said than done. There is no record of what the show was called because apparently the Baker family never discussed it at home. Ben ran the show and sadly it ran down. It wasn't a very good show anyway, but he didn't have the experience to make it work, so it went on what was then called 'the common wealth'. This means that when a company isn't making any money, the company agree to share the takings from each venue, and the theatre gets its cut first. A company is very much on its last legs when this happens and finally the show went down. Hylda's money had been wasted but, worse still, Ben ran off with the girl who had been the leading lady and that was the end of Hylda as far as he was concerned. She was devastated.

Eventually, however, they did get back together again and everything was straightened out. He was her husband, after all, and that meant a great deal to Hylda in those days. It was most important to her. Ben got a job with the Greenwoods Tea Company in Bolton, quite a good job too, and this seemed the answer to all their problems. He did not like work, although he liked to live well and joined both the best golf club in Bolton and the air club. Not long after Hylda came out of hospital after the final ectopic operation, she told her mother that she must get back to work at once because all her husband's earnings were going straight into his pocket and they had gone through nearly everything she had saved. They were poor. Years later she said, "Marriage? It didn't take very well. He wasn't in show business. I gave it up for him, then when he said, 'They've forgotten about you now,' I went ahead and showed him they hadn't!"

She took a job for less money than she would normally command, just to get her foot back in the door. The first work she obtained was appearing in Preston, but one morning there was a set-to at home. Ben was still in bed and Hylda suggested it was time he went to work. In temper he turned on her and said, "Don't you talk to me. I'll decide when I'm going to work!" With that he took the side of the bed and tipped her on to the floor. There and then she made up her mind that she just could not stay there any longer. After the performance that night at Preston there was a party because it was the end of the run. Afterwards, Hylda went to her mother's house because she was afraid there would be another row if she went home. At 2am, the household was woken by a loud clanging on the doorbell. It was Hylda's husband. Words were exchanged and Margaret said she had put Hylda to bed because she had been to a party and was afraid to go home as it was late. Then Hylda came down and Ben asked her why she was so late. She lied and told him that a tyre on her car had blown. He said, "Oh did it? Well, I've just been round to the garage and there's been no blow out, the tyres are perfect. Come and settle this at home.". He tried to pull her through the door but Margaret pulled her back. He then made his final mistake, telling Margaret, "Go on, get back in that kitchen where you belong!" That did it. She replied, "Yes, and Hylda is staying in this house where SHE belongs!" She did and never went back. That was the end of her marriage; it had lasted only four years.

One would think that the Baker family had suffered enough bad luck to last them a lifetime, but yet another tragedy was to darken their life. Eric, of whom there has been a very brief mention, was the second youngest, in his late teens, and Hylda did not really see much of him because she was very much into making herself a star, her mother making the whole family 'kow-tow' to her when she was home between touring engagements. Eric had fallen in love with a girl called Teresa and they had been going out together for some time but broke up, which depressed him enormously. He was so very down; he was so keen on her and felt that there was no one else for him. It affected him so much that he had to take time off from his job. Sadly, the family did not realise the full extent of what was happening to him.

One evening, Mildred and her husband-to-be were in the sitting room when Eric kept coming in and out. He'd chat for a while, then disappear again. Eventually, Mildred said goodbye to Frank, her intended, and went up to bed. Not long afterwards, Eric came into her room saying, "Eh, Mil, have you got a fag?" She gave him one and he left the room singing *For All We Know We May Never Meet Again* — and they didn't. The next morning when Syd went downstairs and into the kitchen, he found him dead. Eric had gassed himself. It was yet another cross for the family to bear and the only reason it is mentioned here is in tribute to that poor young teenager who felt that life had nothing more to offer him.

In 1933, the family moved to 83 Manchester Road, Bolton, then 5 Henry Street; not long after that it was to 198 Blackburn Road, and then 169 Tonge Moor Road. Hylda continued to tour the country in variety, playing dates like the South London Palace (week commencing 3 July 1933). Christmas of that year saw her back on home ground at the Grand Theatre, Bolton, in *Cinderella*, playing Ugly Sister Arabella, with Tom Hulme as her 'sister' Camellia. As traditionally the 'sisters' were always played by men, this no doubt would be quite innovative for the day. Looking at the photograph of this in this book, it is interesting to note that she wears practically the same costume that she wore in *Lucky In Love* four years previously. In July 1935 she was billed at the Lewisham Hippodrome as Hilda Baker (with an 'i', not a 'y', but this was undoubtedly a mistake, as the poster for the Bolton pantomime had a 'y'.). The caption under her name for Lewisham read, 'I Wonder How They Know?' It could be that she was very close to inventing her final catchphrase, although it no doubt came from one of her songs which was *I Wonder How They Know I Come From Wigan*. Top of the bill were G.H.Elliott, 'The Original Chocolate Coloured Coon', and the famous Tommy Handley 'in his latest sketch *Radio Revels*'. She progressed onwards and upwards, in 1936 appearing in variety at the Chiswick Empire, and that same year saw her doing summer season at The Coliseum, Douglas, Isle Of Man, in a show entitled *Round And Round*. The review in *The Stage* of 30 July 1936 went thus:

'Presented by Tom Arnold, it is well up to the standard set year after year by the late Julian Wylie. It is tuneful, spectacular, generously laden with humour, and the talent of principals and other artists is of a high order. George Lacy, a well-established Douglas favourite, is mainly responsible for the comedy side of the show, and his versatility enables him to play many roles in first-class style. Hylda Baker, the Lancashire comedienne, is a big success in novel songs and witty patter.'

December 1936 and she was appearing in Tom Arnold's *Sleeping Beauty* at the Nottingham Theatre Royal. The cast included Billy Danvers, Hugh Rene, Ernest Lester, 'whimsical little Hylda Baker as Trixie, maid to Princess Beauty', Helene Cooney and Eleanor Fayre. The review in *The Stage* pantomime number said of Hylda: 'The wine cellar scene is full of comedy, including the humorous song *I Wonder How They Know*, sung with excellent effect by Hylda Baker'.

In 1937 she carried on touring the variety circuit, including the Bolton Lido, where she was second on the bill to Bebe Daniels, second on the bill to Wilson

Hallett at the Ramsgate Palace (week commencing 29 November), second billing to Reco and May at The Grand Theatre, Clapham Junction (week commencing 6 December), and third billing to Jasper Maskelyne and the Valerio Brothers at the Aston Hippodrome (week commencing 20 December). One point of interest here is that Betty Driver (of *Coronation Street* fame) was also on the bill, but most important is that Hylda's billing was, 'Hylda Baker and Steve'.

This was to be an important time in Hylda's life. She had met Steve, who was a tall, handsome, streetwise East Ender, and fallen in love. She worked out a comedy act, with him playing her stooge. Hylda would be doing her act on the stage and suddenly Steve would come through the audience as the theatre manager, pretending to sell cigarettes etc, on a tray. He interfered with her performance, it became very much a double act and there was banter between them from the auditorium to the stage. The not-so-friendly banter carried itself into their off-stage lives too, for this relationship proved to be a very passionate affair. While they were on tour together, he would do everything for her, doing the band calls and driving them to each venue. He was to be the first of the great loves of her life. She was extremely fond of him, but was afraid to make another mistake. Steve said he wanted to marry her and pestered her about it all the time. Hylda did feel a great sense of guilt over the fact they were not married, because in those days it was a real sin to 'live together', but having had such an awful time with her husband she was adamant. However, Steve was also rather keen to be billed alongside her for the act, and wanted them to continue to be called 'Hylda Baker And Steve', but she would have none of this.

Just a few weeks after the Aston Hippodrome, when they were playing the Stratford Empire in *Variety Show Boat*, she dropped his name from her billing. Heading the list were Leslie Hutchinson ('Hutch') and Billy Bennett, with Hylda down at sixth. *The Performer* review of the show (6 January 1938) said of her:

'A popular comedienne is Hylda Baker, who sings, dances and exchanges scathing remarks with her assistant, who is endeavouring to sell black puddings, "faggots" and the like to the audience. Her lapses from Mayfair to broad Lancashire cause particular mirth.'

In this show 'Hutch' used to sing the number *That Old Feeling*, and then Billy Bennett would come on and sing a parody on it:

'My wife's like the rest, she's lost that old feeling.
Whatever I suggest she gets a cold feeling.
She goes to the pictures when she wants a thrill.
When Robert Taylor's on the screen she can't sit still.
While she's hot and bothered with that old squirming
I go to the pub around the next turning.

There's a pretty barmaid there who's my new sweetheart
So that old feeling has got a fresh start!'

Some time later Hylda would use this parody in her own act, but changed it slightly to fit the female being dissatisfied with her husband!

They played the Hippodrome Portsmouth (week commencing 10 January) with the same show, then a variety tour which included the Lyceum Sheffield and the Hackney Empire (week commencing 27 June 1938), where she was fifth billing to Ivor Moreton and Dave Kay, Dave and Joe O'Gorman, Dick Henderson and Jennie Gregson and her Dressmakers. The review in *The Performer* of 30 June indicates that Steve is still the 'mystery man':

'In the comedy direction, Hylda Baker is seen in both solo efforts and with her partner (unnamed), who "feeds" from the auditorium.'

Then it was the Wood Green Empire (week commencing 11 July), and Chelsea Palace (week commencing 18 July), top billing going to John Longden and Company and Nellie Wallace, with Hylda fourth.

There were understandably many heated arguments between Hylda and Steve over this lack of his name being recognised. One such quarrel resulted in her falling face-first through the french window of the bungalow where they were staying. Steve was horrified and sent for a doctor — Hylda always carried those scars — and he was so sorry and full of remorse that she didn't leave him. Another time they rowed and she cut up all his suits, so he cut up all her evening clothes in retaliation. He did, however, often buy her lovely presents: once it was a diamond wrist watch, of which Hylda said to her sister, "Yes it's lovely. I wonder who owned it first!" It truly was high passion, but as with all these stormy relationships, it finally burned out. Steve did look her up, 30 years later when she was living in London at the height of her fame. He came to see her as he was on his way to a football match. She made him a meal, he sat in the chair and went to sleep, got up, went to the match, came back and wanted another meal! This was the last she saw of him.

Hylda worked with a succession of top show business personalities over the years, and she had built up quite a name for herself in the provinces, but the real stardom for which she craved was still a long way off.

By the end of 1938, Hylda had come a long way from that back door in Bolton, but it was her ability to be focussed with the contained energy of a volcano that was her greatest attribute. When she was down, she always came back up with a joke. This was the woman, she was a show woman first and foremost, and despite the knocks she would always come back fighting. Alas, into the ring would come many a heavyweight who would try to push her back against the ropes.

CHAPTER THREE

Through The Back Yard

THE RELATIVE success with which Hylda met enabled her to broaden her horizons somewhat and around 1939 she decided to set up her own shows. She saw others doing it, performers who often had less experience in the professional world than Hylda herself. After all, hadn't she now been on the boards touring for some 24 years and learnt a lot along the way? She was ready for this change in direction, and had saved enough money to buy scenery and props. No one had ever taught her about the business side of putting on shows, though, or indeed how to produce them, so she had to learn the hard way. Not only this but she would not really be prepared for the attitude of certain members of the male fraternity within the profession, who considered women to be a lesser species and considered themselves to be the dominant ones where producing shows was concerned. Hylda was a woman in what then was very much a man's world, but what those men never took into account was her dogged determination to succeed in that world against all the odds. In fact, sometimes it seems that she became even more of a fighter when she was up against strong opposition than when things were going smoothly.

When she was set up and 'on the road' we have to bear in mind that the theatres she would have played were a mixture of what they called No 2 and No 3 theatres.

The No 1 theatres were the top-notch places, but usually Hylda would be playing the No 3s and some of the No 2s, and generally speaking the former were, to coin a phrase, the real dumps. The facilities backstage would be pretty rough with fairly basic heating in winter — if indeed there was any at all — and conditions were not much better on stage. Imagine, also, that she had to organise the transport of the set to and from each venue, which meant loading it all on to a truck. It was then taken to the railway station, unloaded and re-loaded on to the train, transported to the next town and the whole exhausting procedure would begin again. She would be responsible for absolutely everything, and even if she wasn't she would, more often than not, take charge anyway because she was determined to be the complete perfectionist and highly professional.

The Second World War began in 1939 and the following year Hylda saw the chance to give the public shows that were dominated by females. She starred in a production called *Meet The Girls (The Boys Have Left Behind)*, which was presented by Craven Productions Ltd by arrangement with John D.Roberton. It was billed as 'The first all-women show featuring the original and only crazy gangstress Hylda Baker — 101 per cent pure ...a feminine attack on the black-out blues.' Artists appearing went under such wonderful names as Violet Victoria ('Violently Versatile'), Levanda ('The Wonder Of The Age'), Daisy Dalton and her Rhythm Girls Band, Del Strong ('Just Crazy'), Gladys Church ('The Whistling Songstress') and The Mabs Newnham Clevettes ('Grace! Glamour! Talent!'). The complete show boasted 'Thirty Unattached Females'. Considering the aforementioned superstition regarding whistling, one wonders how poor Gladys Church got any practice for her act, as she certainly wouldn't have been allowed to do it in earshot of any of the dressing rooms!

By this time Hylda had moved to a flat in London's Mornington Crescent district, for she realised that London was where she must base herself in order to get noticed and make contacts. Between 1943 and 1945 she produced another all-girl show called *The Girls They Left Behind*, which title no doubt had been sparked off by the show featuring the whistling Gladys. The title of the show was then changed, as there were men in the cast now, to *Wild Women And Whoopee!*, and was advertised as 'Hylda Baker, Britain's Greatest Comicess, presents her 1943 all-laughter revue'. It featured Renee Dymott, who Hylda used a great deal and who was not only a contortionist but also played the uke. After extensive touring the final date for this show was Feldman's in Blackpool (week commencing 15 January 1945) and Hylda's next appearance was at the City Varieties Theatre, Leeds (week commencing 29 January), where she had top billing as 'Hylda Baker and full supporting company'.

She was once asked for her most vivid wartime memory and replied, "It was about half past ten at night, we were playing Clapham with my own show and there was a terrific air-raid going on outside. We came to the end of the show, but it was impossible to go out, we had to stay in the theatre because the raid was so great. We carried on performing and we finished up at about 4am. We'd played the show three times over and still made the audience laugh. We were still in a terrible state of nerves, but there was such exhilaration that we were still there, with all that bombing! It went quiet, then everyone started to sing all the cheerful songs. That's one of my happiest memories, if you can say happy, of the war."

Then she was back on tour with *The Girls They Left Behind*, billing it as her '1945 Victory Revue. Beautiful girls! Lovely girls! Modern comedy laughs all the way! Latest dances! Pretty scenery! Sweet singing! Enchanting music!' It was an extensive tour with one of the dates being the Woolwich Empire (9 April) and another coming one week after the end of the war, at the Theatre Royal, Loughborough (week commencing 14 May). The cast comprised Gloria Winston ('She'll amaze you'), Molly Braithwaite ('Aiding and abetting'), Yvonne ('Lovely to look at'), Eve Hughes ('Grace and charm'), Zona and Zita ('Will entertain'), Grace Hartington ('Queen of song'), Carol Gray ('Sweetness and allure') and The Three Diacoffs ('Speedway riders').

In June of that year, *The Performer* magazine lists Hylda in a show, presumably with the same wartime theme, called *Joys For The Boys*, one date of which was a week at the Grand Theatre, Brighton (week commencing 4 June). This, no doubt, was a celebration of the fact that the war had ended only four weeks earlier

The Girls They Left Behind continued to tour, taking in The Grand at Luton, Grimsby, Cheltenham, Aldershot, Eastbourne, the Theatre Royal in Blyth, the Grand at Chesterfield, Bedford, Wakefield, Bath, and Southport's Garrick Theatre. In the show was a very young girl called Winona Oliver, who now lives in California. She recalls, "What a remarkable comedienne! She could say it all with her expressions, and her eyes. She came to life over the footlights. I believe that's when her soul was born. Hylda Baker was very good to me. The show consisted of wartime themes, ration books, blackouts, vaudeville acts and sketches. I worked with her in all the sketches, and she kind of took me under her wing. I was very young and the things she taught me I still cherish to this day."

In the show, Hylda once more showed her determination to be 'different', for she did a sketch dressed as a man, in a Spanish flamenco routine, looking rather elegant. Winona, who did this sketch with her, clearly remembers one incident. "I will never forget the big sequinned flower I had sewn on my skirt between shows. I had no idea the stem of the flower hung down between my legs, I just thought it would give colour to my Spanish costume. As I was waiting to go on with Hylda, she stood on the opposite side of the stage, dressed as a man, in a big sombrero and black moustache. She waved her hand to me and pointed. I didn't understand what on earth she was trying to tell me, nothing passed her, she noticed everything. Extremely naive and unaware of the flower's stem and where it hung, I went on, we did some patter together sitting at a table. When I stood up, she looked at me, and then down at the flower, her eyes sparkling mischievously. She looked right out at the audience, wiggled her moustache, and said something that brought the house down.

"In the scene we did a dance together where she swung me up over her shoulders, I slide down her back on to the floor, twist around and knock her off her feet with my legs. After we came off, I was held by two large brown eyes as she said, 'Winona, you put flowers in the damndest places, but keep it there!' So I did. She gave me a box of Cadbury's chocolates. It was my privilege to share the stage with this remarkable woman. She did her own act just before the end of the show, her head haloed against the theatre lights. She was at her best then, playing to her audience, she had an electrifying effect on them. That's how I will always remember her. To me she was kind and good."

There was a sketch in this show where a group of women were complaining about buying clothing and the fact they had to give up so many ration stamps for them. Hylda came on wearing saucepan lids over her chest, saying she wasn't going to give any of her bloody ration coupons for them, she would rather see them swing first! There was one scene entitled 'Six Eves Without Leaves', and most of the songs were with a wartime theme such as *I'll Be Seeing You* and *White Cliffs Of Dover*. The costumes were certainly most lavish, bearing in mind it was wartime, and Hylda must have spent a good deal of capital in order to get such quality.

Then there was the barracks, where all the women were in uniform. Winona, playing one of higher rank, inspected the line up of five women and Hylda. She says, "I was to pick one to take a parachute and jump from a plane. She had joined up carrying Mrs Murphy's washing, and did not know where to put it. Much nonsense was done here, she was hilarious. She did her best to hide her big bag of washing from me, it got passed down the line and then back to her again, she couldn't get rid of it! Not in time to make the jump, which I had decided she would take. In this skit she used to try to dry me up, but she never could. She went offstage, then there was the sound of a plane taking off. I stood looking out of the window. 'There she goes, higher and higher,' I said, giving the countdown, whereupon the lights went down to a purple haze. 'She's jumped'. Suddenly there is the sound effect of a crash and a bang. I find the parachute on stage and hold it up. Someone shouts, 'She jumped with Mrs Murphy's washing.' Blackout."

Always on the alert for new ideas, Hylda did something extremely innovative just after the war, which was that she produced a show entitled *Meet The Men And Me*, but this time it was an all-male revue, except for Hylda, of course. There was also a 'muscle man' contest within the show and at the time she said, "God'll strike me down," probably because the cast was comprised totally of female impersonators. She also dressed as a man for this, smartly and elegantly dressed, suited and sporting a trilby hat. It was very brave for its day and one wonders if she was trying to copy Greta Garbo or Marlene Dietrich as she was always very proud of that particular photograph (which is reproduced in this book). She so wanted to be the glamorous leading lady and although she had been successful as a soubrette in the past, and fate had decreed that she should concentrate on the comedic side of her skills, one gets the feeling that she always knew that making people laugh was to be her forte. In fact, in one part of her act later on she would send up one of her idols by calling her Marlene Dirt Track!

After the Second World War, Hylda's very first big success in the world of producing was with a show called *Bearskins And Blushes*, a mainly all-women 'nude' revue, ('with Six Parisien Models, Eight Blushing Beauties, Renee Dymott, Jack le White and Pauline Simone'). The girls were dressed as Guardsmen and the show was such a hit that it ended up running into three editions over three and a half years. All of this goes to prove that Hylda's business acumen was very sharp, and not only that but she wrote the scripts for her shows and the sketches, often composed the music, did all the bookings, engaged the artists, paid the wages, designed the sets, sorted the technical requirements, performed in them, and once even conducted the orchestra when the conductor didn't turn up!

There is one tale of a conductor who could not read music, which really does sound almost ludicrous, but apparently he used to come into Hylda's dressing room and hum the tunes to her, she did the same and said later, "By golly, could he wield that stick!" Apparently he ended up in a famous musical doing very well for himself too.

She always managed everything herself, putting into practice the old adage, 'If you want something doing, do it yourself', but very often the reason for this was that certain unscrupulous theatre managers would try to cheat a visiting company, and in particular probably felt that, as she was a woman, she would be 'easy meat'. Often they would try to fiddle the box office returns, by re-selling tickets that had already been taken at the door into the auditorium, and pocket the money themselves as there would be no record of the sale. In fact the way she discovered this was happening was quite a stroke of luck, because she happened to be appearing near her home town. She enlisted the help of her brother for the front of house duties as he was nearby, and he caught them red handed. He was standing there in the theatre foyer when they did it right in front of him. She had been trusting to begin with, but they cheated her and she learned the hard way. On many occasions the takings were stolen out of her handbag, but this was usually due to the fact that she stuffed the money into her bag and, being forgetful even in those days, would leave it somewhere. She was actually a very generous woman, but once she learnt her lesson, then in business no one could put one over on her and she was suspicious from day one. She got the reputation of being a very difficult woman, which she carried with her until her death, but surely in the light of what it must have been like for her at this time, is it at all surprising?

Hylda also toured extensively on the variety circuit, to such theatres as the Queen's, Poplar (second on the bill to Leon Cortez and Doreen Harris) in September 1945; and in January 1946 she topped the bill at The Royal, Stratford (London), and the City Varieties, Leeds. In February, down to second billing, she went at the King's Palace, Preston (topping were Harry Mooney and Victor King), and the following week she was sixth billing at the Lewisham Hippodrome (above were Troise and his Mandoliers, Jackie Hunter, Dick Henderson, and the Three Astaires). To give the reader an idea of the varied programme, it is worth mentioning that also on this bill were Locarno's Pigeons and Dogs, and the Ringle Brothers and Rene ('Fun In A Restaurant'). She then spent most of 1946 touring in variety, many of the theatres being the somewhat better class No 2s, the F.J. Butterworth circuit, such as the Kilburn Empire (15 April), Bristol Empire (20 May) and the Palace, Burnley (27 May). The show for these three dates was entitled *Wot! No Men!* and was produced by Leicester Square Productions.

One interesting point to note in the tours was that in April at the Kilburn Empire, Hylda was second billing to Bartlett and Massey, but on 10 June of the same year, at the Woolwich Empire, she was top of the bill and they were fourth, with Alan Melville and Kardoma ('Fills The Stage With Flags') fifth and sixth. However, bottom of the bill in April were Gloria Gay and her Band, but only four months later, on 21 October, they topped the bill at the Bedford, Camden Town, with Hylda only second! The review of the latter production does show that Hylda was definitely making her mark, even though her billing was somewhat erratic:

'It is a well mixed programme with Gloria Gaye and her Girls Band topping ...Hylda Baker makes three appearances and on each occasion (two of which she is assisted) the laughter almost reached the hysterical stage.'

Pantomime that winter (1946-47) was at the Bedford, Camden Town, and was advertised as Frank Pope's *Cinderella* (in association with Hylda Baker). It was a tough one, though, as the shows were three times daily.

She did a considerable amount radio around this time, such as *Variety Bandbox* and many others. No doubt she would remember the days when the Hulme Hippodrome in Manchester was adjoining the BBC Playhouse — they were back to back — where many northern shows were recorded, such as *Variety Fanfare*, and the heating used to run between the two theatres. It is a fond memory of all who worked there that if there was an ice show on next door, the radio theatre would be icy cold and the Northern Dance Orchestra would be sitting there playing in mittens, overcoats and scarves — but if there was a strip show on in the Hippodrome, they would be down to a pair of shorts!

Hylda's love life, too, had its ups and downs during the 1940s, and one particular partner who was with her in the Mornington Crescent flat caused her not a little heartache. She bought him a window cleaning business, and he would get on with this while she was away on tour, but on one occasion when she returned unexpectedly, he had another woman living there! However, it was in 1946 that she met the handsome, dashing Charles Martin (later to be well known as Tex Martin). One person who knew him said, "Oh yes, he was a damned good looking man!". Life began again for Hylda and this relationship was to last for many years.

Touring continued throughout 1947, and by 1948 she was back at the City Varieties Theatre, Leeds (week commencing 19 January), the third week of a four-week season. Top of the bill, though, was the famous Phyllis Dixey, ('The Country's Premier Nude Posing Star'), second was the popular BBC pianist Kay Cavendish ('Kitten on the Keys') and Hylda was third, but very last on that bill was a young unknown called Harry Secombe!

Other notable dates in 1948 were the Tivoli, Hull (2 February) where the was bill headed by the Five Smith Brothers; Wolverhampton Hippodrome (a No 1 Moss Empire venue) with Reg 'Confidentially' Dixon; Empire, Nottingham (1 March). The bill for this makes very interesting reading as to the 'order of merit'. It read: Betty Kaye's Pekes, Donald Peers, Tony Walsh, Reginald Dixon, Hylda Baker, Syd and Max Harrison and Wilson Kepple and Betty! The very next week she was at yet another Moss Empire venue with Billy Reid and Dorothy Squires, and week commencing 15 March played the Empire, Middlesbrough, where the top of the bill was the famous Ivy Benson And Her All Girls Band. Hylda was moving onwards at a steady pace.

Many years later, regarding her vast touring experience, somebody asked her what were the most exciting towns she had performed in, and as usual her reply was shrewd and professional: "Every town is a challenge, and every audience you have to adjust to. You can always learn. That's show business!"

Halfway through 1948 the directory entry in *The Performer* magazine was amended to 'Hylda Baker, New Star Comedienne and Own Show *Bearskins And Blushes*'. She was now well and truly on the road with her own production, playing dates such as the Eden, Bishop Auckland (24 May), Empire, Gateshead (14 June),

King's Palace, Preston (21 June), Salford Hippodrome (28 June), Theatre Royal, Ashton (5 July), Queen's Park Hippodrome, Manchester (12 July), Theatre Royal, Middlesbrough (2 August), Theatre Royal, Castleford (16 August), Hippodrome, Darlington (6 September), Grand, Byker, Newcastle (13 September), Hippodrome, Aldershot (20 September), Empire, Woolwich (27 September), Empire, Tonypandy (18 October), Feldman's, Blackpool (25 October) and the Regent, Rotherham (29 November).

The tour was not without incident and one of the girls desperately needed the work but unfortunately found that she was pregnant. She was getting quite large and was sometimes a bit under the weather, so much so that in one town they played, the theatre manager insisted she go to the doctor. Eventually, she managed to persuade one of the other dancers, who was a good friend, to go in her place and thus received a clean bill of health! However, she still had to go on stage with the other dancers to pose under the Union Jack and as the intro played for their entrance, apparently the audience caught sight of her huge belly long before she herself appeared! When they played the Queen's, Poplar, there were no digs for the dancers to be found anywhere. Wages were small and they couldn't afford hotels, but a solution was eventually found — the local undertaker let them sleep on the slabs in his mortuary!

That's one in the eye for anyone who complains about the state of accommodation on tour nowadays.

Hylda had a female stooge at this time called Mary Radclyffe, who played a rather prim and proper character, and Hylda devised a catchphrase of, "She can take it," whenever she referred to her, and the tag line would always be, "You've got a lot to learn". The banter would start with Mary talking about having done an hour's overtime, throwing it back and forth to Hylda, who ignored most of it, and then she'd finally turn in an exasperated way to Mary and say, "Well, have you ever done four hours overtime?". "No," says Mary, to which Hylda replies, "Oh, you've got a lot to learn". Mary also worked for a time as the secretary of Hylda's company when she wasn't performing with her.

Most of the above tour dates were booked by the legendary Mannie Jay, who was responsible for booking many of the No 2 but more especially the No 3 theatres, and consequently the majority of the above would be the No 3s and therefore, bearing in mind the description of these places earlier in this chapter, conditions would have been less than perfect to say the least. What is so interesting about this tour is a couple of really long journeys that must have been made on the Sunday. For instance Newcastle to Aldershot, and Tonypandy to Blackpool! This is just an example of the kind of stamina that was required for a tour of this nature, as they took the bookings whenever they were available with no regard to geography. With her awareness of the powers of advertising, Hylda put the following advert in *The Performer* on 5 August:

'Calling agents and bookers everywhere. Don't miss this enormous attraction. Hylda Baker in her hit review *Bearskins And Blushes*. Playing to terrific business — refer anywhere played… "Last night saw the usual Monday night audience at the Empire TREBLED, and one can only presume that the reason was Hylda Baker, a perfectly good reason. One of the brightest and snappiest shows seen for a long time" (*Oldham Chronicle*). Vacant 4 October on, with exceptions.'

She did manage to stay in one place over Christmas 1948-49 as she was in *Babes In The Wood* at the Hippodrome, Accrington, but come 24 January 1949 she was off on the road again with her show, until April. The tour included the Collins, Islington (7 February), Theatre Royal, Loughborough (14 February), and the Grand, Doncaster (21 February). Week commencing 31 January they played The Grand, Clapham and the following revue appeared in *The Performer* (3 February 1949):

'*Bearskins And Blushes*, presented by Miss Hylda Baker, is a fast moving colourful review in 14 scenes, with plenty of comedy for which Hylda Baker herself, depicting various male characters, is mainly responsible, although her partner Cyril Hatton gave able assistance. Billie Gibson and Bernard Granville are first-class vocalists, while the Musical Stuarts (two girls and a man) put over a musical act with distinction. The Eight Blushing Beauties, who sing and dance well, are frequently on view, while "Carmen" displays her splendid figure in some nude poses. Sonia Leslie is the musical director'.

In April, May and June 1949 Hylda went off on a variety tour, no doubt feeling it was something of a 'rest' after running everything herself. This time she was playing mostly No 1 theatres, and some No 2s. The dates that follow are of note because of the names who headed the bills. The Palace, Huddersfield (headed by Archie Lewis, the ex-Geraldo singer) 18 April, Alhambra, Bradford (Chico Marx of the Marx Brothers) 25 April, Empire Newcastle and Hippodrome, Birmingham (Joe Loss and his Band) 2 and 9 May, and The New, Cardiff (Bryan Michie) 6 June.

However straight after this she was rehearsing the third edition of *Bearskins And Blushes* and toured with it until Christmas, once again playing many No 3s such as the Attercliffe Palace, Bilston Theatre Royal, and Pontypridd Town Hall. Pantomime then followed, this time at the Empire, Oldham, where she was very popular. This time it was *Aladdin* and the bill was Dan Young, Hylda Baker, Four Graham Brothers, Billy Scott Coomber and his singing Crinnelinnets, Edward Victor, and The Java Brothers. After the panto she did a short variety tour, but by April 1950 she was advertising her show with a slight change of title:

Managers and Agents!
NOW IS THE TIME TO BOOK
HYLDA BAKER
In her new show
BEAUTIES IN BEARSKINS
With strong supporting cast
Introducing a new laughter feature
RECORD RENDEZVOUS
Beautiful scenery and dresses, modern comedy.

The tour went on until June, but this time included Tex Martin in the cast list. Hylda had decided to put him into the 'family business' and even gave him third billing, even though the line-up included her stooge, Mary Radclyffe, who had been with her certainly for some years.

The cast was: Hylda Baker, Four de Lisles, Tex Martin, Jeanne Webb, Mdlle Lydia, Bob Roberts, Mary Radclyffe, Six Continental Jewels, Jack Edlin, Danny O'Dare, Six Bearskin Beauties.

Times were hard, and in Tex's own words in an interview many years later he said, "I was a film stunt man — I've broken every bone in my body doing it. I had been travelling about a bit, decided to put my stunts together into a music hall act, and that's how I met Hylda. She saw the act and asked me to join her road show, and eventually I suggested I help in her act as well playing Cynthia. There was no money in the business then. We fell on hard times, we had a little old car and we kept trying. Finally we started on the up and up, I stopped my stunt work and concentrated on my part as Cynthia. I lived that part and learned not to overdo it. I received hundreds of letters from children and old folk who were a bit lonely. I seemed to touch off a spark of sympathy in them. But after we reached the top, that old bond didn't seem to be there, and now I don't regret having given it up. I did it for ten years and now there are other Cynthias." This character of Cynthia is explained more fully in the following chapter, for her creation of this most unlikely silent friend and companion really did become the turning point in Hylda's career.

In November 1950 the directory of artists lists a new address for Hylda. Prior to this she had listed first her contact address of 101 Hampton Road, London E7, then Syd Elgar at Johnnie Riscoe's agency, 5/6 Coventry Street W1. But now it read, 'New address: 291 Plodder Lane, Farnworth, Lancs.' Hylda had obviously decided to go home!

In fact, what had happened was that the Second World War, coupled with running her own shows, had left her in such a tired and nervous state, that she ran down her own curtain and decided to leave the stage. This was the price she had to pay for keeping up the 'show must go on' tradition which had been such tough going through the London blitzes. One Christmas, just after the war, she had three pantomimes going at the same time, she was starring in one and keeping a professional and business eye on the others. The fact that she was also doing spells of variety in between the tours of her own shows, meant that it was hardly surprising, after 11 years of being a producer, that she began to feel the effects. She became ill with stomach trouble in the summer of 1950 and consulted a Harley Street specialist, who diagnosed nervous dyspepsia. In fact she really was quite close to having a nervous breakdown.

There is something else that has to be taken into account too, and that was the fact that until September 1968, all theatrical productions came under the jurisdiction of the Lord Chamberlain, so the sort of show that Hylda was presenting would naturally come under very close scrutiny. The Lord Chamberlain decreed that nude displays were most definitely not allowed to move, and woe betide any that did. Consequently this rule was strictly observed by the theatre managers, and all Hylda's script material also had to be 'vetted'. Posing ladies had been an integral and decorative part of so many reviews of the time, examples of this being Jack Taylor's *King Revel* in 1939 which featured La Nueda — 'The World's Most Beautiful Woman', and Don Ross's *Don't Blush Girls* in 1941, advertising 'Beautiful Jean Morris in her Sensational and Artistic Scena'. Often they would be billed as 'Poses Depicting The Beauty of Womanhood,' and would be announced on stage as 'We now present, in a series of artistic poses ...Psychic in the court of Venus,' and so on. Naturally this would be something else that Hylda had to take care of when writing and putting together the material for her tours. The responsibility for ensuring that she adhered to all the rules was, on top of the other problems of running the shows, a pretty hard task.

In those days a producer was actually called a 'revue proprietor', and let it not be forgotten that she was the first female ever to attempt to do this. Not only that but she was the first female to set up her own tours, write them and also star in them too. There were comediennes in the 1930s and 1940s, but very often they were appendages to the comedian, for example Freddie Bamberger and Pam, Loll Park and Tina Trent, so Hylda was one of the very few solo comediennes. She was a pioneer in her field.

However, she had constantly encountered very tough times on the road as a result and once, in Lincoln, the stage crew refused to put the scenery up just because she was a woman. They would not take orders from her, so in the end she had to do it herself. Like all the other artists of the day she went back and forth, up and down the country like a yo-yo, constantly travelling, living in digs, never being able to settle and basically living out of a suitcase. When she was running her own shows it must have been exhausting because the organisation alone, getting everyone and everything from place to place, was no mean task. The pressures of this kind finally became too much for her. All her working life she had never put down any proper roots, so she decided that she and Tex should settle down. She had under belt 40 years of hard grind that was the world of show business, and there seemed little chance that her dream of stardom and the 'big time' would ever materialise. The fish and chip shop in Plodder Lane, Farnworth, was up for sale, and it had been in the family for 50 years. This was the answer! They decided to take it over, and make a go of it. Tex, who used various guns as part of his act, hung them all round the walls and from then on it became known as 'Tex's Bar' (it is now a Chinese take-away).

Farnworth people who remember Hylda at that time say that she always had a cheery greeting for everyone and it was, "Hello love, how are you?" and so on. Perhaps it was that she was just 'playing a part' in a way, and as was her wont, she threw herself into it with her usual gusto when she began to recover from her illness. They all remember Tex as being the strong silent type, and Hylda always let people think that they were married, although they weren't. Once again she had decided that tying the knot was 'out' as far as she was concerned.

St Gregory's Church in Farnworth, which was in reality a wooden hut, had an operatic and dramatic society, and they also used the hut for their performances. The stage was at one end and the altar at the other. They were saving up to get a new church built and Hylda would always help them with any of their fund-raising events. How ironic it is to recall that her mother, all those years ago when Hylda was a baby, had also worked very hard for them, and yet the priest had refused to christen baby Hylda because her mother hadn't be married in church. Yet Hylda bore no grudge and was apparently very generous with her time, even appearing herself in one of their fund-raising shows.

This spell of normality was pretty short-lived, however, and one gets the feeling that anyone who knew her could have predicted the outcome. The couple did do quite well in the shop, because Hylda would always make a good attempt to succeed at anything she undertook, but as her Auntie Agnes said at the time, "They won't get rich while they're sharing it with his pocket!" Only six months later, Hylda realised that it wasn't the kind of existence for her. She had also recovered her strength by now, and she knew her life would always be the world of show business.

Over Christmas 1950-51, only six months after vowing to give up the theatre, she was booked to appear in the resident pantomime at the Dewsbury Empire which was Richard Stephenson's *Cinderella*, with Reg Bolton, The Melomaniacs,

The Four Graham Bros, Lucille Gaye, Stella Holles, Jacqueline Boyer, June Lynette, Mollie O'Connor, Dave McMurray, Charles Adley and Dawn, Florence Whiteley's 16 Zio Angels, Peggy Glen's 12 Junior Misses, and Gilbert's ponies. This was a very long run and didn't end until 10 March 1951.

It was back to the normal variety touring schedule once more for Hylda throughout 1951, with notable dates being the Palace, Huddersfield (14 May), Empire, Leeds (21 May), Tivoli, Hull (4 June), where she was third billing to the great Jimmy James and Co, the Hulme Hippodrome (11 June), second billing to Lee Lawrence (also in the cast was Paul Raymond 'Man Of Mystery'), the Empire Sheffield (10 September) fourth billing to Arthur Lucan and Kitty McShane, Cavan O'Connor, and Max Bacon (also in the cast were Hackford and Doyle, Les Mathis, Delaire and Eva May Wong), and the Empire, Newcastle (1 October) being third billing to Bob and Alf Pearson and Albert Burdon. The management of the above tour was K & P Productions, who were an old music hall act called Kimberley and Page. Hylda was billed as 'Tiz she. Hilda "101 per cent pure" Baker, that hilarious girl from the Dewsbury pantomime'. It is fairly certain that her name was spelt with an 'i' by mistake, and was no doubt a great annoyance to Hylda. Her patter in the act would usually open with "I am known as the girl who is pure, one hundred and one per cent. I fought for my honour, while almost a gonner, but I can't keep it up all the time!"

She ended 1951 with pantomime at the Theatre Royal, Rochdale. It was a resident season, for Harold G. Robert, playing Dame Dumpling in *Babes In The Wood*. It was advertised as 'The most lavish pantomime ever staged in Rochdale, with 14 scenes, 250 costumes and a magnificent transformation scene'. Harry Marsh played Simple Simon, but he also played Cynthia! Eunice Joyce (now Odins) was one of the chorus dancers in the show and she distinctly remembers Hylda doing the 'drill' routine with a hose pipe between her legs, dressed in a little striped top and shorts, being hysterically funny. The show then went on to the Spa Theatre, Bridlington. Eunice and the other girls were all invited, one by one, to Hylda's dressing room on the last night, whereupon she shook hands with each one and gave them a bar of chocolate. Bearing in mind that sweet rationing after the war was much in evidence, this was a rare treat. Eunice ate the chocolate, but kept the wrapper for years and years afterwards as a souvenir.

The single variety act which she performed without Cynthia is remembered by her very first fan, Gerry Lammyman, who says that he will always remember seeing her coming on stage in a long green raincoat which was down to her ankles, a red scarf on her head and plimsolls on her feet, which visually was hysterical and never failed to bring the house down. There would be banter such as, "These things belong to our Alice. She's a good sport our Alice, well all the lads in our street say so!" And so on. Then she would sing one of her famous songs of the time which was *I Wonder How They Know I Come From Wigan*, then she would dash off, discard the coat etc, and come back on to the piano in a smart outfit, this change being completed in seconds. She would play the piano and sing, in particular, one of her favourite songs, *A Good Man Is Hard To Find*. At some point in the act she would always break off and have some exchange with the orchestra leader and would mouth at him silently, indicating that they would get together in an intimate way after the show. As yet she hadn't fully developed her act with the famous Cynthia; she was an embryo, although Hylda had been doing her 'hosepipe' drill routine with a tall man dressed as a woman during a sketch in *Bearskins and Blushes*, and it must have been bubbling up somewhere inside her very astute brain.

Later in life she had the most strong superstition against the colour green, but it obviously wasn't with her at this time as this was definitely the colour of the raincoat she wore for her act. But as she explained many years later in an interview, she did in fact collapse while on stage when wearing green, so no doubt her later vehemence towards the colour was yet to manifest itself.

It has been very necessary to list throughout this chapter all Hylda's very varied tours in order to indicate just what sort of background she had, both in doing her own shows and working for others. She really was a very seasoned professional, there wasn't much she didn't know or hadn't experienced at some time, but her 'lucky break' had still eluded her. She was a bookable 'name' on the circuits, but the top place on the bill was rare. Perhaps by taking over the shop, that short diversion from the path fate had mapped out, had not been altogether wasted, for just as 30 years before when she learnt to copy the girls in the clothing factory which was to form the basis of her comedy act with Cynthia, there is no doubt that her observations of the people who frequented the fish and chip shop would be stored up for use in the future whenever she needed new material.

She once explained that she devised her particular brand of comedy from pure observation. "I am a student of life. I take ordinary conversation and use it in a way that makes it appear outlandish, ludicrous and extremely funny, but the truth is that every housewife speaks one of my comedy lines every time she goes out to do the family shopping. There is nothing pretentious or phoney about it, because I watch the people around me and draw the material from everyday life".

Her 'retirement' had been short-lived, her health and her confidence were restored, she was back in theatrical harness, for she was a born entertainer, and from now on it would be stardom or bust! An obvious remark here would be to say that she exploited the latter in her shows, in order to get the former, but the road still had many a twist and turn that was to lead her to it.

CHAPTER FOUR

Through the Alley and Into the Street

THE something that was within Hylda, and within her blood, made her decide to press on, so they sold the fish and chip shop and began planning stage activities for 1952. She decided once again to set up another show, which she called *Frills With Thrills*, which was along the same lines as her previous *Bearskins And Blushes* in that it featured nudity; she was astute enough to know that if she gave the public the spectacle they wanted, she could also do comedy sketches in between using her own skills, and thereby presenting something for the masses. However, there is no doubt that she was determined to use the show as a vehicle for herself, and why not, as she was taking all the risks?

In fact her 1952 tour of *Frills With Thrills* was advertised thus: 'Hylda Baker presents her Scintillating Revue. Laughs all the way! Beautiful girls! It's thrilling! It's spectacular! Modern comedy! Gorgeous scenery!' She billed herself, at the top, of course, as 'The Radio And Television Star and Britain's Only Comicess' and the show opened at the Theatre Royal Bilston on 3 March, and played the Attercliffe

Palace, Aldershot Hippodrome, Southend Regal, Woolwich Empire, Walham Green Granville, Islington Collins, New Brighton Tivoli, Salford Hippodrome, Preston Palace, Stockport Royal etc.

Television was in its infancy but Hylda knew how to market herself, and who can blame her for the odd little white lie? Absolutely everybody did it then, it was a cut-throat business, and Hylda was by no means unknown in the provinces. Having been touring for so long, she was a bookable name and had built a considerable following. The tour went on until September 1952, and also on the bill were Alexandria and Davina ('Novelty Hat Juggling'), Bryan Lloyd ('Nature Boy'), Dale Warren ('A Voice And A Guitar'), Tex Martin ('Sensation Of The Century'), Pearl Moss's 8 Fascinating Frillies, The Lovely Katrina ('Film Stunt Girl'), and last but by no means least: 'First Time In England Syd Baker in the "Muscle Dance" with The Continental Models. The temple of God depicting the ritual of the sacrifice of youth to the God of Gold, introducing the Muscle Dance for the first time in England.'

Hylda's youngest brother, Syd, had been made redundant at work and she decided to employ him in her show, for he had a marvellous skill which was muscle control, very much like that which Tony Holland did later with the *Wheels* cha-cha. In fact it was Syd who suggested to him that he use that particular tune for the act. However, Syd's own act was very spectacular, especially because he was covered from head to foot in gold paint. Hylda had designed all the sets for the show and this scene had huge pillars, the curtains parted, then the scene would begin with him standing like a statue on a plinth, in the middle of a garden setting surrounded by gold and red drapes.

The chorus girls began to dance to the tune *Temptation,* there were two nudes who posed at the foot of the pillars — as we know they were not allowed to move — and as the dance ended and they sank to the floor, the gold statue would come to life. First the arms came out, and gradually the muscles began to move individually in time to the music, the biceps, then the triceps, then gradually the pectoral muscles in the chest would begin to move, then the stomach and legs. This would then be repeated with the back muscles facing the audience, and all in time to the music until the big finish which was a little bit of flash powder in the plinth and an electrically operated flash and the curtains closed. It really was most spectacular and highly skilled.

How sad that Hylda didn't appear to appreciate her brother's efforts and was blinded instead by her obsession with Tex, because she actually paid him three times as much as she paid Syd. Tex was getting his board and lodging, too, as he was living with her, and Syd did a great deal in the show as well as his own act. Indeed, he was hardly ever off the stage. He had to find and pay for his own accommodation, too, but no doubt she probably considered that as he was 'family' she was entitled to get away with it!

She used to open her own spot with *You're Nobody's Sweetheart Now* and followed this with songs such as *Down Yonder* and *Why Worry,* accompanying herself on the accordion and dressed in a crinoline. Then later on there would be the sketches like 'Montgunnery's Mansions', which was a skit on the fact that during the war Montgomery stated that the army should provide better billets for the soldiers. The set was plush and there was the part of a maid. Hylda once again dressed as a man, playing the part of a soldier, with her brother Syd playing the other soldier, the sergeant was played by Brian Lloyd, the captain by Dale Warren, and she did the most amazing bit of business where she would walk a tightrope on the edge of a pair of trousers to get a good crease and then promptly threw them away. Ironically she used the Mary Radclyffe catchphrase for this sketch as the tag was, "Oh you've got a lot to learn," which goes to prove that when something worked Hylda would always keep it and use it again.

Later there would be the scene entitled 'Making A Film' and was described as having 'Three changes of scenery and dresses showing you what really happens on a film set from Broadway to Mexico.' It began outside 'The Diamond Horseshoe Saloon', with Hylda once more playing a man, this time in a Davy Crockett style hat and her brother Syd playing 'The Smart Fella'. Then the scenery was raised to reveal the bar inside and Hylda would rush off to do a quick change. She would then return a little later as a Diamond Lil character, with all the glamour, wearing yet again a green dress (!) and on her head a real stuffed Bird of Paradise with another as a corsage, and one number she sang was *I Didn't Know The Gun Was Loaded.* There were ghostriders and barmen, and Tex played 'Fingers' Orson, a gun slinger with all the trappings and a Stetson hat. (However, he had a rather strong Cockney accent and unfortunately had never quite mastered the American.) There was a mock fight in this scene, with a considerable amount of chair smashing, and it is of interest here to note that the famous boxer 'Gentleman' Jim Lewis was employed to set it. This shows Hylda's professional integrity as she was always taught that 'if you want to show the best, you have to have the best'. One of her favourite sayings at the time was, "I'm not going to work for a packet of fags, or a packet of Woodbines." One performance of the show, at the Grand Theatre, Doncaster, is recalled by Bill Owen (not Compo, but his namesake), who was in the audience. As her Diamond Lil character, Hylda had to fire a pistol in the air to break up the brawl, but being short in the arm, when she fired the blank, the cartridge shot off one of the feathers in her hair. Everyone on stage fell about with laughter and it was apparently very evident that she was none too pleased.

The main part of Tex's contribution in the show was: 'The World's Most Sensational Act. Tex Martin, the Ace Daredevil Film Stuntman and His Hollywood Lovelies. See Tex shoot a cord from a girl's throat while blindfolded with pads of plasticine and a black bandage and featuring the Spectacle of Undressing A Girl With Bullets. The ONLY Act Of It's Kind In The World! See Katrina, America's most beautiful showgirl, first fully clothed, and then shot by shot, bullet by bullet, being completely unclothed by the ace crackshot, while he rides his super-charged motorcycle at terrific speed, using a .45 six shooter.'

In fact Katrina had a string down her arm, and the 'target' on the bra was a little pin with two rings, so that when she pulled one of the strings the pin came out and the bra dropped. Timing here was essential and often Tex would get it wrong. He'd go to shoot and then delay slightly, the girl would have operated the string — and the gun would go off after the bra had dropped! Instead of 'bang! drop!' it would be 'drop! bang!' One of the girls was a bit of a giggler and whenever this happened she got absolutely hysterical and would begin to shake with laughter. Being quite well endowed, one can imagine this was enjoyed by not only the theatre crews but the audience too!

Towards the end of the tour, they were playing the Empire, Tonypandy, in the Welsh valleys, and when it was discovered that one of Tex's other specialities was shooting at candles to put them out (they were in fact perfectly safe retractable candles), the fire brigade arrived en masse to 'stand by' in case of accidents. What had no doubt happened was that word had got round as to the nature of the show and they were looking for some excuse to be in attendance, so there in the wings, were burly men standing by on guard with hosepipes at the ready.

It was in this revue that Hylda developed the 'Drill Routine' which was mentioned in the previous chapter, billing it in the programme as a sketch entitled 'Girls In The Home Guard', which as we know she had first put into her wartime shows. It was an extremely funny scene where Hylda came on with a hosepipe, which she referred to as a 'squirter', between her legs, calling to the squad to 'thread it through, thread it through', which was rather suggestive but very, very funny. The 'new recruits' were Hylda, the very tall Bryan Lloyd (the latter dressed as a woman — the embryo of Cynthia) and two other girls (who were in fact boomerang jugglers in the show!). They would attempt to line up, but the tall one kept getting it wrong and one of Hylda's famous lines in the sketch was, "I'm able, and she's bodied." This sketch with the tall Cynthia had been bubbling inside her for some years, but it was only now that she perfected it, and it was to be the act that made Hylda Baker a household name. The audience found this drill routine so funny, which indeed it was, that Hylda immediately knew she was 'on to something', and from then on began to develop the idea.

It went like this:

(*Enters with hosepipe*) "Psst! Oh! I've lost the squad. There were about 24 of us when we set off. It's the women's section of the Home Guard. They won't have anybody in this lot, you've got to be something. They don't half ask you a lot of questions. (*Enter Cynthia. Picks up hosepipe, pulls it.*) Cynthia! Stop pulling at it, don't look as if you don't know. Thread it through, thread it throooogh. Well, I don't want it do I? I've been lugging it about all day. Go and get the guns, the guns out of the coppice. She's willing enough but it's just not there. We'd better get on with this practice. We only joined yesterday, we've only had one lesson. We're going to do what we did yesterday. I'll be the sergeant, are you ready? From the right number two, one... it's you you're in the wrong place. What did the sergeant say you were yesterday? The second time he said you are one didn't he? Well why don't you go where number one goes? Eh? She knows because the sergeant told her, and then when he thought she might forget it he wrote it down for her on a bit of paper. What have you done with that bit of paper the sergeant wrote it down on? I'll say no more, I know what she's done with it, she's wrapped her sandwiches in it. It's getting too much for me. I'm at that funny age where you haven't got the same patience have you? Don't stand there like wilting Jezebel. You're in the army now, you're defending your country against the invader, God help us. Look pull yourself together, throw your chest out. (*Business. Throws false bust out.*) When I say throw your chest out, I don't mean throw your chest OUT, I mean throw your chest out! And remember we are the girls of the old brigade. (*March off*)'

She loved the instinctive northern comics, in particular those who were great observers as she was, and one of these was Norman Evans. Years later she did an impression of him on a radio programme, saying; "Oh yes, he was so funny. I loved where he used to say 'OOH that cat, OOOH that cat. Tek it away, it does smell. OOOh, I could taste it in't custard on Sunday!'"

Hylda was a tremendous performer and she had a truly original style. She had a great life force, a great fierceness which manifested itself on stage, and off stage she was fierce too, but only with her tongue, as she found it hard to suffer fools gladly. Often when she cracked the whip, she was merely getting her own back for the way she had been treated in the past. For a woman to stand up and be funny is so much more difficult than for a man, because they have to lose their femininity. She bridged all this because she was wholesome but she was never ever 'blue', and anything of that nature was only implied. There were no women around at that time to match her — she wasn't just an act, she was a show, she did everything and was a law unto herself. She worked as a man in some of those sketches so she could cover the male side of comedy, and was clever enough to know that not only could she do it, but that it would work too, and it was only her who made it funny. How brave that she would come on all glamour, in her crinoline, at the end of a section and sing the famous Johnny Ray number *Cry*, the full tear-jerker, then at the finale she would sing *At The End Of The Day*. Laughter and then tears. It was her philosophy that comedy is very close to tragedy, and that if you have a comedic situation and take it to it's logical conclusion it will, almost always, end in tears.

Hylda had the instinct to know how to punctuate a gag, and found her own style by laughing at her own jokes. Every time she delivered a punch line, she would laugh, sometimes a chortle, sometimes a belly laugh, and she would be known as much for this as for any of her famous catchphrases. Also, she had the knack of still being funny if things went wrong on stage and, apparently, to see her when nothing went right (particularly in the days of running her own shows) was a joy to behold. She had a great attribute, though, and that was that she never appeared to bear a grudge. She had a sort of honesty which people who worked for her found hard to understand, in that she could give you the most enormous dressing down, losing her temper completely, and the next minute it was over, forgotten, and she'd take you for a drink as if nothing had happened.

Great music and great poetry have often been created in times of struggle and adversity. Perhaps this can be said of any art form, and in Hylda's case, the world of comedy. The fact that she came through so much, metaphorically fighting her way through two world wars, often not knowing where the next job was coming from, meeting the opposition from her male counterparts, experiencing a broken marriage when she was only 24 years old, and so on, perhaps contributed to her making the final leap which she had to do, in order to find the magic formula.

Hylda's love of animals was well known to everyone around her, for she had this great need for love which maybe she felt she got only from them and her audiences. She was never really able to give love, except to them because she had to trust people first, and this she found very difficult. From the early 1950s when she acquired the first of her 'little men' (the famous monkeys that so many people have heard about) there would be a succession of stories surrounding them and her dogs, too. For a long time she had a dachshund which toured with her in *Frills With Thrills* and who Tex nicknamed 'Shitsie Mitzi'.

One day in September 1951 she had been working hard in variety, travelling around the country. She was very tired and suffering from nervous headaches and she was driving from the south, where she had been playing The Regal, St Leonards, up to Liverpool when she had a slight collision with an army vehicle. She eventually got there, but was shaking so much and in a state of shock, that she decided to go for a walk. She came across a pet shop and there in the window was this tiny monkey, so she went in. He immediately took a fancy to her and clung to her like a baby. Naturally she couldn't resist this, bought the animal and took it back to her digs with him still holding tightly on to her.

As soon as she was indoors he let go, and instantly she had the fright of her life. He went round and round, up the curtains, then up the wall, swung on the picture frames, swung on the electric light, ran under the sofa, shot up the door, ran along the sideboard and nearly disappeared through the window. When she finally got hold of him, he bit her hands, scratched her face, dug his teeth into her ankle and then disappeared into a cupboard. She put some leather gloves on to handle him, but he liked those even less, bit and scratched them, and finally tore them to shreds. She said, "I never had a headache after that actually and I quite forgot I wasn't well!"

"I only knew monkeys as things you see in zoos. He's a Capuchin monkey from Brazil. There are very few in this country, but I'm told that this breed was the original one that the old organ grinders used to have in the streets. Well, people have dogs, cats, parrots and budgies as pets, so why not a tiny monkey?" One day there was another mishap when she was going to Blackpool on a train. He escaped from his box, skipped under the seats, swung on the luggage rack and once again tried to exit via the window. She threw her beautiful new fur coat over him, it went quiet and all seemed well, but finally he came through the coat, there were bits of fur everywhere because he had eaten his way out! Finally, kindness and patience paid off though. About a year later Hylda was back in Liverpool and gravitated towards the pet shop once more, where lo and behold there was another monkey. What could she do? She bought him as well and called him Co Co.

She treated them like the babies she would love to have had, keeping them warm with their own hot water bottles, feeding them treats and even washing them in scented soap. She travelled them around with her everywhere in a large cage, but more often than not they would be found sitting on it, looking for mischief. One of their favourite games was to empty her handbag for her when she wasn't looking, and they loved to imitate her. They often appeared on stage with her, apparently loved the applause, and once even got their own fan mail! On returning from the theatre she would give them their supper and put them to bed in her room, in their own little beds, and the next morning they would not rise until she did.

Hotels, however, were not so keen on them as Hylda would have liked. She was barred from a top Nottingham hotel which flatly refused to accommodate them. The manager said, "We can't have pets," so Hylda said, "Well then, you can't have me!" and off she went to a guest house where the landlady enthused, "Oh monkeys! We love monkeys, they're good fun." Hylda said at the time, "The hotel people were very stuffy. The monkeys are well behaved, and they probably cause less trouble than a lot of the guests. The same hotel allowed a couple of poodles to stay some time ago which belonged to Eve Boswell. I refuse to be parted from them, they're like children to me. We've stayed in the best hotels in London and the provinces and this is the first time anyone has objected."

Some of Hylda's friends, however, were not quite so enamoured of them as she was but would never dare admit it to her. Apparently one person went to see her in the dressing room after a show and said that it was as if an earthquake had struck, the wallpaper was hanging off, there was half a grapefruit sliding down the wall, nuts all over the floor, one of the monkeys was swinging on the light fitting, there were banana skins everywhere, and it was total chaos. To use one of Hylda's famous Malapropisms, it no doubt looked like the aftermath of a very rowdy wedding 'conception'. Also, the scented soap with which she washed them obviously did no good whatsoever, as monkeys apparently urinate on their fingers to mark their territory. This smell went everywhere with them, and one visitor remembers the rank odour even to this day.

During the autumn of 1952 came the biggest turning point in Hylda's career, and she dealt with it the only way she knew how, by being utterly ruthless! *Frills With Thrills* was still on tour and they were appearing at the Theatre Royal, Stratford East. The famous Grade organisation came to see the show, went backstage to see Hylda and said, "We like you, but we don't want the show." Hylda put the notice up that night and the whole cast were naturally extremely put out as they had been booked for some time in advance, and were now out of work. Who can really blame her, though, because she had doggedly sought her dream of stardom for some 37 years since that day she went on stage professionally at Tunbridge Wells in 1915. Hadn't she now earned and been given that one big chance of advancement? She sold all the props and the scenery of her shows and let someone else do all the worrying. It wouldn't be long before her instincts were proved correct and the realisation of everything she had worked for, cried over, and needed with such a passion, was lurking just around the corner.

The next entry in *The Performer* read thus:

'Hylda Baker. 13 October FREE for variety.'

Sole agent: Burton Brown of Lew and Leslie Grade.'

Over the Christmas of 1952-53 she was in Lew and Leslie Grade's pantomime, playing Widow Twankey in *Aladdin* at The Empire Theatre, Sunderland, and the review confirms that she stole the show:

'Most buoyant personality in the show is Hylda Baker. Her caricature of a gossipy woman drew some of the biggest laughs of the evening.' (*Sunderland Echo*, 30 December 1952).

She did a good deal more radio around this time with shows such as *Northern Music Hall* and from now on she was, thanks to the Grade organisation, also playing the quality theatres, appearing as the top comedy support act on bills headed by American or British singing stars such as Al Martino and Lee Lawrence. The Grades saw to it that she was kept pretty busy, and 1953 saw her make her mark in Jack Taylor's *Latin Quarter,* a Blackpool Hippodrome summer season show which starred Max Bygraves and Winifred Atwell and was advertised as having 'a cast of 100'. Max Bygraves did a sketch with her called 'The Honeymooners', with the pay-off being that he had to try to get her up on to the table which always got a huge laugh. He remembers, "She was a most private person whose greatest love at the time was a monkey! What sticks in my memory is the man who played Cynthia. He never said a word but just stared straight ahead while Hylda told the audience, 'She knows etc…' Yet they were ALWAYS REHEARSING …she could have done it with a lamppost!"

Once again Hylda showed that she was capable of consideration for others and, contrary to some reports, was of a generous nature. Gerry Lammyman says that during this show, when he was in her dressing room, Tex, who was polite, pleasant and genuinely fond of her, would always be friendly and entertain him if Hylda couldn't. Hylda would always make time for Gerry, even when she was doing heavy shows. He says, "I found her warm, friendly and considerate, and the proof is that she always replied to letters and took time for me. She was always concerned for my well being if it was late at night and would say, 'Can we run you home, or get you a taxi? We'll pay for it, don't you worry about it.' I know that although she could probably be awkward and difficult, there was this warm and human side to her, but she was a lonely, vulnerable woman."

It was evident, though, that where Tex was concerned she definitely controlled the purse strings because he always had to ask her for money when they went anywhere and she would dole it out. Poor Tex, with the tattoos on his hands, and the aura of a gangster, he was really a 'kept man'.

At this time Hylda was also planning a new act for Tex, and the idea was that they would build a revue based on him doing a super magician, illusionist routine. They'd seen an American called John Calvert doing one very successfully, so they thought this would be an excellent act for Tex, but it never materialised. Bearing in mind that he often had some difficulty in getting his timing right in *Frills With Thrills*, one can only say that it was probably just as well!

My goodness, though, Hylda made audiences laugh — they literally cried with laughter and they loved her — but at that time there seemed little likelihood of her being able to 'set the Tower alight' in the way she had hoped. She then toured for a short period during the autumn in the Blackpool *Latin Quarter* show, with Tex taking over from Max Bygraves. Hylda was top of the bill, headed, 'Hylda Baker and 24 Girls.' The tour included the Hulme Hippodrome (week commencing 23 November) with Alex Munro and Tommy Willis, and Bill Maynard as second and fourth on the bill. It was around this time that Hylda, still fed up of waiting for the real stardom that had eluded her, hit on a plan which she was determined to carry out. An extremely bizarre, outrageous plan it was, too, and one that only Hylda could ever have thought of trying. She planned to go to America and return as somebody else!

Hylda had always been something of a romantic and her favourite book was *Gone With The Wind.* Ironically, there are many parallels that can be drawn between the dramas in the lives of Scarlett O'Hara and Hylda Baker. This may seem a very strange comparison but the clues are all there because their lives, and also their characters, were somewhat similar. Hylda may have been very aware of this, although there is no proof, except she was so very proud of telling people how much Tex resembled Clark Gable!

Her idea of changing her identity was to be that she would go to America as Hylda Baker, on the Queen Mary, and then possibly even without leaving the ship, she would return all glamorously dolled up as a famous Irish American film star called Katy Sullivan. She planned that she would bring with her some lavish brochures describing her triumphs at the Cotton Club in New York and Radio City Music Hall and so on, and firmly believed that if she did this, the agents in Britain would come rushing for her services and work would roll in. What is so amazing is that she was determined that she could pull it off — she who was so very distinctive, both in looks and in stature, and who was already quite well known by so many people, not only in the profession, but by the public in all those touring venues. This must have been seriously planned because she designed a very tasteful letterheading with her new name, and even had the notepaper printed. It was never used, however, as luckily enough bookings finally came in for her, so 'Operation Sullivan' (as she called it) was never launched.

In 1953 she starred in Jack Taylor's pantomime, *Aladdin* at the Queen's Theatre in Blackpool, and by this time her 'Cynthia' routine was well and truly established. In fact poor Tex had some time ago had to give up his days of being the dashing young blade, give up his motorcycle, hang up his guns, don a frock, wig and women's shoes, shave off his moustache and play Hylda's famous stooge! A far cry from the days when he would ride the motorcycle with three scantily clad girls draped about him. One newspaper article during this Christmas show, while praising him, must have made him feel rather embarrassed at their description of his role. It said, 'Tex Martin, Hylda Baker's slow-witted stooge "Cynthia", was not so slow last night when fire broke out in the theatre.'

What happened was that Tex was on his way upstairs with some props at the end of the show when he smelled something burning, and saw smoke drifting down a corridor from the end dressing room. He heard girls voices coming from the next room and very quickly bundled them out and down the stairs. When Tex pushed open the door he found the room was engulfed with smoke and flames, so he immediately fought the fire with an extinguisher while Hylda called the fire brigade. Then Hylda, plus The Slave Of The Ring, Tex, and two other members of the cast formed a chain and threw buckets of water over the blaze while the theatre manager used the theatre fire hose. In the end they had the blaze under control by the time the fire brigade arrived. There was a considerable amount of damage and the roof of the dressing room was destroyed, as were many costumes. As Hylda was to play the Queen's Theatre many, many times in the future, one wonders if this memory was always with her whenever she was appearing there, and that she would reflect on that pantomime season when she had no idea that in just over a year's time the medium of television would make her a household name, and in only 18 months she would be back at the Queen's once more, starring in the summer show and commanding considerably higher wages.

In 1954 she was on the road again, doing the Empire circuit with stars such as Derek Roy (week commencing 1 February Nottingham) and Phyllis Dixey (week commencing 1 March Edinburgh), and in May *Girls In The Home Guard*, (Hippodromes Birmingham and Manchester, and Empires Middlesbrough, Sheffield and Sunderland) followed by summer season at the Britannia Pier, Great Yarmouth where, incidentally, she threw a birthday party for Mickey the monkey! She commented at the time to her fan Gerry, "Who the hell wants to hibernate in Great Yarmouth for a season?" In the autumn she was on the same bill as Al Martino (Chiswick Empire, week commencing 13 September), Anne Ziegler and Webster Booth (Empire, Dewsbury, week commencing 27 September), Guy Mitchell (Hippodrome, Bristol, week commencing 29 November), but she did top the bill at the Palace Theatre Halifax for week commencing 4 October. The reason for this was that at the No 1 theatres she was supporting big stars of the time, but at the No 2s like the Palace, Halifax, and the Palace, Huddersfield, she would be the main attraction. She yet had to conquer being top billing in the No 1 theatres.

During the above tour Hylda also co-starred with Frankie Vaughan at the Hackney Empire, and he remembers her with great affection:

"I have many fond memories of that very special funny lady. She would be just as funny, I am sure, in today's comedienne presentations. She was what we would call 'funny lady' like Tommy Cooper was a 'funny man'. She was funny off and on the stage, she enjoyed being Hylda Baker and was always slightly over the top, and that's how people loved to see her. My first memory of Hylda was when we co-starred together at the Hackney Empire. That was before I really had any big hit records. Seemingly I was doing what they called a good variety popular singing act. I, of course, took a room at some digs, which I hardly remember, near the theatre in Hackney, and my girlfriend, Stella — who I had rung to ask if she would come down to see our last night because I was enjoying myself so much with Hylda Baker and the variety bill — joined us, but what I failed to tell Stella was what sort of a zany person Hylda was.

"On leaving the theatre on the Saturday night, Hylda swept into my dressing room to wish me well and thank me for a super week. Stella, in all innocence, shook hands with the great Hylda Baker and was admiring her fur wrap around her neck, until the fur moved and Stella gave one yell and realised it was Hylda's pet monkey. Stella hit me forcibly in the chest for not warning her. It was hilarious and so was Hylda. We all fell about and Stella was screaming, and from being an admirer of Hylda she hated her. Hylda never got over that and some years later I had started to make some hit records and was about to star in my own show, my first summer season at the North Pier, Blackpool. I had on my bill the great Jimmy James, Ted Loon and other terrific comedians. When Stella came up, pregnant with our second child, Susan, Hylda threw a party, mainly to greet Stella, with all the stars in Blackpool. After our Saturday night show we all went along to Hylda's house which she had rented for the season and we had the greatest party, during which Hylda related the monkey story to everyone there. Stella will never forget Hylda Baker, and neither will I. She was a great comedienne on and off stage."

What a great testimonial from one who himself is a great pro and much admired. Hylda was always a great judge of character, and no doubt this is why she liked him so much.

However, back in March 1955, Hylda was still soldiering away on the touring circuit, but she had no idea what was in store for her when in that same month she was asked to appear once more at the City Varieties Theatre in Leeds. For some time, there had been a very popular programme on TV called *The Good Old Days,* which was broadcast live from the City Varieties. The joy of it was that the audience would dress up in the clothes of the old music hall days, the men would be in evening dress with wing collars and bow ties, the women in long dresses, colourful plumed hats, and all the trimmings. It really was an occasion to go to one of the shows and be a part of the live recording. Barney Colehan ran this theatre, booking all the acts, and having seen Hylda's act with Cynthia decided to give her a spot. The date he booked her for was 11 March and on the same bill was another 'unknown' called Ken Dodd. He had been in the business for only five months and was 25 years old; she was a veteran, and aged 50, although she claimed to be only 45. She once said, "I must have been the oldest overnight sensation in the history of British showbusiness." Overnight success? All that hard work she'd done from the age of ten, and then nearly half a century later, they notice!

Notice they did, though, and one lady in that audience, Laura Viccars, to this day

42 years on, remembers the only two acts in that show which made her laugh were this tiny woman with the funny walk called Hylda Baker, and Ken Dodd doing the gag about eating a tomato through a tennis racquet. In those days there was only one televsion channel, so Hylda was catapulted to fame overnight, after the years and years of playing those seedy No 3 theatres, followed by the relative success in the No 1s. Both on stage and off, she was the little person battling against all the odds, an expert in drollery, with her foil being the tall, bizarre Cynthia.

Much later she was quoted as saying in an interview, "I knew TV might be a turning point, but when the BBC first asked me to appear in *The Good Old Days* I didn't think I was quite ready. In the theatre and the music hall it's before thousands, but in front of the camera and TV's millions I wanted to do something special. But the ideas wouldn't come. I did 'Cynthia' and the same act that thousands of variety-goers in the north knew, but now I was standing in front of about five million people. Really it didn't seem much different to me from all the preceding 30 years on stage — not, that is, until we were off the air, and people began phoning up. Then there were so many calls for me, and to producer Barney Colehan asking about me, that I had to run away and hide!"

The fairy godmother called TV, had waved her magic wand over the tiny dark-haired fireball, opened the doors and catapulted her to fame, for after that memorable night Hylda's life would change for ever. The very next day people were going round uttering her famous phrase, "She Knows You Know!" and Hylda was on her way out of that dimly-lit alley and into the bright lights. It is sad to note, though, that although stage and live performing were what she knew best and where she had learned her trade, it was television — which was later the cause of many old theatres no longer proving viable and closing, or being turned into bingo halls — that gave her the 'leg up' she had needed.

Hylda had hit the jackpot and it was a success story that warmed the heart and gave hope to all those other struggling performers, no matter what their age. On to the stage came this tiny woman, dressed in an ill-fitting checked suit, old fashioned ankle-strap shoes and an ostrich feather boa, and gossiped to viewers about her friend Cynthia. "Have you seen her?" she said, "She's tall and blonde with aquamarine features," at which point her tall, over 6ft gangling companion with a very pale face and a big floppy hat, wandered on at a snail's pace. "Where are you dashing to, I said where are you dashing tooo... full pelt ...come here I want you." The little one kept nattering on and on, talking about the tall one, asking her questions and getting no reply except a fond stare, and a silent, slow nod of the head. It was the sort of performance she had been giving round the halls for years.

There was something about the act that caught the public It wasn't just the contrast of ebullience and silence, it was the comically loveable character that

Hylda had created, trying to be 'posh' and using all the words incorrectly. Her costume meant that ladies in the audience could identify with her lack of sophistication, coupled with her desire to better herself by flaunting the feather boa with a constant shrugging of the shoulders. All her observations over the years had paid off and she was now about to reap the benefits with her creation of this pair of unlikely friends.

Those studies of the factory girls, the over-the-back-fence gossiping, the people in the queue at the fish and chip shop, the people at the bus stops, they were all stored up and now came pouring out. Hylda never stopped listening, though, and once, after appearing at Halifax, she said, "I went into this cafe between the shows and a woman came and sat at my table and said out of the blue, 'Do you know, I've been in that house 13 years and I never knew about the drains. I've had to ask someone I didn't know. I've never had to ask anybody in my life before. I've lost me independence. Eeh, it made me feel quite ill'."

Just one month after that memorable television performance she was playing dates such as the Plaza, West Bromwich, Leeds and Newcastle Empires, and the Palace Theatre, Huddersfield. She toured in a huge caravan which she towed herself and would park it as close to the theatre as possible. Whenever she played Blackpool she would park it at Squires Gate holiday camp. Inside were her animals, too, who always travelled with her, and in Huddersfield she would park just down from what is now the Huddersfield Hotel, across the road in the car park of the Southgate public house. It was no ordinary caravan, but a huge proper living wagon, certainly 30ft long. Tex wasn't always with her at this time, so how she manoeuvred that monstrosity one will never know, but suffice it to say that she did. On that particular date in Huddersfield, Tommy Fields (Gracie's brother) topped the bill, and because of her recent success she was billed: 'TV's newest comedy star. Hylda Baker and friend. Up from the country.' Cyril Hatton played Cynthia and he and Carol Hayes were with her in her own 'Pools Winner's' sketch in the first half.

After seeing her performances on many occasions, and now that she had been such a success on *The Good Old Days,* Dick Hurran, a theatrical producer of the day, asked impresario James Brennan for her to be included in their summer show, *Pick Of The Pack,* at the Queen's Theatre Blackpool, alongside Joan Regan and Ken ('I won't take my coat off, I'm not stopping') Platt. Dick Hurran had put on many shows for Jimmy in Blackpool and had also staged several Palladium productions, and put on all the London Follies Bergere shows for Bernard Delfont. He looked at this tiny, quaint woman, and decided that she was very funny. Ironically, Brennan had only just turned down an application from Hylda, asking to appear in that very same show, but on the strength of that TV appearance he changed his mind and hired her.

Hylda was quoted as saying later, "I accepted such a low salary because I had a good place on the bill!" She is also quoted as saying, "I began to realise what had happened to me. People started asking at the box office if this was the Hylda Baker show, and if I was the same Hylda Baker who was on television. I was only a featured artist. Then I did some more TV during the run and realised that millions were seeing me, and I had to decide what to do about this. I took a chance and insisted on top billing. The bookers said, 'Who do you think you are?' and although inside I was thinking the same thing, I had to go on. I decided to stick out for top billing, but told them that if they let me top the bill for one week and I didn't turn out to be the attraction then I wouldn't ask them for any money. They offered me so much a week but I said, 'No. After the first week when we've seen if I'm the attraction, then we'll talk about money. If I'm not — then forget I ever asked.' Well, after the first week, they paid me £100 more for the second week! I knew then that I was destined for stardom." So did the person who reviewed the show: 'I think she's the funniest comedienne since Nellie Wallace.'

After this Hylda was much in demand, touring followed in the autumn and then at Christmas 1955 she did pantomime, *Robinson Crusoe,* playing the Dame, at the Grand Theatre, Wolverhampton. In January 1956 it was reported that Hylda had gone on in this show with an attack of 'flu and the theatre manager, Peter Marwoode, was so grateful that he presented her with a special bouquet of flowers because there would have been no performance due to the fact that she had no understudy. He was no doubt doubly concerned as another star member of the cast had been 'off' for several days suffering from bronchitis, and that person was none other than Jimmy Young! It was also reported that at the first day of rehearsals Hylda had turned up wearing her mother's shoes. The reason for this was that just before coming up to Wolverhampton she had been Christmas shopping in London and had slipped on the edge of a pavement, suffering a torn ligament which resulted in a broken blood vessel. A few days after her 'flu, she developed bronchitis but insisted in going on against doctor's orders. Having spent so long on the journey to fame she had no intention of letting it slip away just when things were beginning to happen for her.

Hylda so shook up the town of Blackpool in that summer of 1955 that Jimmy Brennan was determined to get her again for the following year's summer season of 1956, this time at the South Pier, when in fact he would now find that he had to increase her salary to £450 a week. She was well and truly on her way and was armed with all the valuable business know-how that her years of experience had taught her. Maybe now she really could set the Tower well and truly alight, and cause that Golden Mile to shine far more brightly than it had done for many a year.

CHAPTER FIVE

You Can See the Golden Mile From Here

AFTER the very successful Blackpool summer season Hylda was much in demand for the touring circuit, but this time under very different circumstances. She was a name on everyone's lips and got star billing on a tour of old-time music hall called *Nights at The Alhambra.* In September 1955 it must have been wonderful for her to have been asked to make a personal appearance at the Bolton Co-op, and afterwards to open the society's 'See For Yourself' exhibition at the Co-op Halls, this time returning to her home town as a big star. She went with her mother and Tex, and the throngs of people outside waiting to catch a glimpse of her would have no doubt given her a great thrill, as did the autograph hunters who followed her round as she toured the departments inside the store calling out, "We love your show. Keep it up Hylda!" She was the main story on the front page of the *Bolton Evening News* that day, accompanied by a photograph of her with her mother and surrounded by fans. The caption, however, may not have pleased her quite so much. It read, not as one would expect something along the lines of 'Hylda, The Star, Returns To Her Home

Town' but simply 'Cynthia came too you know.' Not only that but Hylda was always very anxious that Cynthia's identity, plus the fact that 'she' was a in fact man, should be kept secret. We will find out later that the complex relationship with Cynthia, and how she finally tried to lose the image of her stooge, affected her greatly and caused many a upset.

In 1956 she bought herself a house in Green Lane, Bolton, and a big American car. She loved cars, and changed them frequently, but she did drive ones that were rather too big for her. She had to have the pedals extended so she could reach, and many friends of hers have said affectionately that sometimes you really couldn't see her in the car and that at times it was rather as if 'The Invisible Man' was driving. However, she had good reason for these cars, always having her eyes open for the opportunity to steal some publicity. She was right, too, because every time she bought a new 'flash' model she would inform the press and they would come running. "People say I drive cars that are too big for me, but what they've bought me in publicity!" she said. Cars she owned over the years included Jaguars, Rovers and a succession of very big American models, and the majority of them would have her catchphrase, 'She Knows You Know!' emblazoned on the bonnet and down the wings ...how about that for showmanship, and eccentricity?

The contrast between the shabby little character the people saw on stage and the elegant and expensively dressed woman, which was how she presented herself off stage, was vast. She would eat in the best restaurants, had beautiful expensive jewellery, diamond rings, mother of pearl earrings, and a stunning gold ring watch. She bought designer clothes and was almost like a little child in her joy at being able, at last, to indulge herself. She had earned it! She took her mother to Paris and Monte Carlo as she had always promised she would do, in her own words, 'when I came into my own'. Now she could say, "That time has arrived!" When a reporter from *The People* tracked her down in May 1956, she was staying at a luxurious West End hotel and was late for the interview. The reason? She had stayed too long under her private shower, and said with great glee, "I just can't get used to it all. For years I've looked in shop windows and set temptation aside. Now I really have to push myself into believing that I really can afford to buy what I want."

In March 1956 Jimmy Brennan had booked Hylda to appear for a week at the Wigan Hippodrome prior to the Blackpool season, with the supporting acts including Howard Jones and Reggie Arnold from the Joe Loss Orchestra. The manager of the theatre was Leslie Lightfoot, who had been there since October 1955. He was told by Mr Brennan to go to town and really lay out the red carpet for Hylda, providing flowers and drinks for her dressing room, and that she was to have every consideration as to her requirements. The reason for this was that, having decided to ask her to do the Blackpool summer season, he had heard that she was considering an offer to do the summer season at the Garrick Theatre in Southport for George and Alfred Black, which made him more determined to secure her services! It was also arranged that a young singer, who was a protégé of Hylda's called Alwyn Brown and who had begun to travel around with her, was to be given a good spot in the first half of the show. Hylda arrived at the theatre like royalty and was installed in her flower-filled No 1 dressing room.

The musical director, John Hyland, was told that everything had to be perfect for Hylda and for Alwyn, who was placed halfway through the first half as Hylda herself was going to come on and introduce him. This was her first entrance in the show, which is surprising as one would imagine she would want the big build up, when in fact she just came on and said, "I would like to introduce you to Alwyn Brown, a young man with a phenomenal voice and a great future ahead of him."

Hylda's own act went down a storm. It was a terrific success, the Wigan audiences loved her, the total receipts at the box office were more than double the usual figure, and the end of the week saw 'House Full' signs outside the theatre, probably for the first time ever. However, all was not well at the first house on Friday, at least as far as Hylda was concerned, and she demanded that Leslie Light-foot should be summoned to her dressing room immediately the show came down. Apparently she asked for the musical director to be dismissed post haste, as he had 'exposed' himself in the orchestra pit. As it turned out, many musicians, knowing that only the top half of them could be seen by the audience because they were surrounded by the usual red velvet curtain, would wear their dicky bows and dinner jackets, but often would have just everyday trousers on down below.

That particular evening, John Hyland was wearing an ordinary pair of old brown trousers which had seen better days. The Wigan Hippodrome had no licenced bar and at the interval it was customary for members of the orchestra to dash out of the theatre from backstage to the Shakespeare Hotel next door for a quick drink. Naturally there were many occasions when speed was of the essence and drinks frequently got spilled down the trousers. This had happened once too often for the ones that John was sporting, the fabric had weakened and they had split, revealing white underpants which of course were visible to the artists on stage. Hylda was such a staunch professional that she could not accept this and, although to others it may seem a harsh and extreme reaction to insist that he should be sacked, it was the way she had been taught by her father and the only way she knew.

John was told to make himself scarce for the evening show, Leslie promised him he would try his best to calm the situation and save his job, but in the meantime the first violin would take his place. It was to no avail because when

Jimmy Brennan was told what had happened, he was so keen to have Hylda for the summer that he agreed to her request without a second thought. On the Saturday night, after the packed house, Jimmy went backstage to see Hylda and some time later came out of her dressing room, having got her to sign the contract for the summer, so for him it had all been worthwhile.

A few weeks later there was a very bad fire at the theatre and a good deal of damage was done backstage: there was a huge hole in the roof and rain poured in overnight, engulfing the stalls and the circle. The front of house was now ruined, too, and eventually it was sold to a large supermarket company. Jimmy Brennan then asked Leslie to manage the South Pier show as he had got on so well with Hylda at Wigan, and he began to work on the publicity straight away. She was to top the bill with a supporting cast of The Dandy Brothers (an Italian comedy and music act), singer Billy McCormack, soubrette Vicki Emra, Albert and Les Ward, and Renita Kramer, a German novelty act.

In the spring of 1956 she continued to do the touring circuit with artists such as Hollander and Hart ('Vocal Duo'), Nenette Mongadors and Anne ('Continental Juggler'), The Lane Twins, Benson Dulay & Co ('The Sorcerer and his Apprentices'), The Falcons ('Dancers In The Roar'), Rey Overbury & Suzette ('The Musician With the Twinkling Feet'), Renee Dymott ('The Unusual Girl'), Lionel King ('Joker-Ace High'), Frances Duncan ('Glamour In The Air'), and Paul and Peta Page ('With Their Puppets'), playing No.1 theatres such as the Bradford Alhambra. Whenever she could, Hylda would use Renee Dymott, who she had included in her shows in the 1940s. She loved her performance which was a 'spesh act' in which she walked up and down stairs on her hands, being something of an acrobat. Some seven years previously *The Performer* magazine (3 February 1949) reviewed her act thus: 'Renee Dymott scores a big personal success with her very well presented acrobatic contortionistic turn, notable for some difficult twists and turns, most gracefully carried out.' On 9 April 1956, at the Empire Theatre, Newcastle, it is very interesting to note that the bill included one Des O'Connor who was described as a 'New Style Funster'!

Hylda's roots, as has been mentioned before, were important to her, so it is no surprise to learn that the people from her past were too, which is shown by one little incident in Bristol when she was on tour. Alan Burton, a young man from Farnworth who was a member of St Gregory's Opera and Dramatic Society, had got a job in Bristol and saw that Hylda was appearing at the theatre there, so he went to the stage door very early before the show. He was shown to her room, knocked on the door and said, "My name is Alan Burton and I come from Farnworth." Immediately it was, "Come in love, sit down and have a cup of tea." She treated him so well, chatting away all the time, and then suggested that he might like to sit and watch the show from the wings rather than go out front. When he said he'd rather watch from the front, she appeared very disappointed but said that he mustn't go after the show, and that he was to come backstage afterwards, which indeed he did. This incident shows how much the theatre was a part of her history and her life, because for Hylda it would seem natural and much more exciting to watch a performance from the side of the stage. She certainly expected others to consider it a great treat.

Hylda still continued as a revue proprietor, though, and presented for the same week as above (week commencing 9 April 1956) a production called *Davy Crockett Comes To Town* at the Regent, Rotherham. The cast comprised Phil Strickland, Ernie Shannon, Joy Gibbs, Jean Thatcher, Polly Sander and Glynn Croft, and it was just billed as 'Hylda Baker Presents'. She still wanted to keep her hand in with the producing game, but it was short-lived; this was her last production and she became busier than she could cope with at times.

She was also asked to do a radio series which began on 3 July 1956 and was entitled *She Knows You Know!* She wrote a song with the same title (which was later released by Decca, in November 1961) and that now very famous catchphrase was also the title of her summer season show at Blackpool. When she was asked how she had invented this, she said that while doing the act on a radio show some time before, and because she often improvised, she had turned to Cynthia, nodded and said knowingly to the audience, "I know every move she makes. She doesn't make many, but I know them all. I've been a good friend to her, I have, I don't care who hears me say it, I don't, because I know I have, and when you know what you know then you know it don't you ...and SHE knows you know!" It caught on and from then on that was it.

Not only did she have her own radio series, but she starred, along with Billy Daniels, in *Sunday Night At Blackpool* on television, having already appeared in *Sunday Night At The London Palladium*, and all this had happened in just twelve months. All those years ago her grandmother's prophesy 'the film people should have you' was proving that it wasn't such a silly remark after all; she was correct and maybe Hylda was on the right track this time.

Hylda didn't sit back and let it all happen, though. Always the business woman, she was constantly searching for new ways to stay in the public eye and during this 1956 Blackpool season she published in a paper that she was looking for ideas for a new domestic TV comedy series. She would be a widow, Cynthia would be her friend, and there would be a man in the upstairs flat that she was very keen on. She asked for husbands and wives to write to her at the South Pier, relating in detail any funny or sad domestic scenes they had experienced. 'Letters not usable I will return immediately, and those that I keep for possible use I will pay for, from one guinea,' she advertised. The promenaders and holiday makers were also all going around the town wearing paper hats with 'She Knows You Know!' slogans on them. The hats were being sold at the South Pier and the profits from this were going to two local charities. The show was so successful that it broke all records for the theatre with total receipts of £56,000, a fortune in those days.

In August *The Stage* reported, 'Hundreds of fan letters came in after Hylda had been seen in *The Good Old Days.* Strangely enough, reaction to her previous television work had been only moderate. In fact reports of her TV debut from Collin's Music Hall in 1947 made her wonder whether, so far as she was concerned, television could ever prove a profitable medium. She had to wait another eight years for the public to convince her. Blackpool audiences for the summer season are making that point perfectly plain.'

Their review of the show had said, 'Hylda Baker's gossip mongering with her dumb partner with the drooping eyelid and sly nod is extremely funny.'

Hylda arrived at the theatre in style, driving her huge black and yellow Ford Fairlane with her slogan on the bonnet, and as soon as she saw her dressing room she set about making it her own, insisting on a kidney-shaped dressing table, a large stand to accommodate the monkeys' cage, and her own personal telephone, all of which she got because she was now well and truly a star. The management organised a rented house for her in Stanley Road, and the owner agreed to be housekeeper for the season, with one of her most important duties being to bring the two monkeys to the theatre just before the first house, and to collect them after the show and take them home again. Hylda could not bear to be parted from them.

One night Mickey was getting rather agitated in the dressing room, the noise was deafening and Hylda announced to a visitor, "Baby's having tooth problems, nurse him for me there's a good lad." The 'good lad' took hold of the monkey with a good deal of trepidation, whereupon it immediately stopped screeching. Hylda said, "You two little monkeys get on very well together." That 'good lad' who was left holding the baby was none other than Charlie Naughton of the Crazy Gang.

Dick Hurran, who was responsible for Hylda being booked in the first place, directed the show, but right from the very start there was a clash between him and his star. The main problem was that he had a London West End theatre background and upbringing which contrasted greatly with Hylda's forthright northern attitude, one of her favourite sayings being, "I call a spade a spade. You can put a ruffle round it but you can't hide it." She was also not at all familiar with taking orders, because for so long it was she who had issued them. This caused a few problems between them and one morning during rehearsals, Dick had set up his table in the centre aisle, about 15 rows back from the stage. Hylda was sitting in the third or fourth row, when Dick suddenly said, "Hylda, come here please," at which point she exploded and said, "If you want me, you can come down here and see me!" This then erupted into a huge row. When Jimmy Brennan got to hear about it he insisted that Dick Hurran should leave — and that was very much that. Jimmy was not prepared to risk upsetting his star, but how ironic that the person who had fought for Hylda to get the job in the first place was the one who fell by the wayside.

A few days after all this, the current Cynthia was replaced by Ricky Morecambe, who was over 6ft tall and a very experienced artist which really pleased Hylda as this would always be a problem with her 'stooge'. By this time she had had a succession of them, some good, but some unable to understand that to play Cynthia you needed almost as much comedy technique as Hylda herself, because knowing how to time the nods, the looks and the walk were vital. It is very possible that perhaps she, too, was often not really aware how very much she relied on the technique of the men who played the part, because being such a natural comedienne she would consider the 'basics' of timing etc to be relatively easy, although it is maybe somewhat unfair to say this as it would be to insult her intelligence! When she found a good one, though, things always went much more smoothly and peace would generally reign. She and Ricky were a good partnership; he was very easy going which no doubt helped enormously, but he also saw through her tough exterior to the generous woman that she was underneath.

The opening number of the show was the whole company with Hylda in old-time music hall period costume doing the main spot where she sang a medley including *Oh Oh Antonio*. But after a few weeks she cut herself out of this and did just two spots, her Cynthia act and a sketch she had written herself which was always rapturously received, called 'The Pools Winner'. Once again, as she had done so many years ago, she dressed as a man and played the part beautifully, with one of the girls in the show as her 'wife' (she was in fact Leslie Lightfoot's wife) and Ricky Morecambe as the man next door. This no doubt was once again Hylda's determination to show that she could act, so that her career could expand along those lines, and she certainly proved it. It is very interesting to note that in the very first issue of her fan club magazine (October 1956), she says, "When I give my stage act in which I dress as a man, I feel as if I am portraying my father as he was when he used to be on the stage." Such was her admiration of him that she was determined to emulate him.

The fan club magazine was started when a lady called Norma Cartwright was given the chance to visit Hylda backstage at the Birmingham Hippodrome earlier that year, where she asked Hylda for details of her fan club, and was surprised to find there wasn't one. Hylda asked her if she would like to start a club for her and Norma, who incidentally was only 19 years old, says in the first issue, "I nearly fell off my chair with amazement."

Membership was just half a crown (12½p in today's money) and for this they got a personally signed photograph, a year's membership and a badge. In that very first issue of the fan club magazine was a most interesting item which shows how much Hylda's comedy appealed to all ages.

It read, 'Walter Gooch of Middlesbrough is certainly an enterprising member. He has enrolled three new members in the past few weeks, including our youngest member, Miss June Kershaw of Birmingham, aged ten, and her mother.'

The oldest member at that time was Mrs M. Parton of Luton, who was 66 years old. She sent Hylda a cape, skirt and bonnet, all of which were 100 years old, which were invaluable to Hylda in her act, and Mrs Parton is quoted as saying, "I don't want anything in return, but what would please me, would be if you had a necklace or some beads, if they are only from Woolworth. The value doesn't matter, It's just because they will be from you."

Every Saturday night during the Blackpool season, the entire company were treated by Hylda to a champagne and fish and chip party on stage after the show, and once they gave her a wonderful surprise to celebrate the greatest achievement in her career so far. She was given her first booking to star in London's West End, and Ricky and Billy McCormack went to all the trouble of getting a 'prop' crown and then perched her up on a mock throne and had a solemn ceremony in which they crowned her 'The Queen of Blackpool'! This is a wonderful indication of her relationship with fellow members of the company and proof enough to those who, at the time, liked to think otherwise that Hylda was not always difficult but so very often respected and liked by her colleagues. They even presented her with a cake to mark the occasion — and for those who think Hylda had little sentiment, it meant so very much to her that she kept that cake and it is now in the museum in Preston, although 40 years on the smell around it is quite strong!

Her stamina knew no bounds, too, during the summer of 1957 and every opportunity for publicity that presented itself was taken up. For instance, a performer at the North Pier had been taken ill and Hylda agreed to take their place. It was to be some feat, to perform twice a night in two places! After she'd done her spot at the South Pier, she dashed out to a waiting taxi, changed her clothes during the short journey, and there was so little time to spare that a wheelchair was kept waiting at the North Pier gate. By running with her all the way to the theatre at the end of the pier, the person designated to do the pushing ensured that Hylda had enough breath left to leap through the stage door into the wings and on to the stage. For the second show she would go through this all over again, but never complained and was heard to say, "I have more energy than a girl of eighteen." She was in fact 51 years old, but under no circumstances was she going to show it or admit it! Ricky played Cynthia right through the season, but turned down the offer from Hylda to tour in the autumn, so yet another one was found to take his place. By now the Cynthia 'count' had reached approximately seven, but things would get progressively worse and there would be many more to come.

After it closed in Blackpool on 6 October, the show was taken to Manchester's Hulme Hippodrome for three weeks, but one can understand the great elation she felt every day, knowing that she was to make her West End debut as a star — at the top of the bill — in a variety show running for two weeks at the Prince of Wales theatre. She opened in London's West End on 6 November 1956; only 18 months earlier she had begun to think that her dream would never be realised.

It was reported that she was so nervous about the London show that she booked an hotel room just across the street from the stage door. She was described as a homely little woman with twinkling eyes. "I thought it wouldn't be far to carry me if I fainted with fright," she said. As it was such an important milestone in her career, it is important at this point to quote the reviews for the show, which no doubt filled her with glee at the time.

The headlines read, 'They Laugh and She Triumphs', 'Hylda Hits Town', and 'Hylda Approved'.

'A little woman with a load of humour parked beneath her yellow checked costume won West End applause last night.' (*Daily Mirror*).

'A little, funny woman who has toured the halls for 38 years blinked back the tears as applause signalled the fulfilment of her greatest ambition. A bunchy little mill town gossip, she stands on the stage by the side of a vast mute friend, Cynthia. Her task is to interpret, explain and, incidentally, malign. It is expert characterisation rather than riotous clowning.' (*Daily Mail*).

'A roly poly little lady from Lancashire shuffled on to the stage of the Prince of Wales theatre last night, to inject a warm new spark into a variety tradition increasingly strangled by crooners, swooners and disc stars. Her name is Hylda ('She Knows Y'Know') Baker, and her arrival in Town represents a double first. It's middle-aged Miss Baker's top-of-the-bill debut in the West End and it's the first time in many years that a woman has starred in a West End variety production. She is assured of a real welcome to the big time. Her humour — a sort of back-fence gossip routine, is superbly timed.' (*The Star*).

To be the first woman for many years to be top billing was probably even more of an accolade than the reviews, and it is interesting to note that beneath her on that bill were Derek Roy, Morecambe and Wise, Joe Church, and Charlie Cairoli with his brother Paul.

Following this success, she went off on the road again, playing the Empire variety circuit including her home town Bolton (Grand Theatre week commencing 28 January), Chiswick, Sheffield, Nottingham and Sunderland, where in March 1957 she received an injury on stage during her act. This was to be the beginning of a series of incidents which would continue regularly throughout her life and which could be described as sheer bad luck, although the regularity of such occurrences would make it appear to be much more than that. She had her share of good fortune, but equally as much of the opposite, and certainly more of this than most people would experience in their lifetime.

During her act at the Sunderland Empire she was suddenly aware of a sharp, agonising pain in her thigh but thought no more of it until she got back to her dressing room, when she found that she had actually been hit by a ball bearing. How could this have happened? It was from a catapult used by some idiot in the gallery of the theatre, and one or two of the other artists had a similar experience, The result of this was that she had contracted calf muscles and damaged veins. One wonders if this put her in mind of the days of her youth when she was terrified out of her wits at Glasgow with similar missiles being hurled on to the stage.

The variety show she was doing at Sunderland was obviously a very varied programme because she said after the incident, "Thank heaven it didn't hit anybody on a high wire or trapeze. It might have caused their deaths." In April she went home for a few days' rest and, unusually you might think, sought treatment from the Bolton Wanderers FC physiotherapist at Burnden Park. She knew what she was doing, though, and had already had some treatment from Wolverhampton Wanderers' masseur, Dick Bradford. By the end of May she was proved correct; she had recovered and ceased the treatments. "Football trainers recognise the importance of speed in clearing up this type of injury," she said, "I cannot afford to lay up when I have contracts to fulfil."

That same month saw her appearing on ITV's *Val Parnell's Saturday Spectacular,* and the review in *The People* the next day was a glowing one.

'Hylda Baker scored a hit as a very funny sketch actress. It was clear that these sketches owed their funny lines to Eric Sykes, who played with her, but in this guise Miss Baker might well provide ITV with a good comedy series.'

It was in this year, too, that Hylda proved her generosity once more after an awful disaster occurred in her birthplace of Farnworth. At 9.15am one quiet morning in Fylde Street, near Moses Gate, there was a great rumbling from under the ground and the whole street just fell in. Every house was reduced to rubble, they had completely disappeared, and the cause was mining subsidence. The miraculous thing was — and it is hard to believe but absolutely true — that not a single soul was in one of the houses, workers were out working, shoppers out shopping, and all the mothers had gone off with their children for the 'school run'.

The Mayor of Bolton, John Glanville Seddon, had no sooner announced that he was setting up a disaster fund to help the families, than Hylda was on the telephone straight away offering her help. She arranged to get the Grand Theatre in Bolton, rustled up many other well-known artists who gave their services free, and put on a huge show to raise money. Jack Featherstone, whose wife Molly was the mayor's daughter, remembers the concert and the reception afterwards when Hylda was obviously on good form. The law prevented the theatre bar being opened on a Sunday, so a small private reception for just the mayor and the other four guests of honour was held in there, and of course Hylda was invited. She spoke to the mayor about her house in Blackpool and was lightheartedly commenting on the crowds who gathered regularly outside 'gawping' as she put it. She was asked why they did that and, not unnaturally, she retorted sarcastically, "I've no idea." There followed a very long pause and then she said, "Unless it's because I have a name plate on the gate which says, 'Be Soon,' (another very long pause) "...and a flagpole in my lawn." She thoroughly enjoyed sending herself up on that occasion and completely forgot her slight annoyance with the crowds.

Another Cynthia was on the scene around this time, Alan Barnes, who was first employed not only to manage her affairs but also to play 'The Manager' in one of her sketches. She would be playing the piano and he would come on in full evening dress and complain. There followed banter and an altercation, but this particular act wasn't so successful for her; it had originally been the basis of the act with Mary Radclyffe and, although it worked then, it had not stood the test of time and so she eventually got Alan playing Cynthia when she needed one. She really was the master of the ad lib, and on one occasion they were doing the act in front of a cloth on which was painted a lake scene. Hylda turned to the audience and said, "For two pins she'd be in there. Mind you, she can only do the breast stroke, but she can only do it with her hands."

Alan was to experience various none too happy incidents with the monkeys. Once he got back to the dressing room to find that they had delved into the make up and eaten all the sticks of greasepaint, but then 'passed' it some time later, in various colours! As was always the case, Alan was called upon to clean it up. It's also probable that he had to clean up on another occasion. too, when Hylda decided to make him one of her famous meals with the pressure cooker. It blew up and there was steak and kidney pie all over the ceiling!

For the summer of 1957 she was back in Blackpool for the season, this time at the Palace Theatre. The production was called *The Hylda Baker Show* because apparently the previous year they had thought her name didn't carry so much weight, and so used her catchphrase instead, but now with so many TV and radio performances under her belt, her name was well and truly 'there'. Also on the bill were the Tanner Sisters, Sonny Roy ('TV's Funny Boy'), The Impero Brothers ('New Style Acrobats'), Boliana Ivanko Quartet, Janet Gray, Odette Crystal ('The Parisienne Nightingale'), Martin Granger and his Puppets ('A Circus On Strings'), The Joan Davis Ballerinas, and last but not least The George Mitchell Singers. In July she had bought herself an £8,000 house in Blackpool, she had a £3,000 American car and was drawing £600 a week plus a share of the profits. She also got a new pet, an Alsatian puppy called Inga, to keep her company along with the monkeys.

The review in *The Stage* for this 1957 season was glowing:

'Hylda is at the top of her form, with the best of her well-tried material retained and some rollicking new stuff added. Cynthia is as dumb as ever, and Hylda slides into half a dozen character sketches in easy vernacular. Her musical burlesque at the piano is a genuine humdinger. She comes over big, and is at her diverting best. "What's Winifred Atwell got that I haven't?" she asks. Quite a pianist our Hylda! She also teams up with comedian Sonny Roy in a melodrama wrecking routine from opposite stage boxes.'

The house that fame bought Hylda was in Cleveleys, a cream pebble-dashed residence with a high wall all around it. She had always dreamed of having a home by the sea, and it was the last one in the road leading down from the main Blackpool thoroughfare to the promenade, the Golden Mile. There follows a more detailed description of the aforementioned famous flag, for at the front of the house was an enormous sort of flagstaff, like the rigging on a ship, and contrary to popular belief Hylda did not put it there; it was already installed. She did make very good use of this, however, by having her own personal flag designed and which was always flown when she was in residence. She really was living the image of Queen of Blackpool and there are no prizes for guessing what the slogan on her private flag was — 'She Knows Y'Know!' Hylda was beginning to prove herself a real eccentric and was genuinely upset when some neighbours complained and signed a petition to get her flagpole removed as they considered it unsightly. Poor Hylda, all she was doing was showmanship in a town that was made famous by glitz and glitter, illuminations, circuses, fun fairs, booths, side shows, 'kiss-me-quick' hats, donkeys on the beach, candy floss, toffee apples, and fortune tellers. The whole place was one enormous exercise in marketing and publicity, and she knew only too well the value of squeezing every ounce of these out of every opportunity that presented itself.

She did a considerable amount of work to make her home something special, knocking two rooms into one to make the main sitting room, the main feature of

A 'glamour' photograph taken during one of Hylda's wartime reviews.

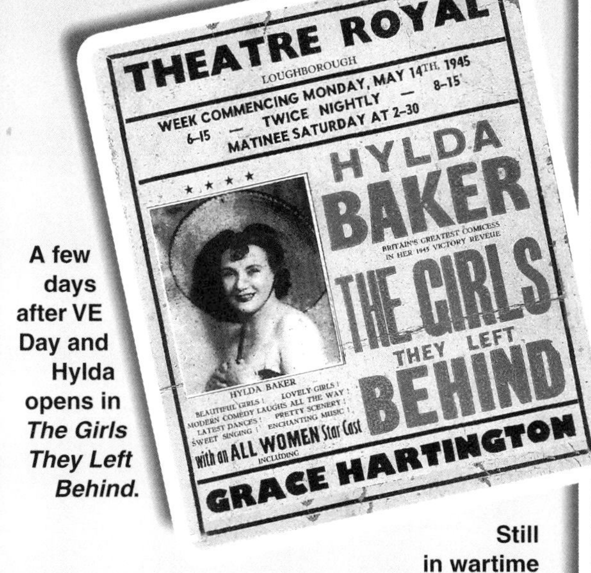

A few days after VE Day and Hylda opens in *The Girls They Left Behind*.

Still in wartime review but this time the embryo of "Be Soooon I said!!"

Another publicity shot from the 1940s, this time a slightly more sophisticated Hylda.

"There was a little girl, who had a little curl right in the middle of her forehead ...and when she was good, she was very, very good – but when she was bad, she was horrid."

1945: On stage as a man in *Wild Women And Whoopee!*

Hylda with her female stooge, Mary Radclyffe, in *Wild Women And Whoopee!*

A trio of dancers from the all-male (except for Hylda) revue *Meet The Men And Me.* "God'll strike me down" she said!

Hylda was especially proud of this photograph taken for *Meet The Men And Me.*

A daring pose by 'Yvonne' in *Bearskins And Blushes*, no movement was allowed so the chorus drew the curtains.

Hylda signed this picture for Tex: "To My Dearest Charles, With Love, Hylda."

Another scene from *Bearskins And Blushes.*

Mary Radclyffe, Hylda and Frank E. Wayne in *Bearskins And Blushes.*

1952: Brian Lloyd as the embryonic Cynthia, in *Frills With Thrills*.

Hylda on the right, brother Syd on the left in "Montgunnery's Mansions" from *Frills With Thrills*.

Outside the Diamond Horseshoe Saloon in *Frills With Thrills* with brother Syd as the 'smart fella'.

Inside the Diamond Horseshoe Saloon. Tex Martin (right) is 'Fingers' Orson.

'The Girls in the Home Guard' from *Frills With Thrills*. The start of the famous 'drill routine'. Dale Warren (left) is the sergeant.

"THE ACE FILM STUNT MAN"

DARE-DEVIL **TEX MARTIN**

AND HIS HOLLYWOOD LOVELIES

featuring

"UNDRESSING A GIRL WITH BULLETS"

THE ONLY ACT OF IT'S KIND IN THE WORLD

SEE !—"Katrina," America's most beautiful Show Girl being unclothed bullet by bullet by Tex Martin, the crack shot, whilst he rides his super charged motor-cycle at terrific speed and using a .45 six shooter.

SEE !—Tex crashing through the 30-foot long "Corridor of Fire."

SEE !—Tex shoot a cord from a girl's throat with a rifle whilst standing up on a motor-cycle ! ! !

SEE !—Tex jumping over a girl's body at full speed on a powerful motor-cycle.

SEE !—Tex performing daring stunts on his motor-cycles whilst blindfolded with Pads of Plasticine and a black bandage.

BOOK THIS BOX

You have seen Tex Martin's stunts in films—on Television

SEE HIM IN ACTION

UNDRESSING A GIRL WITH BULLETS

Tex Martin's promotional leaflet.

The blindfolded Tex Martin and his 'Hollywood lovelies'.

From dashing blade to bashful maid! Eventually Tex had to do his stint as Cynthia, "Go on. Set off from there!"

Hylda's brother Syd Baker as 'The God of Gold' in the 'Muscle Dance'. *Frills With Thrills* 1952.

The *Frills With Thrills* finale. Syd is on the extreme right of the front row. The man with the guitar is Dale Warren.

which was a red quilted cocktail bar in one corner with a canopy over the top; her suite was a matching red, the walls were yellow and the ceiling was in dove grey. Her bedroom was the height of luxury with soft mauve curtains, a matching bedspread, and her built-in dressing table occupied three quarters of one long wall. Hylda loved to cook. Her kitchen was two smaller rooms knocked into one and sported two ovens, one gas and one electric. The monkeys, however, didn't seem to appreciate the fact that this was all so special, for when a member of the orchestra from the show at the Palace Theatre called at Hylda's house, the monkeys had been allowed to roam free and one of them was in the sitting room frantically chucking coal out of the scuttle all over the new carpet! When asked if this house would be a tie for Hylda with her busy life, and would she consider moving, she replied, "I'm here for the rest of my life, and it'll probably take that to get the garden just as I want it. As you can see, it's a very large garden and in part of it I intend to have a glass fibre swimming pool. I have never gardened, so I don't know if I've got green fingers, but when I get the time I'll find out!"

Her professional and home life seemed to be giving her all she could have wished for, but as always she would find that to achieve satisfaction of a permanent nature was constantly to be beyond her reach.

During the summer show of 1957, Tex was once more back playing Cynthia, but things came to a head in the September and he walked out, saying, "After what she has said about me, I've finished with the theatre." This relationship had been becoming a bit of an 'on-off' situation. Indeed, Tex had relationships with other women to which Hylda's reaction was, "He's taken up with some dancer, but it's nothing." Her long association with Tex was finally over after 11 years. David Kirk was the next one to take the job, completing the summer show season with her. He, too, was soon to discover that sharing a dressing room with the monkeys was not an easy task. He was in charge of what went on in there, looking after all the props etc, but the monkeys used to be running around loose. One day while she and David were on stage, the monkeys got into her make-up box and flung things about in their by now habitual fashion. There was loose powder everywhere, bits of make up strewn around, the whole room was in a terrible mess, but it now fell to David to clear it all up — and not surprisingly he was unimpressed.

Dorothy Bickerdike, who was Barney Colehan's production assistant for many years, remembers them, too, and says that on one occasion she went to Hylda's dressing room for a drink and was suddenly aware of something chattering near her ear. She looked around to see that the monkey was right beside her on the back of the settee, just staring at her. "I thought, any minute now it's going to pounce. They were funny little things, they were alright, but a bit strange, and you had to be very careful with them." Perhaps Hylda's sense of humour was very much to the fore when she named these little creatures, because of those famous sayings 'taking the Mickey' and 'I should Co-Co'.

She had recently decided to have a base in London again and had rented a huge mansion flat in the West End, just off Tottenham Court Road, 97 Ridgmount Gardens, although she did keep her Blackpool house as well for the time being. She even had two hooks fitted on the floor in the kitchen to tether the monkeys when she was out, for they could create such havoc that they were only allowed to roam at certain times. What a pity this wasn't the general rule in the dressing room too! Her reasoning behind having the London base was that a trunk call (who remembers those will show their age!) could cost 2s 6d, but a local call was only 2d, therefore managements wouldn't be keen to spend that just to see if you're available, so you might end up losing that important job you want so much.

David Kirk also went on to work with Hylda in her new BBC television series in October. This series was called *Be Soon,* another one of her sayings that had become part of her repertoire. It was a domestic comedy with Hylda as an ordinary little Lancashire woman and Cynthia as her silent friend. She reputedly devised the basic formula for the series, no doubt drawing upon the stories she got from her advertisement during her summer season, and it was to be centred around the homely happenings in the houses, pub and corner shop of a Lancashire street. It was fitting that Barney Colehan, the man responsible for her rise to stardom, was to produce the series, and the *Radio Times* wrote, 'If Hylda is at all superstitious, this fact alone must assure the series will be a success.' One of the most telling things that Hylda admitted to reporters at the time was when she showed that underneath there lurked a fear of failure, and that she wasn't always so confident as people might think. She said, "You're at the top and you wonder whether you can live up to it. You fight for a thing for years, and when you get it, it frightens you."

Barney had no doubts about her talent, though. He said, "Hylda doesn't set out to tell gags alone. People laugh at her because she's funny in herself, even to talk to. The sort of gossip she delivers is heard in the north on every day of the week."

At this same time Hylda also made it clear that she would love to play a straight role, something heavy, and was desperate to do a play about everyday situations and people, saying that many comedies had casts of unbelievable characters. She was extremely nervous during rehearsals for the series and seemed to have great difficulty remembering her lines. She also became quite ill and developed a nasty chest once again, possibly brought on by nerves. Once she insisted that she played the accordion in one of the scenes, which had been second nature to her only five years before in *Frills With Thrills,* but once again she was very nervous and worried about remembering the tune. Her solution was to put chewing gum on each of the keys she needed so she could feel where to play. It sounded fine, but it was very difficult for the camera not to pick up the gum on screen.

The first episode of *Be Soon* was rehearsed on 23 and 24 October 1957 and shown on Friday, 25 October. Sadly, superstition did not save the day and the series was panned by the critics. For the first time in two years, since her amazing success story, Hylda had to take quite damning criticism which must have hurt her greatly at the time. No one likes it, but in this case she would no doubt be terrified that fame, which had eluded her for so long, might slip away from her; and not only that, her dreams of being an actress could be dashed. The newspapers came up with headlines reading, 'Poor TV Lines and Situations,' and even worse, 'Hylda Baker Flops'.

The *Daily Telegraph* reviewer said, 'Hylda Baker came near to destroying her established television reputation as a comedienne when, last night, she began her own series. Seldom have so many poor lines and half-hearted situations been contrived to provide half an hour's intended comedy. Miss Baker runs a grocer's shop and decides to take a lodger in the shape of Guy Middleton. The rumour spreads to her back yard that he might be a murderer, which provides some Bakerish quivering and a decidedly amateur bedroom scene. Flashes of her humour did come through, though, when she was given lines close to her stage act. The rest would have improved with the sound off.'

The *Evening Standard* was equally unimpressed, commenting, 'Miss Hylda Baker is a twitching wrestling midget of a woman with a unique gift for character comedy. Sad, therefore, to say that the first programme in her TV series was a flop. The script was simple minded, and Miss Baker, whose timing is usually masterly, seemed quite out of her stride. She mistimed or forgot her lines. She seemed ill at ease. She was no more ill at ease than I, an admirer, watching her reputation dwindle.'

Although hampered by ill health brought on by overwork, the determined Hylda pressed doggedly ahead with the series but it only had the one run. Some years later she was said to be very much aware of the irony of the fact that another series, based on a similar idea, had a great deal more luck — it was called *Coronation Street.* Poor Hylda, she must have been very upset; she had been hoping that acting in a successful series was to be her next rung up the ladder, but luckily it did not have a lasting effect on her popularity and she was on the road touring again.

One incident which happened in early December, while the series was on the screens, shows Hylda's extreme nature — she reacted to everything in an instant, a sort of 'add water and stir'. She was in Glasgow and had invited Barney Colehan, Dorothy Bickerdike and an associate for a meal at her hotel. They were seated at a table right bang in the middle of the vast dining room, having all ordered the same meal, roast beef and Yorkshire pudding with all the trimmings. The food came and Hylda looked across at Dorothy's plate and said, "Oh, you've got more than me," whereupon, because she is polite and also because Hylda was the hostess, Dorothy said, "Well by all means you must have mine then." Without a second's pause, Hylda said, "Thank you very much," and they exchanged plates. To those who think this is not the way to behave, it is yet again an example of Hylda's strange character, in that were she questioned about it today, she would no doubt defend herself by saying, "Well, she shouldn't have offered to give it to me!"

At the end of the meal, the head porter suddenly appeared at the door of the dining room, very tall and imposing, and bellowed, "Is there anybody here by the name of Baker?" Dorothy says, "He knew full well who she was because she was not only a celebrity but was staying at the hotel. However, Hylda rose up with great dignity, gathered herself together and off she went right across the dining room, this little tiny figure, to answer the telephone. That is one of my very happy memories."

By early 1958 Hylda was to have lost the two people who were most dear to her: Mickey and Co-Co. During the *Be Soon* series Mickey became very ill. Hylda was very upset and eventually he died. Poor Hylda couldn't accept this and tried to give him the kiss of life; it didn't work so she sent for the vet. She explained to him how precious he was to her and that she needed to be absolutely sure her pet would have a proper burial, giving him suitable funds to ensure this was done. The vet remained suitably obsequious and, reverently picking up the monkey in his bag, he left the dressing room and shut the door. Once outside he looked at everyone waiting, gave them a little wink and swung the bag gaily around in the air. Off he went — and that was the end of Mickey. It was such a shame because Hylda really did love him and it was certainly not the lack of love, or of great care, that caused his death; presumably, being so small, their life span is short. No one knows what actually happened to Co-Co, who died very soon afterwards, but no doubt he was pining for his mate and when they had both gone Hylda was devastated. She spoke about her lonely dressing room when starring in *Val Parnell's Saturday Spectacular* on TV in May 1958. "Yes, they were really like children to me. I'm missing them terribly," she said tearfully.

She had just returned from a holiday in Majorca but had almost had second thoughts before she went because she was so happy trotting between her London home and her Blackpool house. The air was bracing there and she said she felt she didn't really need the sunshine as she'd treated herself to a sun lamp.

A wonderful example of Hylda's determination to get her act right and to strive for perfection came that same month of May which saw her driving all the way to

Wolverhampton from Blackpool. She booked into a hotel for the night and promptly used her room just to watch TV. This was all because they were showing a repeat of a programme she had starred in but was only to be broadcast in the Midlands area. She said at the time, having seen herself as others saw her, "I came to look for my faults, and I think I have found where I can improve myself."

For the summer season of 1958 she was once more back in Blackpool, at home base for the fourth year in succession, and this time it was *The New Hylda Baker Show* at the Winter Gardens Pavilion, with yet another new Cynthia! She had advertised and received somewhere in the region of 300 applicants (with a lot of wives recommending their husbands), but in the end she employed Victor Graham. Also in this production were Rawicz and Landauer, Harry Bailey, Tamara and Orloff, Mary Millar, The Joan Davis Dancers, and The George Mitchell Singers. An excerpt from the show was televised on 20 June 1958. It is of great interest that she decided to revive one of her *Frills With Thrills* sketches too.

The Stage reviewed it thus:

'It is built around Miss Baker, and it well justifies the adjective "new", for though some of the material has its origin in the remote days before Hylda reached her mass public, it has been streamlined. Cynthia, for this edition, takes on the role of a hospital nurse, and it says much for Hylda that she feels confident enough to venture into quite new fields, deserting the piano for a workmanlike attack on the accordion, and to take up no less than a third of the show's total time. Two first-rate artists are seen together in a most diverting military skit "Montgunnery Mansions". Harry Bailey is, of course, very slick-witted and a master raconteur.'

That summer, Victor Graham spent one very hot day in particular on the beach, and he tells of the repercussions on stage in the evening. "When I got on stage at night under the lights, I passed out in the middle of her act, with mild sun stroke, and when I came to I was lying in the wings. Apparently Hylda had dragged me off-stage — how she managed my 6ft 2ins I'll never know — gone back on stage and said something like, 'She gets like that sometimes; it's her age y'know,' with all her characteristic business, and then finished the act by herself!"

Also, around that time it was mentioned in a newspaper that the Duchess of Kent did her shopping in a famous chain store, so Hylda, no doubt thinking it would help to get as much press coverage as possible, promptly got her publicity people on to it and they sent a letter to the paper:

'Following your recent disclosure about the Duchess of Kent shopping at a chain store, I thought you would like to know — exclusively — that Hylda also uses them!' The newspaper's reply caption was: 'Thank you — Queen Hylda.'

In order to keep up her star status she decided she needed a personal assistant and, advertising in a newspaper once more, found John Kirby, an 18stone 6ft-tall ex-Guardsman. To her surprise, joy of joys, she struck lucky because he had Royal connections. One day as he was packing negligees for her holiday in Paris, he said to the press, "If only the Palace could see me now. What would they say at Clarence House." The last lady he had worked for was the Queen, when she was Princess Elizabeth, now it was the Queen of Blackpool!

He told a reporter, "They were days of great discipline, when I'd have to run errands for the Princess. I was like an unglorified private secretary. If there were tickets to be collected for the Royal Family, I was sent to get them. Any messages that had to be delivered in London, then off I was sent. So when I read an advertisement from Hylda saying she wanted a personal manager with experience of dealing with temperament, I thought I was just the man."

Helping her pack, he apparently looked very uncomfortable and rather shy — a far cry from the strapping Grenadier Guardsman — but as Hylda bustled around in her element she said, "I must have someone who can understand my moods. Since he left the army, John has worked as a clown in an Austrian circus... he'll be just right for me. I'm often very dictatorial, and I'm so busy I'm often rude to people." There was such a great honesty in her that she would even mention her temperamental nature in the advertisement, and also admit to the press about her rudeness. Many people felt that she went through life totally unaware of it.

That autumn of 1958 saw Hylda off touring once more, this time in her own game show called *Strike It Lucky*, but it was totally the wrong vehicle for her, and she was visibly lacking in confidence when she was giving out the prizes. She was a comedienne, not a quiz show host. The opening of the show saw her going around the auditorium in a maroon dress she'd worn in pantomime the previous year, desperately trying to show enthusiasm, with lines such as, "I am the usherette extraordinaire. I've got monkey glands for old cow hands." Business was not good, she finally collapsed and became very ill with bronchial pneumonia and was admitted to a Sheffield nursing home in November. She was due to appear at the Empire in Leeds, but Issy Bonn stepped in and took her place. She had suffered from shingles during the summer and in fact, trouper that she was, had worked with a scarf covering the unsightly rash on her face, which no doubt hadn't helped her recovery.

Hylda was kept in the Sheffield nursing home for two weeks because, along with the bronchial complaint, she was also suffering from congestion of the lungs. She said later that after the shingles she went back to work too soon. "It was August Bank Holiday and people expected to see me. I ought to have rested for some months, and going back to work must have lowered my whole resistance." From Sheffield they took her back to Blackpool in an ambulance, and when she had finally recovered, she was told that the pneumonia had left her with a strained heart. Three doctors, plus a specialist, all agreed that her health was in a very bad state and warned her that from now on she must lead a quieter existence. This, of course, made her very low because things looked black for her where her career was concerned, particularly as she had always prided herself on being able to withstand all the demands on her time and energy. How could she give up now, when she'd fought so hard to get there? As luck would have it, she decided to consult another specialist who discovered that her problem was actually a thyroid condition, gave her two months' treatment, and from then on she was a new woman. Once again she was able to do all the things she loved — dancing, playing golf — but above all she could get back to her first love — work. Another crisis in the colourful life of this bundle of energy was over.

Hylda spent most of 1959 recuperating, but by the autumn she was on the road once more, and the programme of the Leeds Empire, week commencing 28 September, states that on the bill were Burke and Kovac ('Artistry in Rhythm'), The Shermans ('The Act With a Gimmick'), Dave and Joe O'Duffy ('The Genial Giants'), Alexis Troupe ('Springboard Acrobats') and Howard Jones and Reggie Arnold ('Radio and TV's Singing Personalities').

By this time Hylda was doing her Cynthia act to close the first half as 'Hylda Baker and Her Friend', and closing the whole evening with comedy and music. It may seem to the reader that these lists, which crop up every time there is mention of a tour or a show, are unnecessary, but it is so important to name all these artists, particularly as it is an indication of the social history of a time when television still hadn't quite taken over from the spectacle of live variety. In 1959 TV was still something of a relative novelty, but at that time it was also a great help to artists, a case in point being Hylda's own rise to fame; she was certainly beginning to get the television work too. Having been ill, though, she had lost a good deal of confidence. Gerry Lammyman says that when he saw the show in Leeds, he went backstage and said, "Oh Hylda, you were good tonight. You were spot on!" She beamed and replied, "Yes, I've got my timing back haven't I? I'd lost it." She was having a bit of a struggle to keep on top, where she needed to be.

In August she had appeared on Granada TV in a sketch called *Emergency Ward 10 and a Half,* playing a nurse with Cynthia as her side-kick. She said that this was her ninth Cynthia, and that everyone thought he was her husband. "Not true, of course, as I am a widow," she said. She was certainly not going to tell the truth to the press, although once or twice in later life she would slip up and admit that she had a broken marriage behind her, which is quite telling as it was usually at a time when she was feeling lonely, and it was perhaps a way of getting some form of sympathy without begging for it.

Her love of animals came to the fore again at this time and she lavished her love once more on a tiny Chihuahua dog called Cha-Cha. "They are very obedient dogs of Mexican origin, the smallest breed of dog in the world. They have to be fussed and treated gently but one must not forget that even though they are small, they are as lively and as perky as any other dog and will get away with all kinds of mischief if they are over pampered," said Hylda at the time. She did, however, always clean his teeth for him, saying, "Dogs with dirty teeth are dangerous if they nip anybody!"

Earlier that September she was supposed to be resting after her hectic six-week tour, when Max Miller was taken ill with a heart attack and was in hospital. Her rest was broken by a telephone call from Moss Empires to ask if she could step in, which she did, and found herself starring again at the Finsbury Park Empire in his place. It must have made her feel rather proud, the little lady from Farnworth, to be considered as the top of her profession and to step in for someone who was a legend in his own lifetime. It no doubt proved to her that she had been right, and having a London address was going to prove valuable — that cheaper phone call had been made and she was 'on the spot'.

Pantomime in December 1959 saw Hylda back up north, though, at the Empire Theatre, Liverpool, playing Dame Trot in *Jack And The Beanstalk* with Morecambe and Wise as The Giant's Henchmen, Jimmy Clitheroe as Jack's Brother, Lorrae Desmond as Jack and Tony Melody as The Squire. She was still doing her Cynthia spot, with Victor Graham, because this act was the one that the audiences loved her for, and by this time all her phrases were in everyday usage in most households. "Be soon, I said," was quoted by mothers to their children, and "She Knows You Know," chanted by the crowds wherever she went. However, she knew she would have to fight to maintain her star status. She had achieved sudden fame but she was a seasoned trooper who was only too aware that she would have to strive to keep it, constantly searching for new angles and material, hence, no doubt, her mistaken attempt at a game show.

Victor Graham, who was destined to be the Cynthia who was to be with her the longest, remembers her with great affection. He worked on and off with her from 1958 to 1963 and says of her, "Hylda could be difficult, but she could also be extraordinarily kind. It wasn't all sweetness and light, but I admired her gutsiness and I had a lot of sympathy for her. She was very much alone when I knew her and she hated being alone. I often had to go out with her after a show because she didn't want to go home to an empty flat. Despite all her theatre life she often seemed happiest at home, cooking and being a normal little north-country 'housewife'. When I worked for her she was past her first peak of popularity and had to fight to get back. And how she fought! Above all things she fought to keep her top-billing. A lot of what people saw as her being difficult was her determination to get things absolutely right, so that she was seen at her best."

Also working on the pantomime *Jack and the Beanstalk* at Liverpool in 1959 was the stage manager Brian Howard, who went on to become a very successful director. Hylda would have supper with him at least three times a week over the period of 14 weeks, which was the length of the run, and he vividly remembers how lonely she was, desperately seeking someone to talk to. Most of the conversations would be about her past and of a serious nature. Once during the show, she had to fall backwards in a mock faint and be caught by Jimmy Clitheroe, but he mistimed it and she fell badly and banged her head. She came off stage in a real state and was genuinely shaken. It had really knocked her for six and she suffered bad headaches for some time afterwards. She went to her dressing room, her understudy was summoned, but when she came out of her room and caught sight of this girl all dressed up and ready to go on for her, she instantly became well again. Brian says he will never forget this remarkable recovery, for nobody was going on in her place! 'Doctor Theatre', as it is called in the profession, had come to her aid. Brian says he had never seen anything like it and there was absolutely no doubt that Hylda had been genuinely injured. She always blamed Jimmy and said it was deliberate, but it wasn't, he had just mistimed it, the scene being somewhat busy and the whole cast including Eric and Ernie on stage at the time.

At the end of her opening patter she would sing a song which required audience participation: "Clap your hands and laugh, ha, ha, ha, ha, and sing toodle, oodle, oodle ooh!" It really got the audience going and apparently had been taught to Hylda by her grandfather. Her act, however, was somewhat erratic and Brian had all her scripts in the wings, never knowing which way she was going to go (and indeed neither did Cynthia) because she would change it mid-stream if she felt it wasn't going well. One night she went through four routines, which was a bit of a problem as there was a timing on the show which had to be adhered to, and it turned out that it was always Hylda who over ran, such was her determination to get the accolade. However, there was another problem if it wasn't going well — she would blame Cynthia, it would always be her/his fault! On one occasion she sent him off stage saying, "Go on, get off you, your dress is torn," simply because the audience weren't laughing at the character. Never in a million years would she be prepared to admit that she was the only one responsible, for she was the one telling the jokes.

There was also a scene where Hylda had to come up through the trap on stage in a sort of 'Sputnik' (older readers will remember this as being the first man-made satellite to orbit the earth, which was launched by the Russians in 1957) and this was how she got up the beanstalk. Everyone on stage had to keep absolutely still and away from the trap before it could be opened, but for some reason Lorrae Desmond would back towards it, Hylda would be down there under the stage waiting, and the cue could not be given if anyone was standing over it. Hylda was totally unaware that Eric Morecambe was sitting in the wings with Brian, whose job it was to give the cue, doing his utmost to make him miss it and trying to delay him by telling him dirty jokes in order to keep her down there!

The pantomime ran until mid-March, for they had very long runs in those days, but after her patter, which as we know was often never-ending, Hylda would still be wishing people a Happy Christmas, to which Eric Morecambe would mutter, "It'll be Easter before she's finished!" The reason she tried to battle so hard with her act was because Jimmy Clitheroe was a real pantomime expert and knew the style inside out, Eric and Ernie had a more surreal act at that time than the one they developed later, and Hylda's style was so different that she was somewhere in the middle of these styles and had to combat this.

As always she was determined that people shouldn't know what her salary was; it was her own business and when the company manager, Martyn French, asked her for her insurance number she got very irate saying, "Oh no, he's not having it. He's far too keen." Of course, it was a requirement that everyone had to give. She had been so used to running things herself that she just couldn't or wouldn't accept it when others were in charge.

Times had actually been quite happy for her, though, as she had become very close indeed to John, her personal assistant, the former Guards officer. In fact they were very much a partnership and seemingly very much in love. However, this too was not without its stormy incidents and the final blow came in the house in Blackpool. Hylda was convinced that she had heard John flirting with the lady who came in to do the cleaning, and who apparently always arrived all 'dolled up'. Hylda had gone to run her morning bath, but she heard him talking to this woman, apparently in an intimate way, so she tackled him about it in the only way she knew, for she was fiercely jealous. She later said to a member of her family, "I could see he liked her and I just couldn't contain my jealousy when I heard him messing about with her. I went for him, he went for me back, and he said, 'If you feel like that I'll go!' And he did. It upset me terribly because I was very fond of him."

John wrote to her after this and apparently the letter was very sloppy and sentimental, but Hylda's pride would not let her back down. He went to America in 1960 and wrote from there, too, with lines such as, 'Our love was too great for both of us, we couldn't contain it. We're so much in love it wasn't possible to live together.' But she didn't relent and that was that. For all her bravado, though, until her death Hylda kept all the letters he'd ever sent her. Ten years later she rather sadly admitted to a friend that her one big regret in life was that she had ignored his pleas for them to get back together, settle down and get married.

Although her private life was still less than perfect, workwise the 1950s had been very good to Hylda and she was now a star, but the 1960s were going to be an even bigger challenge, for it was now five years since she had made such an impression on TV and she knew the struggle was to continue. In her own words, "A woman who makes her name must fight more than a man to keep at the top. People have tried to push me back a few times but I haven't let them. I've had to be a bit of a battleaxe or I'd have been trodden on. I don't want people's sympathy, just their laughter, and, if possible, their affection. Then I'm a contented woman."

In order to attain this she knew that out on the open road she would have to choose her parking places with care and keep her eye very firmly fixed on the driving mirror, for those who sought to overtake her.

CHAPTER SIX

It'll Be Sooon!

ONE particular performance, which happened to be at the Chiswick Empire, was once more to bring to Hylda's mind the words of her grandmother, for who should be in the audience but the film producer Karel Reisz, just at the time he was looking for someone to play the part of a tough little woman — Albert Finney's aunt Ada — in the film *Saturday Night And Sunday Morning*. Reisz liked Hylda so much that he offered her the part. Here, at long last, was her one big chance to demonstrate that she could transfer her talent to the cinema screen, not as a music hall comedienne, but as a straight actress, and in what proved to be a very controversial box office blockbuster.

The chance had come to her by 'doing the rounds' of the variety theatres, at a time when perhaps she might have been tempted to give up the long hard life on the road to concentrate on getting TV work, for who could have predicted that topping the bill at Chiswick would lead to this? She said, "I'd been doing sketches in my shows for years, and I played them as if they were short plays. Karel Reisz saw me doing one of these sketches and he knew from that, that I could act. It was a very wonderful thing for me."

Three years earlier, she had talked about films when asked if she had any plans in this direction. She said, "I would dearly love to make a film, but too many northern comics have been pushed into them. They may have made a lot of money, but have the films enhanced the stars' careers? I'd rather wait for the right story than be pushed into a film with a string of variety acts for support." Ironically, it was Hylda who was supporting in this film, which not only starred

Albert Finney, but Shirley Anne Field, Rachel Roberts and Avis Bunnage; but what a powerful performance it was, and 1960 was to be a memorable year for her.

She earned for herself a Critics' Acclaim award, and when it was announced that she was to play the part, the *News Of The World* said, 'Little Hylda Baker the comedienne needs *Saturday Night And Sunday Morning* so much. In many ways her character role is a return to the world she knew in almost 40 years of trouping. Her straight part is the only way she can relive the past. The old halls, where she learned her trade, have gone."

When the reviews came out Hylda must have been thrilled to read:

'Hylda Baker brings fine strength to her part in a film that opens new hope for British pictures.' (*Evening News*).

'Let me finish by handing a bouquet to Hylda Baker for making me sit up when I watched her in the film. I always knew Hylda could act, but this straight, serious performance was a revelation. It certainly made the film for me.' (*The Stage*).

'Here is exciting down-to-earth drama, wonderfully acted by three principals and with a scene-stealing performance from variety comedienne Hylda Baker.' (*Woman*).

'Hylda Baker puts over a polished performance.' (*Yorkshire Evening News*).

'With this showing, Hylda Baker proves that she is an actress of promise, much more than a female Charlie Drake.'

In January 1961, while she was starring in pantomime at the Theatre Royal, Bolton, with Dave Allen, there was a big disappointment in store when her request to adopt a child was turned down. An official of the National Adoption Society in London said, "It is very doubtful whether any single woman of 52 would be able to adopt a child. [By this time she was in fact aged 56!] There is nothing legally that would stop her, but most societies have a waiting list and always give top priority to married couples, and we don't accept any applications from people who are over 40 years old." Hylda said, "I've always wanted children but have been told it would be difficult to adopt a boy of my own. I'll even consider getting married again. It's not just a question of loneliness, but I want to share my success with someone not so fortunate." She went on stage that night, hiding her heartache, playing, under the circumstances, the rather aptly-named title role of Mother Goose, and hundreds of children in the audience roared at her antics.

Seven weeks later, at the end of February, she still hadn't given up, as she asked the Actors' Orphanage to let her adopt. She said, "I haven't given up hope. All my adult life I've wanted a little boy. Being childless has left a large hole in my life, and the older I get, the greater becomes the desire to fill it." Strangely enough, she had a few private offers when people read about her disappointment, and it appears they were genuine. One mother told her, "I have 13 children and you can take your pick." Hylda replied, "I could not accept a child from a family, but one who has no home of his own."

Finally, Hylda had to give up the search for someone to satisfy her acute feelings of lonelieness and she concentrated once more on her animals. (Quote of the week in the *Daily Mail* for 7 October that year: "I find it safer to shower my affection on animals. They are more reliable than men," says TV star Hylda Baker.) She really was a complex person, who could have had a much more fulfilled life if only she had learned to trust, but she just couldn't; nor did she find it easy to give love, possibly because it had never really been given to her when circumstances decreed that she should grow up too soon.

She never gave up anything easily, however, and as had been so obvious throughout her life, she would fight when she was thwarted. A year later, in July 1962, there was a big article published in the *Today* weekly magazine with the headline, 'The Law Won't Let Me Have A Child Says Hylda Baker.' The feature was called 'Mark My Words' and the idea was that people in the public eye could have their say in their own words — and she did!

"I was walking along the street one day a long time ago with my two tiny pet monkeys chattering away on my shoulder. A woman turned around as I passed and said very loudly to her companion: 'A bloody pity she didn't have a kid instead!' The taunt stung me very hard, but I walked on making no reply. She didn't know how cruel she was being, people never do. In my eyes were tears of anger and misplaced guilt, for my two little monkeys were more than dearly loved pets. They were my one great consolation for not being able to have what I wanted more than anything else in the world — children, either my own or adopted.

"Since I was 29 I have known I could not have any children myself, and it was a great shock, because I had always wanted them. When I was 24 I got married and more than ever looked forward to my first child, but four years later I found out that I would never have any. A year or two after that my marriage was dissolved and I went to live with my mother again. Years later I began to wonder about adopting a child for myself, but the only obstacle to this at the time, though, was that I was so often away on tour. Then I hit the jackpot with television, which eventually led to my own series *Be Soon* and later the lead in *Our House*.

"Now I was at home more or less all the time, not really a very rich woman, but at least I was comfortable, without any money worries and in a good position to give a child all the material things it would need. Most importantly I knew that I had the mother love that was necessary. I made enquiries, first of all with the Children's Society, was asked firstly was I married and then how old I was. I explained I was over 45 and divorced. They turned me down. Next to the knowledge that I could have no children myself, it was my greatest disappointment ever. I knew that there were thousands of children who needed the love I longed to give.

"I had always believed that if you want something badly enough there's a way of getting it, but here I was faced with an irrevocable 'you can't have children either through birth or adoption'. However, a friend gave me fresh hope with the suggestion that I might be able to become a foster mother, but this hope, too, was dashed when I learned that a foster mother has no permanent right to the child she takes in. I knew it would break my heart to take in a child, become attached to it, only to lose it. So I turned my back on this.

"The news of my wishes got around, and one morning I opened an emotional letter from a man who said his wife had run off with another, leaving him with two boys aged three and five that he wanted me to adopt. My heart leapt at first but then I realised they weren't his to give. His wife was still their mother and they were hers as well his. How tempting it was, but I had to write to him to say no. This letter was followed by many pathetic ones from unmarried mothers offering me their babies. Some sent photos of lovely children. It was almost too much to refuse."

Her final comments show that she hoped that by writing this article it might put a better light on being able to win her case with the authorities.

"I still live in the hope that some day I will hear of an orphan child I can care for and love for life. I dream that one day I shall find a child who has neither home nor parents and that I shall be there at the right moment to make both the child and myself happy."

She was by this time 57 years old and really had no hope at all. There are some who say that she led such a selfish sort of life that, even if she had been able to adopt when she was a bit younger, it would never have worked out, but who knows what would have happened had she found her dream in some form of motherhood? There are certainly many instances which show how she dearly loved to listen to, and look after, the young people she came across. On many occasions she 'mothered' the young stage management members of various companies she worked in during her later years, taking them out for meals and listening to their problems. Often she would invite the drama students from the Royal Academy Of Dramatic Art round to her flat for tea, as she lived just around the corner, stuffing them with cream cakes and the goodies they couldn't afford on their grants. She would insist that they did their audition speeches for her, and she obviously got a great deal of pleasure out of this. She was really very intelligent and extremely well read, as we know, and so clever at writing sketches, scripts, all her own material and many synopses for stories and screen plays. At these tea parties she would love to talk about acting, and once admitted that it was her ambition to play the Nurse in *Romeo And Juliet*, a part for which she was absolutely tailor made; there is no doubt that she would have excelled in the role.

It is very interesting that she announced, early in 1961, that she was determined to get rid of Cynthia, for in her eyes Cynthia had become her Frankenstein's monster. She didn't really regret her past, but she had created this character, using it to the full extent, getting every ounce of comedic opportunity out of the union, which ended up making her into the star that she longed to be, but with the slow demise of vaudeville and the rise of television, she felt she needed to get away from this image.

Before starring, without Cynthia, in BBC's *Showtime* in February, she said, "I'm fed up with Cynthia, with people talking about Cynthia, with Cynthia dominating me, and I want people to see that I can be just as funny when I've buried Cynthia. It's my showmanship and artistry and — shall I be big-headed? — my skill which have made her a laughing stock. Anybody with the right build can play her. I can make anyone into a perfect Cynthia if I could have an hour to rehearse them before a show." It was apparent that nothing short of a national outcry at that time would have brought poor old Cynthia back into the limelight, but Hylda was to discover that it wasn't quite so easy to kill and finally 'bury' her 'monster' as she so obviously believed. We also know that it often took her more than an hour to get the perfection she required!

At this point, perhaps, should come Hylda's own detailed explanation of how her 'friend' came about in the first place, and how and why she developed the character after writing and developing the 'Drill Routine' in her own shows way back in the 1940s. Originally it was a slow process, for the sketch worked well and she didn't feel any need to expand this, but in two interviews in the 1960s she said, "At first I tried women Cynthias but that didn't work. Anyway, it's so much easier to malign a man — especially when he's got up as a woman! You see it in everyday life. A tall person and a small person — the same as with a man and a woman. They don't actually choose, it just seems to happen, and I think this is what makes the population the proper size eventually! You see, six foot and four foot ten brings out a five foot eight!"

Victor Graham's comments on what it was like to work with Hylda in the act are very telling. He says, "Hylda had created this character which was so popular at the time, and in a way she became jealous of its success. We opened a shop somewhere and the crowd gathered round me rather than her. She was horrified at this reaction and the fact that Cynthia was so popular. For the act we had to rehearse the walk-on over and over again. It had to be absolutely right, this slow measured cross of the stage to arrive at the spot, because it was terribly important and immediately established Cynthia's character. Then for the exit you had to go so far, turn round slowly and look at her, but this was vital, for it was then she would say, 'Ah yer bonny!'

"She would be so very nervous in the wings that she would constantly fiddle with my costume to try to occupy herself, because she didn't want to stop and think about going on stage, so she just had to do something to keep her busy. It wasn't so much that she was worried about forgetting, but she had got to be good. She knew she'd got to be good, they expected it and so she had to find a way of working herself up. She was so determined to be good. Even in the early days, in 1958, she would go off at a tangent in the middle of the act. It wasn't clear whether she was buying time as it were, but she'd sometimes do two or three minutes patting her hair, adjusting her feather boa, hoisting herself up and getting the costume right. It could take an enormous amount of time while she decided what bit of material she was going to do next, but the audiences went wild. They loved it."

Hylda also based part of this act on her Aunt Agnes, whose husband was deaf, so she would tap him on the shoulder, make frantic signs at him, mouthing in an exaggerated way and talking in a very loud voice. One day they were watching a zoo programme on TV and she turned to her husband, saying, "Look at those lions, can you see them? Look at that one there, laid lying down all alone, by itself, with nobody with it." He would just nod slowly and Hylda would be in stitches. "The funniest thing was when she'd ask if the milkman had been and waggled her big bosoms to show what she meant ... I never dared use that on stage," she said. One day when her aunt came to see one of Hylda's performances, she said afterwards, "Eee, that were right funny. Wherever did you pick that up?"

"Of course you have to talk when you're small. I mean everybody can see tall people can't they? They don't have to exert themselves to make themselves felt but small people do, and I've noticed this. The small one talks and asks the tall one for corroboration and the tall one lets it go and lets the small one talk — and of course she is entitled to!

"Calling her Cynthia is part of the joke. It's a contradiction, a pretty name, an ugly woman. It looks right because Cynthia is big and I have to do all the talking, otherwise nobody would know I'm there. That's how you put your face about when you're little — you make a noise! Anyway, it's so much easier to malign a man, especially when he's got up as a woman."

These final remarks are so very interesting when trying to find the truth inside the woman, and the phsycological reasons that underly her character. Yes, of course she was very clever in creating Cynthia and there is no doubt that it was a stroke of genius and the result of years of observation, but surely the above paragraph serves to show that maybe there was something deeper that also contributed? It seems to indicate that she always harboured a deep resentment over the fact that she was small, and perhaps underneath she still bore the scars and the hurt of the days of her youth when she was pushed out of the way at the band calls, and even when she was older was looked down upon by her professional male rivals. She had had to fight, and it was hard not to get bitter about it. Perhaps, too, this was her way of getting back at all the men who had treated her badly, and it gave her the opportunity to make a man look stupid. It is certain that she always longed to be tall, and wanted very much to be glamorous, but this was not to be, except for that brief spell as a soubrette and leading lady when she was young. All her life she would only want to have relationships with tall men, especially if they were over six foot.

She is quoted once as saying, "I always wanted to be tall, and my father used to say, 'Why do you want to be like everyone else? You're unique.' He was on the short side as well you see." Other comments she made about her height throughout her life also serve to show this unrest, by the very fact that she was constantly on the defensive about it, even though she appeared to be, and no doubt was, proud that she had made the 'big time' by using her lack of stature to great advantage.

Her act was also full of references to Cynthia having had an accident, being hit on the head or some such disaster, and ending up on the 'pieciatrist's' couch. It is not difficult to link these dark happenings as being a sort of reflection on her own deep fears, and the fate of her father.

There is a retirement home for people in the profession in Twickenham, called Brinsworth House, and it is a wonderful place. What could be better for members of the entertainment profession who are no longer able to live at home, than to spend their last years among their own kind. It was started by the Entertainment Artists' Benevolent Fund, and they had a special celebrity day when Princess Alexandra was the guest of honour, on 20 April 1961. There were many important guests invited to the function, of whom Hylda was one, which pleased her greatly because to have been especially asked to attend was proof once again of her own celebrity status.

After the great success of *Saturday Night and Sunday Morning*, Hylda began working on her second film in July 1961, a domestic comedy with a Lancashire background called *She Knows You Know* which was made by Eternal Films at Twickenham studios. She had been booked to star in another film, though, with Bruce Forsyth at Shepperton, which was due to begin in March, entitled *I'm In Charge*, but sadly Bruce was taken ill so it had to be cancelled. The producer asked Hylda if she had ever had any ideas for a screenplay, and she immediately thought of a comedy she'd written herself some time before. To her great delight the suggestion of a film based on this idea was accepted. She had originally called it 'The Reluctant Grandmother', (and research shows that, even before this, it was a play she had written called 'Born In The Vestry'!), but it was decided to call the film *She Knows You Know* because of the popularity of her catchphrase. The film was set in the north, and apparently Hylda had to make a trip to her home town, Bolton, to borrow or buy authentic clothes! She said, "I discovered that the sort of cardigan, shoes and skirts worn by the type of woman I portray in the film are not available in London."

One interviewer, who somewhat tactlessly talked about her having been so successful as a northern character, and therefore no doubt more popular in her home town, was treated to a wonderful reply, "Oh, I find you are very rarely a prophet in your own town. They say, 'Oh I don't know, she used to live next to our Nellie, you know. She went to the dancing classes there. She's come on a bit since, you know, but I know that Lily Hilthorpe, she could dance her off that stage . . . and she's not even in the business, you see. She doesn't get paid for it. They all get paid you see, these people on the stage.'"

It is reputed that while she was filming she caught sight of a beautiful, brand new gold Rolls-Royce that Kenneth More had just treated himself to, and insisted that she much preferred her own huge American car, whereupon the newspapers leapt on this saying, 'She doesn't know you know,' but it is fairly certain that this was once again her defence mechanism coming to the fore, coupled with her desire to grab whatever publicity there was going! Around the same time she got another little Chihuahua dog called Bella, as she felt Cha Cha needed a companion, so now she had two tiny dogs instead of two tiny monkeys.

The film was quite well received, being a second feature in both London and the provinces, but it never really hit the big time, with one or two reviews being pretty lukewarm:

'Lively, if unpretentious, low life comedy unfolded against industrial town backdrop. Hylda Baker is amusing as an aggressive and possessive Mum . . .' (*Kinematograph Weekly*).

'Everyone's hoping this popular little person will be put on the map with *She Knows You Know*.' (*Parade*).

On 16 September that year Hylda began her comeback in a series called *Our House* for ABC television, which had originally been a Sunday afternoon series and returned for a Saturday evening slot. The cast included Hattie Jacques, Charles Hawtrey, Leigh Madison and Bernard Bresslaw. While working on this series, she was given a chance to further her ambition to do more serious roles when she was asked to do a new television play, which was filmed in the autumn and screened on Friday, 15 December 1961.

The play was called *Where The Difference Begins* and it was a first for Wakefield-born author David Mercer, who was destined to go on to much greater things. This was to be Hylda's TV drama debut, playing the part of Aunt Beatie, the sister-in-law of Wilf Crowther, an engine driver on the point of retirement, with the plot centred on something which is much discussed even today, the 'north-south divide'. It starred Nigel Stock, Leslie Sands and Barry Foster and Hylda's character was not unlike the character she played in her first film *Saturday Night And Sunday Morning*, but she was determined make it her own. There is one memorable scene where she is darning a sock in camera close-up, and never once does she succumb to the fact that the camera is there, she just carries on darning and talking, giving a very low-key sensitive delivery, and it is utterly riveting. There is no sign of temptation to overplay, in fact just the opposite, and it all came completely naturally to her. She put everything into winning the praise of the critics once more, and once more she succeeded:

'Congratulations must go to Hylda Baker who, playing Auntie Beatie, showed her fine talent as an actress. Verdict: A masterpiece of TV drama.' (*Television Today*).

Hylda's career had well and truly taken off in the direction that she most wanted. She was in her element and was riding high, on course for even bigger success, when once again disaster struck. She could not have had any idea that a visit to The Talk Of The Town in London's West End was to end the way that it did, and to have a devastating effect on her. She was quite literally stopped in her tracks, the street lights began to grow dim and she could no longer see what was around the next corner.

CHAPTER SEVEN

Downhill, Uphill and Back On Course

IT was 11pm on Christmas Eve 1961, the lights were up in London's Regent Street, everything was bright in Leicester Square, the night life was buzzing — and Hylda was looking forward to having a wonderful Christmas. She had been to the Talk Of The Town and was standing on the edge of the pavement, about to cross Charing Cross Road, when someone called out to her, so she stopped. A man came up to her and asked, "Are you Miss Baker and have you just been to the Talk Of The Town?" Thinking him to be a fan, she replied that she was, whereupon he threatened her, asking for money, and when she refused he said, "Come on, don't give me that, you've got plenty."

There was no time to call for someone to help her because at that moment she heard a screech of brakes and an almighty crash. There was a car coming towards them and the man turned tail and ran, but Hylda was too late. The car hit her, she felt a bang on the chin and knew no more until she woke up in hospital. What had in fact happened was that a taxi had smashed into the back of a car which had then been shunted on to the pavement right where she was standing. Apparently one of the cars had practically climbed over the other, which shows the force of impact. Having just been threatened by a prospective mugger, Hylda was in a state of shock even before the accident. Now she had received an injured hip, a fractured toe, was very badly bruised and suffering even more from shock, but indeed she was very lucky to be alive under the circumstances. From her hospital bed she was typically cheery and said, "I never thought I'd be a Christmas accident statistic!"

On 27 December she was admitted to the London Clinic for further treatment and as a result of all this she was unable to film the series *Our House*. During the following months her toe gave her great pain, she had dreadful backaches and headaches, movement was difficult, and for a time she was frightened of traffic. In fact she was in and out of hospital three times for operations, the latest one on her hip being in March 1962, which meant that she had been off work for three months and it would be a little while yet before she recovered from the latest treatment. She said later, "I was in delayed shock for a long time. It wasn't just a question of stopping my performances but I couldn't even write new material." And all of this came at a time when her ambitions were beginning to be realised, and the many fights and struggles she had experienced in her past were bearing fruit.

She went on holiday to Portugal to revive her flagging spirits, and just to get away from it all, but she was in for a big surprise when she arrived at her hotel. The waiter who served her dinner excitedly said, "Ela sabe, ela nao, e tola!" which turned out to be Portuguese for "She Knows You Know!" Apparently when he was studying in England, he had been a great fan of hers.

When Hylda felt well enough to start work again, she would think all was well and once more throw herself into it with gusto. After her first TV appearance since the accident, on 28 July 1962 on ABC's *Big Night Out* with Stubby Kaye and Janie Marden broadcast from Llandudno, she admitted, "It took an awful lot for me to pull myself together and face that performance." It would not become apparent until much later that the accident had a lasting effect upon her, and was possibly the root cause of the many problems she experienced in her life to come.

November of 1962 saw Hylda decide to buy another car, but this time she chose an English one, a Jaguar, showing once again her need for a big showy vehicle. On the defensive once more (probably remembering the day she saw Kenneth More's car), she said, "Of course I could have afforded a Rolls-Royce as well, but a tiny woman in such a big car would have looked damned silly." She was determined to get herself a personalised registration number, and what else but HB 1, which she traced to Merthyr Tydfil in Glamorgan because all cars registered there had the letters HB. However, she discovered that the desired registration was on the mayor's car, so Hylda wrote to him asking if he would mind changing, and he curtly wrote back to say that yes, he would mind!

That same month came her next big break, and not before time because she hadn't really worked much due to the effects of the accident, and the latter certainly made her think twice before she signed the contract for the job. It was a new television series called *The Best Of Friends* and there were to be 13 episodes, but she had been so beset by both the accident and her previous illnesses that she refused to sign while it specified that most unlucky of numbers. "I have decided not to tempt providence. I've always been superstitious and have had so much bad luck lately that I have got to take precautions," she told the TV bosses, adding, "I know you know!" They finally agreed to her demands and she signed one contract for 12 episodes and another contract for one episode. It is ironic to note that 13 is often known as a 'Baker's dozen'!

The first episode of the series was shown on 28 April 1963, and Hylda played a cafe proprietress, her business being next door to an insurance office where Charles Hawtrey worked as a clerk. The two stars, of course, knew each other well as they had just been together in *Our House* and the idea was that the two of them would band together and go on insurance assignments with hilarious results. Hylda was back to her cheery self by this time and quipped to reporters, who at the time got a good deal of mileage out of the fact that Hylda herself had once run a fish and chip shop. She said, "Oooh, I'll tell you what I'm like when I'm feeling extravagant. I like a nice roast pheasant, followed by a crepe suzette. Not that you can get them in my cafe in *Best Of Friends* — but we do a very nice line in Lancashire hot pot!"

When she began rehearsals for the series, she was still in a good deal of pain and in fact had great difficulty in learning her lines, which would turn out to be the beginning of even bigger problems for her. Her main complaint, though, was that she couldn't do the 'twist' properly, although she was normally a great dancer. As we know, she loved music and around this time The Beatles were all the rage and one certainly wouldn't imagine that a trouper like Hylda would have appreciated their kind of modern music, but when asked who she admired in show business at the time she replied, "Anyone who's good. The Beatles for instance. They're professionals!"

The series was a success and it seemed that all her past problems were fading into the distance as more work started to flood in. She became a regular performer on ATV's *Big Night Out* with appearances in July 1963 and also in 1964. On 23 October 1963 she played a character part in the ground-breaking police series *Z Cars* but it certainly wasn't to be comedy, it was a straight role as a blowsy, ageing ex-theatrical landlady called Ma Mills. Among her lodgers was Gus, an old layabout who was suspected of stealing from offertory boxes and passing dud cheques, a part played by Dermot Kelly. "I do love straight parts," she enthused, "but that doesn't mean I'm giving up comedy. I would dearly love to run acting and comedy side by side, and mix them both."

Christmas 1963 saw Hylda starring with the legendary Tommy Cooper in the pantomime *Aladdin* at the Wimbledon Theatre, presented by Audrey Lupton and Arthur Lane. Hylda played Widow Twankey, and Tommy was Abanazer, Lauri Lupino Lane and George Truzzi were the Chinese policemen, Barrie Gosney played Wishee Washee, with John Hart Dyke as Suliman, Lord of the Rings.

Hylda always prided herself that she never 'corpsed' on stage, which as most people know is laughing when you shouldn't, and during the run she told John Hart Dyke, "Oh no, I never do that." One evening, however, in the scene where Abanazer has 'frozen' the whole company on the stage she certainly looked like she broke her rule. Tommy had to come down the stairs, wearing those rather upturned pointed toe shoes which were statutory for the Lord of the Djinns to wear in panto, but which are in fact rather dangerous, as the following will prove. The two toes got entangled and he tripped, but somehow or other he managed to stay upright and did a sort of bumpy glide down the rest of the staircase, ending up just beside the 'frozen' Hylda. Needless to say there was not only just a twinkle in her eye, but quite a bit more than that.

Pantomimes are always fraught with unseen danger, though, as there are so many quick changes of both scenery and costumes. On another occasion Hylda was to come unstuck. There was a very quick change for her at the end of the show, as she and Tommy Cooper had just done the song sheet with the audience, (this being topically *All I Want for Christmas is a Beatle*). The finale was a full medieval scene with girls in the long pointed hats and flowing sleeves, and naturally the dame has to have a very outrageous concoction. The fanfare sounds, on comes Hylda to a huge cheer from the audience, she starts to descend the staircase when her veil catches on the scenery, and off flies the hat, off flies the elaborate panto wig, leaving Hylda standing there with a tight stocking top around her head. (To the uninformed, when wearing a stage wig it is always advisable to keep your own hair tight to your head under one of these, as it gives something to pin your wig to, and also stops your own hair from looking a mess when you want to go out quickly after the show!) Needless to say she recovered her hat and battled on!

One review for this pantomime showed how much by this time Hylda had been very much accepted as an actress:

'Whenever Aladdin's mother asked the children in the audience to call out to her, in order that the number of her friends might impress the woman next door, whom she couldn't 'get near to', it was as real, you might say, as *Saturday Night And Sunday Morning*, since Miss Hylda Baker, who took the part, ensured that.' (*The Times*).

Unfortunately she was ill during this production, which provided a few problems for the company, but all was well in the end. The matinees were at 2.30pm and one Saturday at ten minutes to one, the telephone rang in Arthur Lane's office. It was a friend of Hylda's who said that she was very ill, had been coughing blood all night, and she wouldn't be coming that day to do the show. They had only an hour and a half before curtain up, and unfortunately rehearsals for the understudies had been thin on the ground. There was a panic because there was not much time, but her understudy was summoned. She was a young actress who had been working with the same production company in their repertory season. The company always tried to employ their cast members but there was no part for her in the pantomime so they suggested that she work in the office and also understudy Hylda, although there would be little likelihood that she would ever be called upon. Arthur put down the telephone, went straight to the actress and told her, "Hylda's off and you're on." She replied, "I'm not!" before grabbing her coat and hat and disappearing out of the theatre and up to Wimbledon station as fast as her legs could carry her! And who could blame her?

In the end Arthur himself had to do it, but there was the problem of clothes because Hylda's were tiny. The wardrobe store turned up a large dress that had once been worn by Fred Emney, and a large pair of shoes, but realised they hadn't got any wigs that would fit Arthur. At that very moment the Cynthia walked in and was quickly told that he could have the rest of the afternoon off as his wig was snatched from the dressing room. So Arthur went on in Cynthia's wig and Fred Emney's dress.

After the matinee, which got a great reception, he was coming off stage when the stage doorkeeper told him he was wanted on the telephone — it was Hylda saying she felt a lot better and would do the evening show. Arthur, who had got a taste for it and was thoroughly enjoying himself, promptly said, "Oh no, dear, no, you have a jolly good rest this weekend, and come back on Monday. You'll feel a lot better." He had a whale of a time with the full house that Saturday night, it was in his blood, never mind that it was a case of 'employer versus artist'. Hylda returned on Monday and it was back to normal.

The same year, Hylda worked for them again doing summer season at the Alhambra Theatre, Morecambe, but not before she had a battle in the High Court over compensation for the Christmas Eve accident. The newspapers covered it extensively and the headlines included, 'Accident lost me £9,170 says Hylda

Baker,' 'Hylda Baker sues over 1961 accident,' and 'Hylda Baker and the cost of bumping into someone'. On 30 April 1964, both the car driver and The London Cab Company, who were responsible for the other driver, admitted negligence and the action was contested on damages only. Hylda was claiming for loss of earnings, because although her injuries were not of the greatest seriousness they had proved troublesome to treat and while she was 'out of action' that sum of £9,170 was what her gross earnings would have been. It was also quoted that even in 1957 she earned £13,000, but that her expenses were £8,000, and her agent at the time, Mr Harry Foster, said salaries in show business had doubled since then and this was due largely 'to television, the competition of television, and the popularity of artists built up by television'.

Hylda had lost ten weeks in the TV serial *Our House* at £150 a show, and a 12-week tour in a play at £250 a week, as well as needing a cruise on the Mediterranean to restore her confidence, and she had been unable to run about as usual in her next TV series, she said. The judge asked her age, which we know was something she would never reveal, and it was reported in the newspapers that she was allowed to sit down in the witness box and write it on a piece of paper (by this time she was eight months away from her 60th birthday). Another example of the high earnings of celebrities as a result of television was that after singer Kathy Kirby did a Sunday night show, her salary went up to four times the amount she earned previously.

Three days later the headline read, 'Loyal Fans Cost Hylda £2,000,' for she was awarded only £2,921 minus costs totalling around £1,000, and it transpired that she had turned down the sum of £4,000 which had been paid into court in offer of settlement on 1 April. It was reported:

'One reason why Mr Justice Roskill's award was less than 54-year-old [it is to be imagined that she thought that if she wrote it down it wasn't a direct fib!] Miss Baker expected was that he considered her fans more loyal than she believed. He did not consider her eight-month absence from the television screen after the accident had done any great damage to her career, "for she evidently continued to hold the affection of her admirers." He did not think that her injuries called for heavy general damages, nor did they make treatment in the London Clinic essential enough to justify payment by the defendants of the full scale of fees there.'

On 17 June battling little Hylda announced in the *Evening Standard* that she would ask the Appeals Court to rule that the damages should have been much higher. She was not going to take this lying down and had got the bit firmly between her teeth. It probably reminded her of how, all those years ago, the men used to put her down, and she wasn't going to stand for it. Sometimes adversity can be character-building, and it certainly contributed to Hylda's. In February 1965, over three years since the accident, she won her appeal and was awarded £4,073 with costs! She must have been over the moon at the headlines this time: 'Hylda Baker Crash Award Too Little', 'Damages For Hylda Baker Increased,' and 'Hylda Wins By A Photo Finish.'

The final paragraph of one of the articles is worthy of mention because it is so indicative of her life that comedy came out of nearly everything, even a court case. If you put this in a play, people would say it could not be anything other than a clever author's cheap gag:

'Her counsel told three appeal judges his accountants had reckoned damages at £4,073, but counsel for the defence said HIS accountants worked it out at £3,992 — eight short of the magic figure that decided costs. The judges conferred — then decided that Miss Baker's lawyers had done their arithmetic correctly and she should have £4,073 damages WITH COSTS.' Her smile outside court said it all.

Her ability to see the marketing and publicity opportunities in whatever she undertook was apparent once more when, in the summer of 1964, she was doing a comedy play called *What A Joyride* at Blackpool. The theme was topical at the time as it centred on a railway station which was threatened by the 'Beeching Axe' and Hylda was playing an angry stationmaster's wife. She sent a personal invitation to Dr Beeching, direct to his Sussex home — 'to avoid all that railway red tape' — offering him free seats for the show. She said, "If he doesn't come, he'll be missing a really good outing." However, he wrote back saying, "The calls upon my time are so great that I think it very unlikely that I shall find the time to visit Blackpool. I'm sorry," to which Hylda said to the press, "It's a great shame. We were looking forward to giving him a good laugh about the railways for a change." No doubt she wasn't really bothered either way, but it did the show a lot of good, with coverage in two national newspapers, as the closure of railway stations at the time was big news and Dr Beeching was not the most popular of men because of this.

In the September of that year Hylda would be reminded of her father's advice all those years ago, when he had said to her, "Let others impersonate you!" because they did and she was none too happy about it. She discovered that somebody had stolen her act — in Australia! She was furious because, apparently, an 'unknown' over there had pirated her whole material, and as Hylda supposedly had a long tour of Australia lined up with star billing and big money, the deal had fallen through.

"Every single thing about my act — the act I first started building up in 1940 — has been stolen. They've even pinched Cynthia, the big gormless lump I use as my stooge. My material, which I wrote myself, is being splashed all over Australian TV, and now I hear this other act may be booked for America, so I am asking Equity to take up my case. In Australia I could have been earning up to £1,000 a week." The chairman of the Variety Artists' Federation, who at the time was none other than comedian Jimmy Edwards, said, "We've had trouble in the past with Australian comics lifting material off British artists, but never anything like this."

Apparently 'joke poaching' had even plagued the Blackpool summer season show strip that year, but in fact it really is nothing new for comics to use each other's material. It is reputed that many a beer mat has been split in half to enable jottings to be made on the cardboard in dark corners of night clubs, and used at a later date. It has been going on from the year dot! However, to actually copy someone's entire act would never happen, and anyway what would be the point as the 'real' one would be doing the rounds too and nothing would be gained, except, of course, if you were far enough away — and you can't get much further from Britain than Australia. One wonders, though, just how well Hylda's humour would go down there, or even in America, as it was so typically British. Perhaps this is why no more was heard of this unfortunate incident.

Hylda was so popular at the time, though, that people loved to copy her, and on one memorable occasion she was appearing at Blackpool's Grand Theatre, a few years after the Australian incident, when she agreed to meet two ladies who had asked for her at the stage door. They came into the dressing room, one dressed as Hylda, the other as Cynthia, whereupon they proceeded to do her routine, and said afterwards, "Do you know, we go round all the clubs doing this!" Needless to say Hylda shrieked loudly and evicted them both post haste.

Since the accident in 1961 she had not been as busy as she would have liked, but Christmas 1964 saw her starring in pantomime at the New Theatre in Huddersfield, playing Nurse Hylda Double Joy in *Babes In The Wood*, and Allen Sykes, who played Little John, remembers well the first day of rehearsals.

"She arrived accompanied by her Aunt Agnes, driving her own car which was an enormous Jaguar. We could see from the rehearsal room window. She was perched in the driving seat on three or four cushions to give her some height, she got out, went to the boot and took out this huge carrier bag which contained individual portions of fish and chips, which she'd bought on the way, thinking we might all be hungry because we were all members of the regular 'rep' company. Fortunately we had salt and vinegar in the theatre, so before we started rehearsals we all sat down to fish and chips, which was wonderful.

"Nearing lunchtime Hylda said to Nita Valerie, who ran the theatre [and who also devised, produced and wrote the pantomime] 'Where are we going for lunch?' Nita said, 'Well, I hadn't quite decided how long we might have.' Hylda promptly said, 'Look, we'll call at the butchers on the way to your house. I'll buy some steak and we'll cook it, we'll have a really good steak lunch!' Which is what they did."

A Cynthia had to be found for this show, and an example of how Hylda used to employ them was that the box office girl happened to have a very tall husband, who was consequently roped in! Unfortunately, the business wasn't very good, mainly due to the fact that Jimmy Clitheroe, who had a current series on TV, was appearing at the Alhambra Theatre in Bradford, which is very close to Huddersfield, and consequently he ran away with the audiences. She probably blamed him yet again, remembering that unfortunate incident when he dropped her in the pantomime five years before! Hylda had yet to get back her popularity and the last couple of years had not been easy.

Allen stayed friends with Hylda for many years afterwards, and he fondly remembers Sunday evenings in her London flat, where they'd hack the chops out of the freezer, and settle down for the evening in front of the TV to watch the Sunday night play. Apparently, Hylda was constantly commenting on the performances, analysing every inflection, and criticising if she felt it was wrong. She was constantly questioning and Allen praises her for this. He also remembers — and he's by no means the only one — how good she made sausages taste. "She would sprinkle a good layer of salt over them while they were cooking," he says, and although it may sound excessive perhaps this was the secret!

Regarding her work he comments, "Hylda sensed when things were not quite right. That is something which I admired her for. I had the greatest respect for her emphasis that 'i's should be dotted and 't's crossed. That is what made her a star because she knew without any hint of doubt, what was right. She was an absolute genius and it was all the years of training in the provinces that made her like that. I could never accept any statement from anyone who thought she was awkward. Never, ever. She knew what was perfect, and her timing was absolutely spot on, every time."

They often went to Schmits' excellent fish restaurant, off Tottenham Court Road, and one evening when they were there Hylda had ordered plaice. They knew she loved two portions, having a healthy appetite, but this particular evening she couldn't eat the second one, so she decided she would take it home for breakfast. The napkins were of the best Irish linen, but nonetheless she folded the plaice in one of them, leaned down and slipped it into her handbag. When they got back to the flat, after Cha Cha had had his walk round the block, and spent his usual two minutes circling his customary saucer of tea before being put to bed, Allen suggested she take the fish out of her bag, but it wasn't there, it had obviously landed on the floor. They never went back to that restaurant.

Pantomime in 1965 was *Mother Goose* which toured to three places, Ipswich, Doncaster and Hanley on the Gaumont circuit, which was a little bit of a come-down for Hylda after the Moss Empire theatres. She was still a big name, but at the back of her mind it would cause her concern, because she had yet to find the right niche for herself, either with a TV comedy series or the right stage role in order to keep her name at the very top of the best bills. The choreographer of this show was Pauline Stringer, who became a very good friend to Hylda, a friendship which lasted for some years, and this period certainly wasn't without its share of amusing incidents.

The first weeks at Ipswich were pretty memorable as accommodation was very hard to find and the whole company were having problems. Finally it was suggested by the company manager that the best they could do would be to rent some caravans, the company who hired them out being only too happy to transport three of them to a theatre car park for the winter. Although Hylda had booked herself a room in a small pub/hotel, she decided to get one as well, hers naturally having to be the biggest, and they were all conveniently parked right by the stage door. Pauline still remembers the smell of the Calor gas, and the dampness, but in spite of this they had a wonderful time, and Hylda gave hers the full Christmas treatment with balloons and decorations everywhere, giving the company a party on Christmas Day! One gets the feeling that this was a happy time for her. Ann Emery, who played the principal boy, remembers it as being great fun, for Hylda was a great cook. She also remembers that Hylda talked a lot about her father and once even entertained them with the 'drill routine' and the bringing on of the hosepipe between her legs.

William Owen, who had been invited along by the 'Brokers Men' to see the show at the Doncaster Gaumont, remembers going backstage to meet her. She was dressed ready for her Cynthia routine, and he was struck by the fact that although it looked so very tatty from the front, it was immaculately clean. She was very charming, even though she appeared to be suffering badly from a sprained finger which she had trapped in a door on the set the previous night. (Yet another example of how she was constantly beset with accidents). However, his lasting memory was that at the end of the performance, she put her outdoor coat on over her finale costume and went outside the stage door to sign autographs for the many people waiting, including many children. He says, "It was snowing, but despite the cold and sleet Hylda gave a lot of pleasure to a lot of people that night." One wonders if she allowed herself to remember that it was in this same town 35 years earlier, and on just such a snowy night, that she had walked home alone to her new husband?

Pauline Stringer travelled with Hylda in her car to the next dates, and vividly remembers one particular journey when it was bitterly cold. They were in the middle of nowhere with snow piled up on both sides of the road. Hylda got rather worried and so crawled along at a snail's pace. There wasn't a soul to be seen and no other cars anywhere, so she promptly told Pauline to get out and walk in front saying, "Just wave if you see any black ice!" After half an hour the lookout decided it wasn't such a good idea, for not only was it freezing, but she was understandably concerned as to the outcome if Hylda's foot had slipped — and how can you SEE black ice anyway?

On arrival at the hotel, no doubt a welcome sight after the caravans, there would be the inspection of the room, but with Hylda there was always something wrong with it: either the bed (which had to be a double) wasn't in the middle of the room, or it would be too dark and so on. The satisfactory choice would finally be made after an inspection of four or five different rooms, and Pauline would be shown to hers, often on a different floor, whereupon the whole process would begin again because Hylda insisted that her friend must have a room on the same floor!

The touching thing about all of this was that Hylda really did show her need for reassurance at this time and would say to Pauline after they'd had a night out, "Stay with me. Don't go until I've fallen asleep." She'd get changed into one of her luxurious pink or white negligees, and flow off to bed, with Pauline always doing as she asked for she realised that this was something Hylda needed, and it was almost as if the child that was within Hylda had never grown up. Hylda's love of colour was reflected in her cars in the late 1960s, for she drove a shocking pink Cadillac, which is vividly remembered by Pauline, along with a shocking pink bolero jacket which she wore for her cabaret routine.

Something that is still remembered all these years later is that whenever Pauline poured out the tea, she was ordered not to fill it too full. "It's not etiquette," said Hylda, "you'll burn your guest's lips." Another memory is that one of Hylda's favourite accompaniments to salad was mandarin oranges sprinkled with celery salt and chopped mint. When the pantomime was over they remained friends and often Hylda would ring Pauline and say, "I've just put two chops under the grill, come round," not thinking that Pauline was actually in Brixton doing the ironing and having just had a meal! When she replied to this effect and asked, "But why didn't you tell me?" it would be to no avail because she could feel Hylda's tension over the phone and just had to drop everything and go!

They would often go shopping together, particularly to Boots in Tottenham Court Road especially to stock up on Hylda's false eyelashes as she would not be seen without them. In fact she would very rarely be seen without make-up, often going to bed with it on, particularly in hotels. Once when she saw that Pauline wasn't wearing any she said to her, "You do realise that you're in the theatre? You didn't let the maid see you without your make up on?" Her nervousness was very apparent at this time and she would constantly be wringing her hands, then wiping them with a handkerchief. This nervousness would aggravate her bronchial complaint and so she wheezed very badly. However, she apparently never missed a performance and always went on, even if she staggered.

In 1966 Hylda was so determined to continue trying to play serious roles that she placed advertisements in newspapers to draw attention to all the straight parts she had played on film, BBC and ITV, because producers still saw her as a variety artist. It is strange to note that having tried to 'bury' Cynthia in 1961 for that very reason, in 1964 she was so angry that someone else had stolen her act, presumably because she had to continue with that or be out of work. She was once more determined to try to get the parts that she craved for. She planned the campaign and it worked, for in 1966 she played the cameo role of 'Gran' in Bill Naughton's play *Seeing A Beauty Queen Home* for Granada TV:

'Gran was played with the right shrewdness and gusto by Hylda Baker.' (*Television Today*).

'Hylda Baker is capable of much more than a series of she-knows-you-know gags. Occasionally she goes legitimate and produces a straight acting performance that delights the critics.' (*Evening Standard*).

Also in this year she appeared in another TV play, *A Catching Complaint*, and judging by these ecstatic reviews she must have really been saying to herself, "I told them so."

'There was a memorable monologue from Hylda Baker.' (*Sunday Times*).

'Hylda Baker as a domestic acted spots off everybody else. I'd like to see her in Beckett or Pinter.' (*Sunday Citizen*).

'Action and interest shot up sharply when we moved into the kitchen and met Mrs Wiltshire (Hylda Baker). The kitchen scenes were the best in the play, for which most of the credit must go to Hylda.' (*Television Today*).

'The only character who came within a mile of being human was the cook, a part which Hylda Baker played in a way which made me wish she could have had a major role in the production.' (*Western Daily Press*).

'Seldom has a 'dramatic' actress put such lines across so successfully as this comedienne.' (*Ipswich Star*).

There was also a part in *Emergency Ward 10*, with the same result:

December 1953, in *Aladdin* at the Queen's Theatre, Blackpool.

Hylda and her mother pictured at Bolton in September 1955 when she made a personal appearance at the Co-op and was greeted in her home town as a big star. Behind Margaret Baker is Hylda's niece, Ann Turner.

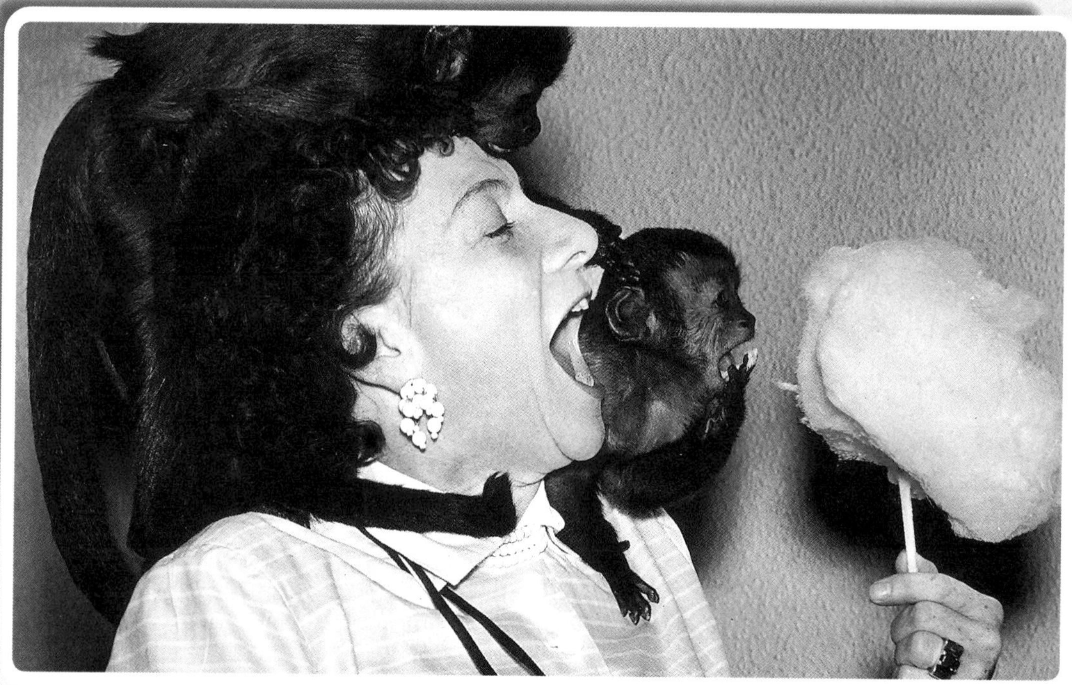

1955 summer season with her 'little men', Mickey and Coco. "There are sights to be seen that shouldn't be seen, because they're obscene, if you know what I mean!"

Topping the bill at Newcastle in April 1956.

This dress is preserved in Preston Museum.

Dorothy Squires, getting full mileage from the camera, congratulates Hylda on her summer show *She Know's You Know!* in 1956.

Hylda in 1956 with her two pet monkeys, celebrating her topping the bill in the West End for the very first time.

Celebration cake for Hylda's top-of-the-bill debut in the West End. The cake is still in existence, in Preston Museum, although no longer edible!

Hylda as 'The Man' in her famous 'Pools Winner' sketch, in March 1957.

With *The Good Old Days* producer Barney Colehan, who made Hylda an 'overnight' success.

"Here! You must get a little hand put on your watch!" Summer 1957 and Hylda is dashed by wheelchair from one pier to another at Blackpool to perform not twice but four times nightly.

"Don't be rickie-doodle-ous! I can't get my handicap down to 12 like this." Hylda, a keen golfer, is pictured at Blackpool in 1957.

Her Ford Fairlane. Too big for her? Oh No! Hylda knew how to market herself – her name and famous catchphrase were painted on the bonnet!

Ex-Guardsman John Kirby helps Hylda to pack for another tour in 1958. She was to fall deeply in love with him.

Publicity photograph from the late 1950s.

A sad and haunting picture. Hylda's father (right) in a Whittingham Hospital production of *Cinderella*. His fellow ugly sister was one of the wardens.

Three interior views of Hylda's new home at Cleveleys in the late 1950s.

Hylda in costume familiar to thousands of her fans, from TV. "Oh she'll have you in stitches. I mean she has had lessons in execution you know."

'Hylda Baker was superb. Who would have imagined her acting ability was equally as good as her comedy.' (*TV World*).

'It was a real treat to see Hylda Baker in *Emergency Ward 10*. She is still the dynamic personality she has always been. I think she deserves a permanent place in the programme to give it more zip — just as Ena Sharples does in *Coronation Street*. (*The Viewer*).

'Hylda Baker was really a bag of hate and spite. Well done Hylda, everyone in our house hissed each time you appeared.' (*Dundee Courier*).

Her very determined crusade to be given the opportunity to play these kind of parts was, in her words, "No laughing matter, as during the past months it has cost me a lot of hard work and a little money." But it had certainly paid off. This is also indicated in what happened just before the episode was due to be recorded. The cast list was rolled on the screen at the start, and suddenly Hylda shouted, "Stop! Where's my name? It's not on the list." The usual procedure was that it was only the regular stars of the series who were billed at the opening, and when it was explained to Hylda that it wasn't part of the contractual arrangements that her name was to be there, she wouldn't accept it. How very brave of her (although some would say foolhardy), to make such a stand when she was merely 'guesting' on the show with a cameo role. Her father's advice was still ringing in her ears.

At Christmas 1966 she was appearing at the Granada Cinema in Shrewsbury with Clinton Ford and Fred Emney, with her next TV role on 1 May 1967 being Mum Nesbitt in a two-part *Z Cars* story called 'The Nesbitts are back',' and completely different to the part she had played on the same programme exactly four years previously. This time she played the mother of a family of small-time crooks, who plans the jobs, but doesn't actually do any of them herself, and the culmination of the episodes is that she eventually comes face to face with Sergeant Bert Lynch (played by James Ellis), gets drunk and makes a few passes at him. One can assume that Hylda would not have let this scene pass by without giving just a little glimpse of her comedic skills.

Apparently her reputation within the BBC had been helped around this time by the fact that she gave a great performance that would never be seen. They were experimenting with colour techniques and she was engaged to do an excerpt of a play for them in front of the cameras. She did something she must have revelled in, the Duchess in the Jacobean thriller *The Revenger's Tragedy*.

The end of May and she was opening at the Golders Green Hippodrome, for a short tour, playing the mother in Shelagh Delaney's *A Taste Of Honey*, working once again for Audrey Lupton and Arthur Lane. She was becoming even more eccentric, too, for when she made her first entrance she got an enormous round of applause, but instead of carrying on with the scene she turned to the audience and said, "Oh, I didn't think you'd recognise me in the hat!" Nonetheless, actor Patrick Duggan, who was also in the play, said she was brilliant in the part, but he found her offstage to be rather sad; there was a façade of toughness although she was never unpleasant, and therefore he never really got to know her. Unfortunately, though, around this period seems to be the start of a big problem for Hylda. She had always been absent minded, but lately she had great difficulty in remembering her lines, and this was going to get no better as time went on.

In one scene she completely 'dried', so Valerie Newbold, (incidentally, she was the girl who was her terrified understudy in the pantomime four years previously) who was playing her daughter, tried to help by 'feeding' lines to her. Hylda carried on but got stuck once more. Valerie helped her again but it was obvious to the audience, so Hylda looked at them and said, "She knows you know!" and received a huge round of applause. Later it happened again, whereupon Hylda came forward and sang, "I give the springtime to the flowers, I give the... etc," going into the full number. The musical director of Audrey and Arthur's company was watching with them from the back of the stalls and remarked, "I didn't know this was a musical play, I should be down there in the pit." They, who by this time must have had their hearts in their mouths, said, "Of course it's not, she's racking her brains to think what comes next." Audrey said later that Hylda was such a brilliant actress, and was so clever that she could always get through on a wing and a prayer.

These anecdotes about her forgetfulness, and there are many more to come because it became much worse, whilst being very amusing in retrospect, were not funny at the time, either for Hylda or the people on stage with her. It is every actor's nightmare that you are in a play and the lines just won't come, and Hylda was destined to relive this nightmare many more times. Imagine being in a theatre full of people, they've come to see YOU, but you can't remember anything and you don't know what you're doing. What a pity that it was to begin just as she had got the kind of parts she had been seeking for so long.

One of these parts was, at last, to see her star in a West End play, at the Vaudeville theatre no less, alongside Sheila Hancock, Harry H.Corbett, Helen Cotterill, and Ken Wynne. It transferred from The Royal Court Theatre, a black comedy called *Fill The Stage With Happy Hours* by Charles Wood, and it opened on 6 September 1967. The setting was that of a provincial theatre, with Harry H.Corbett and Sheila Hancock being the manager and his wife. The scenes which everyone was talking about, and those who saw it still do, were the ones between Hylda as a rather simple, middle-aged usherette, and Sheila Hancock. Hylda's character got everything wrong, dropping chocolates and ices, and Milton Shulman in the *Evening Standard* said in his review she had 'some of the funniest dead-pan lines I've heard on stage for a long time'. He added, 'It is both touching and hilarious.'

The reader must forgive yet another list of the reviews, but it is what Hylda would have been most proud of and therefore it is essential that the praise she received is given full measure, for all the critics were unanimous:

'Hylda Baker, gnome's head over squat little body over short legs terminating in white bobby socks and sandals, is one of the most laughable sights I've seen for some time, and she uses the impeccable timing she has learnt in variety to turn in a smashing performance.' (*Financial Times*).

'The one absolutely authentic note is struck by Hylda Baker's portrait of an elderly programme girl, grotesque, pathetic, and treated like a half-witted child.' (*Evening News*).

'And then there's Molly, a stage-struck retainer, dwarfish, incompetent, played with comic genius by Hylda Baker.' (*The Observer*).

'Hylda Baker turns in a performance of grotesque hilarity as a stage-struck usherette longing to act but not knowing how.' (*Daily Mail*).

'Particularly Hylda Baker as the half-witted maid-cum-usherette who commands laughter with every scamper across the stage.' (*The Sun*).

'The best comes from Hylda Baker, a gauche, devoted dogsbody given to lunatic malapropisms'. (*The Times*).

That final review does show that Hylda could not get away from these, and one assumes she put them in at rehearsals, but none the less she had certainly run away with the honours. In the programme notes for *Fill The Stage With Happy Hours* the biography of the author, Charles Wood, could almost be a picture of Hylda's early life, and perhaps this play touched a few chords in her heart. It read, strangely with very little punctuation, thus:

'Father was a stage director and stage manager and actor with lifts in his shoes. He married my mother against grandfather's will and was told never will you work for me which he did later. Grandfather was Albert Harris and I never knew him because he died before I was old enough to know him from all the uncles and aunties in the dressing rooms, and taking me back to the digs, and sitting with in trains on Sunday mornings when we all changed towns to go to another theatre with a large gasworks somewhere near. But he did leave a memory of the Foreign Legion which I have with me still, I don't know why, perhaps I saw *Desert Song* with him, but I didn't, that was my father, who later swung through a french window on a rope in the Dumb Man Of Manchester, in Castleford, where they had a big iron door I wasn't tall enough to open and the stage manager wore evening dress and had stinking feet. Mother was a dancer before she got to be beautiful and a good actress. They all enjoyed it.'

In January 1968 came what would prove to be the final turning point in what was already a long and chequered career — Hylda was by now 63 years old — and which was to make her even more of a household name. She was given the now legendary part of Nellie Pledge, starring alongside Jimmy Jewel as Eli Pledge, in Granada TV's new comedy series *Nearest And Dearest*. This spurred her on to do something she'd been meaning to do, and that was to lose weight! Very often this will happen when a new and exciting venture beckons, and so she went on what was a diet that the Aga Khan had apparently used with success. She said, "I want to reduce to eight and a half stone, as I am only four foot eleven, and it's not a starvation diet just common sense, with a cup of tea and an orange for breakfast, a steak for lunch, lamb chops and salad for supper. No bread and no drink." She achieved her goal and when she appeared on the *Eamonn Andrews Show* on 4 February, she had lost 11lbs in ten days, and this was the final day of the diet. Her obvious excitement at her forthcoming television series was most apparent, but she would find that this was not to be plain sailing, for there were choppy seas ahead.

CHAPTER EIGHT

Nearest But Not Dearest

THE series revolved around Nellie and Eli Pledge, played by Hylda and Jimmy, a brother and sister who were the reluctant bosses of a run-down pickle factory, having inherited it from their father. The very first episode was shown on 15 August 1968, and once again Hylda stole the critics' praise. The *Sun* newspaper said: '*Nearest And Dearest* should really be watched wearing a kiss-me-quick hat, with a chip butty in the interval. It is the purest Blackpudlian summer season humour. Central Pier with the rain bucketing down. It's basic, broad and bawdy, and good taste is something it thinks comes from tripe and onions. It assumes there's no point in trying to keep 'owt from the neighbours, as they've got lug 'oles like dustbin lids anyroad. Hylda Baker is so Lancashire you can smell the smoke and salt. She's the blood in this fairly assembly line black pudding.'

The series had come about when Peter Eckersley was Head of Light Entertainment at Granada TV. Writers Vince Powell and Harry Driver were working at Thames TV, and Peter rang them one day and said he was doing six separate comedy half-hours and could they write one of them for him. They then devised *Nearest And Dearest* but actually wrote it for Jimmy Jewel who was a good friend of theirs and for whom they had written before. In this they gave him a sister, but she was something of a minor character, the main one being Jimmy, and they sent the script off to Peter. He absolutely loved it, rang them back and said that he wasn't going to do six separate presentations after reading this — he wanted to do six of these if they would write them. At the time Vince and Harry had signed an exclusive contract for Thames, so they went to the head of the company and asked permission, explained the situation, and he said he would be prepared to allow them to do four as they were paid considerably for the fact they were exclusive. After this, when the series took off, it would be billed as having been 'devised by Vince Powell and Harry Driver'.

The read through of the first episode went well and Jimmy and Hylda appeared to be getting on very well, but the problems began in the second episode, in the middle of rehearsals. There was a scene where Jimmy's character was pretending to be ill. He was doing his best to avoid doing the stocktaking in the pickle factory, and Hylda's character had to keep coming into the bedroom, almost catching him having a crafty cigarette or a beer, and then going out again. Being very shrewd she noticed that Jimmy was going to get all the laughs, so she stopped in the middle of rehearsals and said, "Just a minute, I'm in and out of this scene like a fart in a colander!"

That, apparently, was the moment that Jimmy began to hate her. It was to be the beginning of a long, much talked about battle between them, which would not only affect their working relationship, but all of those who worked alongside them.

During the first recording, at the end of the show, Hylda noticed that the final 'tag' line was Jimmy's, so while they were still recording she stepped out in front of the cameras and said, "Just a minute," and the result was that Vince and Harry had to go backstage with Peter and re-write it so that she was in the final 'pay off' as well as Jimmy. It is somewhat understandable, though, because they were both the stars of the show, and Hylda was quite a name after all.

The fact that Hylda was cast in the series came about because, at the same time as Vince and Harry submitted their very first script idea to Peter Eckersley, one was also sent to him from another very successful writing partnership, Roy Bottomley and Tom Brennand. This one was based on Roy's mother who had been a pub landlady. It was set in a pub and he thought it would be an ideal part for Hylda and so suggested this when they sent it off to Peter. He came back to them to say that he loved the script, it was very funny, but he had already commissioned a pilot script from Vince and Harry and asked if they would mind if he extracted Hylda from their idea and put her into *Nearest And Dearest*. It turned out that, as the exclusive Thames contract prevented Vince and Harry from continuing to write for the series, Roy and Tom ended up writing at least half the episodes during its five-year run. Five years! Such was the success of the stormy brother and sister relationship of Nellie and Eli Pledge in that factory making Pledge's Purer Pickles.

The series was a great hit, the characters were so real that it was almost like those old Blackpool McGill postcards. There was Walter (played by Eddie Malin), who in fact probably had the best part as he never spoke, and often when Hylda was trying to communicate with him it was very reminiscent of her 'Cynthia' routine; the famous line everyone remembers, even today, was "Walter, have you been? . . . Yes, he's been." His wife, Lily, was brilliantly played by Madge Hindle, Joe Gladwin played Stan, with thick glasses which meant he was always peering at everyone, and to Hylda it was always, "Hello, Miss Nellie."

Even today, nearly 30 years later, people say to their children as their parents did to them, "Have you been?" and they imitate Hylda's inimitable style of delivery. Mention her name to anyone and they immediately come back with, "Oh, I must get a little hand put on this watch," for this was Hylda's main catch-phrase in the series, along with "Oh, you big girl's blouse." This originally came from Roy's mother, who used it to customers she didn't like. He wrote it into the script but once Hylda got hold of it she made it her own, and even changed it sometimes to things like, "You big flea's armpit!"

It is very sad that she and Jimmy didn't get on, but one wonders whether the on-screen arguments between their characters would have been quite so funny if they had! These scenes are always very highly-charged, very aggressive, and as a result, very funny. One particular phrase he would throw at her which was, "You knock-kneed knackered old nosebag," would never fail to set the sparks flying. Such was the feeling between them that once when Jimmy was driving back in teeming rain to the Midland Hotel in Manchester, where Hylda was also staying, he caught sight of her walking along the pavement, soaking wet, so he stopped the car, wound down the window and offered her a lift. There are no prizes for guessing that she refused in no uncertain terms! It is also common knowledge that on many occasions he had complained that Hylda was killing his laughs in the show, but in truth they were both at it, it was a battle royal and they would fight to the death.

Nellie Pledge was a wonderful character, a sort of extension of her own self, and she would add many of her famous malapropisms from her stage act, which was full of them. Many people think that they are merely accidental, but this was the cleverness of it, because she worked at and thought about them very carefully. However, she didn't bring all the new ones and the writers would be constantly racking their brains because they had to be created to work within the context of the plot. Remarks such as "I'm not menthol, and I am not suffering from illuminations," "She's nothing more than a nymph of a maniac, with her see-through blouse and her see up skirt," "The condescention was running down those walls," "It's my derrogative," and on meeting a rather handsome new male character, "Oh hello, I don't think you've had the pleasure of me yet."

There is one incident that is worth mentioning because it concerned her attitude to Mrs Malaprop. There was a great feature at the time in the Ogden household in *Coronation Street*, and that was the 'muriel' on the wall with the three ducks, one of which was always slightly out of line. Hylda complained to Bill Podmore that they were pinching her material and that she was going to sue them, and when he said, "But Hylda it dates from way back, it's Mrs Malaprop," Hylda replied, "Well, I'll sue her too." She is also reputed to have said once, "I'm fed up of hearing about that Mrs Malaprop. I thought them up long before she did!"

Five or six years later, she was still going on about it, because Vince Powell and Harry Driver wrote a series called *For The Love Of Ada* with Irene Handl in which she did many mispronunciations. Hylda rang her agent one day and said, "Have you seen that series that they've written for Irene Handl? Well, she's pinched my act. They've given her all those mispronunciations. I'm going to sue them." Her agent said, "You can't sue them." Hylda said, "I am, I'm going to sue them." He replied, "You can't, they were started by Sheridan in *The Rivals*," to which she said, "Well, I'll sue HIM then!"

Hylda was a very clever, intelligent woman and it is highly unlikely that by this time she didn't know about Sheridan's play. She might have said it once, but after that she would seize the opportunity of making a gag. She certainly would have had no idea that even after her death these stories would be trotted out and used against her, but they would still be very amusing tales.

The writers of the series were absolutely spot on, the characters, the situations they created were hysterical, the pay-off lines were priceless; they were definitely the main course and Hylda would add to the scenes her own brand of 'salt and pepper'. On some occasions she would add them without warning, though, which could be somewhat disconcerting for the other artists, and often this would be because she had completely 'dried' and was desperately trying to get herself out of it, for her memory was getting steadily worse.

It is so hard to tell, though, when watching those episodes, whether she has just made something up on the spur of the moment, or whether it was scripted, such was her comedic skill, but just occasionally you can catch a glimpse of the terror beneath, and then it's gone in a flash when she has recovered. Sometimes sheer genius would come from these moments, but it was inbred in her from those variety days, and in the dark recesses of her mind was the ability to survive by what appeared to be a casual ad lib.

Jimmy Jewel, however, was none too happy on these occasions, particularly if she 'brought the house down', which she often did. He would say, "Has that woman been at it behind my back again?" Once, there was a scene where Jimmy had been out to get some fish and chips, and when he got back Hylda had some dialogue which was full of pretty complicated malapropisms. She was having great difficulty with this section, so Roy Bottomley suggested that they write them inside the paper of her fish and chips and they would be there for her to read. Jimmy bursts into the room, smacks down a parcel of fish and chips in front of her, she opens it but the lines aren't there. She gives him a look, marches over to his side of the table, smacks down her fish and chips in front of him, grabs his and says, "Wrong fish and chips!" It made no sense to the live studio audience, but as was often the case, she got away with it.

Everywhere on the set, there were the 'cue cards' or 'idiot boards' for her, and once when they were doing an outdoor scene, they couldn't hold the boards close enough when they were filming a long shot, so her lines were written up in big letters on a furniture van at the end of the road. It may seem very cruel to mention all of this, but so many people have so many stories about what went on that it is very important that the true facts are known. At the time, many suffered because of Hylda's problem, but none of them as much as she herself because she was terrified underneath, and is it not true that when an animal is frightened it will either cower and hide or it will attack? As we have learned, Hylda was always taught that you must stand up for yourself, and never show that others have the upper hand, so it is only natural, after all the hard times, that she should choose to fight and not admit to having any weakness. The sad thing is that she did in fact believe that she was going mad, which made her fear even worse, but this she would never ever confide to her colleagues.

Bill Podmore, who produced the series, would often howl with laughter at some of the lines in the scripts when he read them, but would then say, "That really is very funny, but they'll have to go you know, she'll never remember all that." He'd put a 'box' around it, and the secretary would block out that section before the scripts were duplicated. Hylda, however, was not stupid, she would come to rehearsals and say, "I've seen your boxes, you can't kid me. What was there in that space, that I've not seen? What's he cut out?" She didn't appreciate the reasoning behind the action.

Roy Bottomley's own reasoning for this was very astute. He said, "No doubt it was also something to do with that to some degree every performer, particularly stand-up performers, have really deep-rooted feelings of insecurity, as anyone who has worked for, or with them, has to be aware of, sometimes almost bordering on schizophrenia. Hylda's feelings of insecurity were obviously exacerbated by the fact she was a woman, but to stand up in front of an audience at the Glasgow Empire, a little lady of four foot nothing, to come on and make me laugh, oh they were very few and far between. Frankly I don't know of another one. She was a one-off, for at that time it was almost immoral for a woman to be doing it. The secret of success with comedy is that wonderful line between pathos and belly laugh, and she could do it. It's how I remember all my Lancashire relations — you smile through the storm don't you? We all know it but it's so very difficult to get. She was a comedy genius in her own way, because she was unique. Yes, there's no doubt about that!"

Hylda never 'bitched' people behind their backs, and of Jimmy the most she would say was, "Oh, that man!" And she would sometimes ring Roy and say, "I've just read this, he's got 24 laughs and I've only got 16 in that scene." Yet she often gave lines to Jimmy without him knowing, and on one occasion said, "This line isn't funny if I say it, it'll be funnier if he does it," and she was right. However, it is true to say that she really did know which was a line for a man, and she didn't like being masculine (when she wasn't doing her act as a man) because she was actually a very feminine woman. She didn't deliberately want to, or set out to be horrid, but she became obsessed with being a star.

The atmosphere on the set was icy when Hylda and Jimmy were together, but it was really only Jimmy who didn't speak to her. Madge Hindle got on with her, she was very generous and had a great deal of patience. Her description of Hylda is really rather touching. She said, "With her it was always the 'walk down' and you had to 'queen' her. She had the gowns and everything, but she was always wary, she couldn't believe you were being nice for HER. You couldn't dislike her, how could you dislike someone who made you laugh so much? In spite of herself, and all her problems, she couldn't help doing it well." Hylda also once told Madge that when she was young she'd wanted to learn to play the saxophone, but her father had said, "You never put anything in your mouth, you talk with your mouth!"

The year 1968 was certainly a memorable one for Hylda because as well as the series, she made two films. The series was actually top of the TV ratings that year and again in 1969. The first film was *Up The Junction* with Suzy Kendall and Dennis Waterman, and the second was playing Mrs Sowerberry in *Oliver!* In the first of these she played an abortionist, which was what she had also played in *Saturday Night And Sunday Morning*, and as was her wont she got a gag out of this saying, "I thought, soon everybody will be asking me for my address!" Suzy Kendall remembers with great affection that morning they filmed the scene in *Up The Junction*, and has such good memories of Hylda. It was obvious that poor Hylda was having great difficulty with her lines. She was all over the place, so she just made up her own. The situation was supposed to be traumatic for the characters that Suzy and Adrienne Posta were playing, but it was apparently extremely hard to act this as they were helpless with laughter. Hylda was so funny and eccentric that it became a rather bizarre morning, for anything she did was left in the scene as it fitted with this rather dotty character, and it took the sting out of the sinister side. It was remembered as being 'a great fun morning!' What a lovely tribute.

In *Oliver!* Hylda once more showed how clever and inventive she was. She had to do something with her part, as it wasn't very large, and her main scene was when Oliver is brought before her and she has to inspect him to see if he's healthy and suitable to employ. She said, "I delved you see, I delved," and she came up with the idea that if you're inspecting an animal, the first thing you'd look at would be the teeth, so in rehearsal she went straight up to him, pushed his head back and lifted his top lip. The director told her it was a wonderful piece of invention, saying he would never have thought of that, whereupon she replied, "I'm Hylda Baker!" Her cameo role was much talked about when the film opened in September, which led her to make this comment: "I was very excited about it when I went to see it, and I got a round of applause, yes, in the cinema, and a friend told me it has happened since too, which was rather fabulous wasn't it?"

The Guardian published this article about her in 1968:

'Hylda Baker's dog had a bare patch on its stomach from running through the gorse bushes and could not have a bath: a story which you'd think the owner had invented if you hadn't seen the unwashed dog, which did look rather sad. This is Hylda Baker's stock in trade, the warm and human gag about a dog which can't have baths and the shoes which all fall out (as hers do in her flat) when you open up the cupboard, and landladies and marriages and lack of late night buses. She is a funny woman who can keep it up for ever.'

In an interview she gave in August of the same year, there are some comments she made which are very indicative of her attitude to her work, and there is also an insight into her ability to hide her true feelings because apparently when she was talking she couldn't keep still, her world was always a stage, even in her own flat while she was having lunch. One minute she's sitting at her fireside table looking small, tough and rather lonely, and the next she has dropped her knife and fork and begins an animated conversation with the imaginary Cynthia in order to prove a point.

She starts off by saying threateningly, "Don't ask me how old I am. My age is my own affair! Look, I learned my business the hard way — that's the only way there is. It makes me mad when I see people in the theatre who think they can drift in from a finishing school, and because they're Lord So and So's daughter or

Mrs Hyphenated Blank's niece, they'll be an overnight success. It's not that easy to be an entertainer. An artist is a special person and not just anyone can be one. I've been learning all my life, and I don't think I know it all. If I am a success — and I never think of myself that way — it's because I keep on trying. If I fall down, I fight back. I took one look at that box [TV] and said, that's my medium, I'm a visual comedienne. Take my Cynthia act, basically it's a funny situation, and it's funny because it's true. When you're small you have to make your presence felt, but when you're tall you don't need to talk because you're THERE, people can't ignore you. Everybody laughs at Cynthia and her friend because maybe they recognise themselves or somebody they know. They don't always laugh either, sometimes they're close to tears. Charlie Chaplin knew that very well and he's the greatest. Comedy is based on a heck of a lot of observation. I look and listen all the time, because your material is all around you."

Even though she was busy with the television series, Hylda also found time to do her variety spots and toured the club scene. She even did something very rare, and that was she had a woman playing Cynthia. She had once used Claire Ruane in the past, as she was very tall, but this time it was none other than Gaye Brown! It was at The Golden Garter in Wythenshawe, where Gaye remembers vividly that they got to the dressing rooms via the kitchen, and of course people would ask for autographs. Hylda told her that she must never sign her real name, the identity of Cynthia was never to be revealed. Needless to say, undaunted Gaye signed her own name. Her memories of Hylda, though, are wonderful. "I was mesmerised, she was extraordinary, she had that Piaf quality. I learned so much from her and it gave me a great education. That period was my university, she was a great influence, such a talented woman, and drama students today should study her, for there was nobody like her. The sheer genius of her was the marvellous moment where she would leave the stage, while the band played the intro to *I Wish You Love*, I would walk slowly round, hold out my hand, and exit. Then, having done a lightning quick change, Hylda appeared singing her heart out in a silver lame dress with a 1950s style huge white fox fur. It was just fabulous!"

Gaye also remembers the opening song for the whole act was *A Good Man Is Hard To Find* and it being just as electric. It was a case of 'eat your heart out, Ella Fitzgerald!' One of the most amusing moments, though, was when Hylda dried, as she did so frequently. It was during one of her most famous gags about the elephant.She 'went' completely, changed the dialogue to another joke, then suddenly remembered it again, turned to Cynthia and said, "You've remembered haven't you?' and carried on with the first joke. She always turned it round so that it was Cynthia's fault, never hers!

In August she was offered yet another challenge, to star in a new West End musical *Mr And Mrs* which was based on two Noel Coward plays, *Fumed Oak* and *Brief Encounter*, and was written by Ross and John Taylor who were also responsible for the highly successful *Charlie Girl*. Before she began rehearsals she treated herself to a holiday in Majorca as she had suffered yet another attack of bronchitis, taking with her a tape recorder to learn the four songs she would sing in the show. One of the songs, which was called *If The Right Man Should Ask Me*, contained the lyrics, 'I'm so tired of going home to an empty house,' and she said at the time, "I am too. The words of that song are very close to home. At my time of life you need somebody to share your life with. Sometimes I have been very lonely." She must have been unusually off guard that day!

Rehearsals began in October. Hylda played Honor Blackman's mother-in-law and a railway station buffet manageress, Alan Breeze was the ticket collector, and John Neville also starred in the show. It was a first West End musical for both Hylda and Alan, and she did confess at the time that she had quite a few butterflies about it. They had a great reception in Manchester at the end of November where the show was 'run in', and it opened at The Palace Theatre in London on 11 December 1968. It ran only until the middle of January, and one review was headed, 'It's all Mr and Misses,' and they went on to say:

"It's a certain divorce in the new year, when the honeymoon is over and the friendly guests have stopped cheering ...Hylda Baker sings (quite extraordinary) like Noel Coward and the chorus have legs that could inspire no man other than Joe Davis. Yet there are two show stoppers (despite the fact that any stoppage was a blessing) in *I Feel I Want To Dance* and *I Want To Wet My Whistle*. (*Daily Sketch*).

Perhaps Noel Coward took the above review rather badly, as apparently he said of Hylda, rather cruelly, 'I'd wring that woman's neck if I could find it!"

Gordon Pleasant, for whom Hylda would work much later in the 1970s, saw the show and remembers one scene in particular which was electric. Alan Breeze had a very long speech lasting three and a half or four minutes, with Hylda on stage saying nothing. She didn't upstage, but just stood stock still and listened, and as Gordon says, "She took every eye in that theatre!" What a presence she had.

Alan Breeze's dresser at the time, Jonathan McNicholl, remembers that Hylda used to sit in Alan's dressing room night after night because she never liked being alone. She'd be there before the half-hour call and then again after the show, too, but one thing he recalls shows how many problems she had with injuries; indeed, it seemed to be the 'norm' for her. He says, "During rehearsals for *Mr And Mrs* she was rehearsing with John Neville. She was due to make an entrance, but the backdrop came down and hit her on the head. She was bleeding, too, and she came on to the stage staggering everywhere. The director thought she was drunk and called her a name or two, and she absolutely threw the book at him: 'Nobody gives a damn about me, I could have been killed!' I saw it happen, and she could have been, too. She was known for being accident-prone, but this must have been one of the worst and was certainly not her fault in any way."

Just before the show came off, Hylda, interviewed on radio, said, "I just think it's not the best time for theatres, just after Christmas. Even the shopkeepers this year are saying there's not as much money about and people aren't spending. Perhaps they're doing what the government wants them to do for a change!" Suffice it to say that the show was not a success.

While she was in this show there was a reunion with Pauline Stringer, someone whose friendship had meant a great deal to her but with whom she had fallen out in 1967, over something very trivial. Pauline had been very ill with appendicitis and when she came out of hospital Hylda had insisted that she would look after her and she was to recuperate at Hylda's flat, but this was not what Pauline wanted. She wanted to go home to Exeter to be with her family, and when she categorically said this was what she was going to do, Hylda was so hurt and put out that she cut off from her completely. This is such a pointer into Hylda's character — she always wanted her own way. In this instance, however, she wanted someone to look after and couldn't understand that it wasn't always what others wanted. As someone who knew her well in the early days said, "There were no half-measures with her, she wanted your life!" However, during the short run of *Mr And Mrs*, Pauline went to see her, taking a huge bunch of white flowers, and made it up because, in her own words, "I missed her, she was an anchor and she was part of my life. We laughed so much."

Sadly, Hylda lost her other companion during the run of the play, for Cha Cha died in very unfortunate circumstances. One of the girls in the chorus offered to take him for a walk between shows and decided to treat him to a piece of sponge cake. Well, these dogs are so tiny, you don't give them a piece, you give them a crumb! Sadly he choked on it and died and this poor girl had the unenviable task of going back to the theatre to break the news to Hylda. The happiness that little dog gave her far outweighed everything and she had lavished all her affection on it. Naturally she was devastated, as she had been many years before when her monkeys died. All of them had been her family.

Desert Island Discs, which, of course, is still popular on radio today, was a programme on which only very big names were invited to guest. On 12 February 1969, Hylda was asked to choose the eight records she would take to her desert island. She was introduced as an 'actress and variety artist', which indicated that she had indeed been accepted in the field she most desired. She could not have been more pleased when her introduction put the 'actress' bit first. No longer were the headlines to read, 'Hylda Baker, variety artist, tries to go straight.'

Her choice of songs was extremely varied and was indicative of her love of music of all kinds:

Look To The Rainbow (from the film *Finian's Rainbow*) sung by Petula Clark/Don Francis/Fred Astaire

Be My Love sung by Mario Lanza

All's Going Well, My Lady Montmorency sung by Margaret Rutherford/Frankie Howerd

One Fine Day (from Puccini's *Madam Butterfly*) Maria Callas/ Philarmonia Orchestra

Supercalifragilisticexpialidocius (from the film *Mary Poppins*) sung by Julie Andrews/Dick Van Dyke

Lara's Theme (from the film *Dr Zhivago*) played by Los Paraguayos

This Is My Life sung by Shirley Bassey

Give Us A Kiss (from *Mr And Mrs*) sung by Hylda Baker

How very typical of her that she chose one of her own records! She was ever controversial, and very unpredictable. It is not certain — and now we will never know — but it is possible that she actually meant to choose *Tara's Theme* from *Gone With The Wind*, and not *Lara's Theme*, simply because it seems that, considering her great love of that film, it was her memory which made the mistake, and we know how forgetful she had become. If she did indeed make a mistake, it would have been wonderful to have been party to her reaction in the studio. It is only a theory, but what makes one feel it so strongly with no proof whatsoever? The luxury she chose to take with her was a family photograph album, and for the one book she was allowed to take she chose *Gone With The Wind* by Margaret Mitchell! Actor Patrick Duggan, who had worked with her in *A Taste Of Honey* in 1967, remembers even now that when he listened to that broadcast what came over so very strongly was her loneliness, sadness, and a great sense of longing which she couldn't disguise. His feelings were tinged with regret that he hadn't taken more time to get to know her when he worked with her, but she really was so difficult to get close to.

She also hit a high spot in 1969 when she joined Frankie Howerd, Frankie Vaughan, Ronnie Corbett, Ronnie Barker and Peggy Mount for a special Army Royal Variety show. She was extremely excited at the prospect of meeting the Queen, as Peggy Mount, who was sharing a dressing room with her, remembers. Hylda had bought a new dress for the occasion, all frills and sequins, and a beautiful fur cape. She was over the moon with anticipation before the show. All she talked about was what the Queen would say to her and Peggy didn't see her until after the presentation line up when she went back to the dressing room. She found Hylda in floods of tears, mascara streaming down her face, very distressed. The reason was that she hadn't managed to shake hands with Her Majesty after all. Why? When she calmed down she said that the Queen got to her in the line up, went to shake hands, Hylda did the same, but she couldn't — her hands were stuck behind her back. Apparently she had to do quite a quick change just beforehand and the dresser had put her cape on upside down! It could only happen to Hylda.

Six years later, in an interview for the *Sunday Times*, she appears to have forgotten this awful incident, or maybe got her meetings with the Queen mixed up, because she did do other Royal Variety performances, certainly one before this when Antoinette Sibley, the ballerina, topped the bill. She told the interviewer: "I've appeared before her Majesty you know. Oh yes! Much better than the Command Performance, much, because you see I had all four of them. I had Queen Elizabeth, Prince Philip, Prince Charles and Princess what's-her-name? Anne! It was some charity, something to do with the army. I think I was introduced to them later, like you are you know. I did my curtsy and I said, 'Excuse me Queen, but did you happen to see my friend? She was in the taxi after yours.' That's from my act with Cynthia you know. I heard afterwards they fell about. 'Most enjoyable,' the Queen said, so now in my act I always say, 'As the Queen said to me, most enjoyable!'"

She certainly didn't tell her escort actor Allen Sykes, who she had still kept in touch with after the Huddersfield pantomime in 1964, about not being able to shake hands, for his memories are as follows: "It was splendid, the audience were wonderful, and Hylda was so excited. The ovation she had was roof-lifting. Wonderful. Afterwards I was standing in the wings, the Queen passed me, followed by the Duke of Edinburgh, then Princess Anne, and as she passed me she said, 'I'm starving, where are the sandwiches?' Hylda looked wonderful, her eyes were sparkling and she looked magnificent in her gown."

The second series of *Nearest And Dearest* was commissioned, Hylda and Jimmy began rehearsals for it in April 1969 and the two warriors were locking antlers once more. It is really not surprising that there should be problems between them because they were both stars and how do you gauge one getting better billing than the other? Not only that but Jimmy Jewel used to work with a partner, his cousin Ben Warris, before he decided to 'go it alone'; and Hylda had reached her fame by working with a partner (she would never admit this, though, and always insisted Cynthia was her 'assistant') before doing her utmost to be taken seriously as an actress. What happens? They both end up in a popular series, but they are now a brother and sister 'double act' who are always together and rely upon each other all the time. It was inevitable that sparks would fly.

For one episode they went to Blackpool to do the publicity and the following description in the *TV Times* is a wonderfully accurate one of the town and an indication of the atmosphere of the series;

'Blackpool ...5,000 boarding house and hotels open their doors to eight million holidaymakers every year, tripling the town's population in mid-season. Grannies, mums and dads and lolly-licking toddlers bask in up to 30,000 deck chairs every day, leaving a mess which has a gang of men sweeping up at five in the morning. At night 400,000 coloured lights burn up the off-peak electricity while visitors drop an average £2 each into the one-armed bandits and pin machines, guzzle draught champagne at 3s 9d a glass and lighten their wallets by between £30 and £60 per week.

'But when you've been bottled up in a pickle factory for nearly a year, Blackpool is THE place for the works outing. Hylda Baker, Jimmy Jewel and all the regulars from *Nearest And Dearest* turned up on the Golden Mile for an episode. Jimmy, who plays Eli Pledge, playboy boss of the pickle firm, headed for the lights, splashed all his money on champagne, cigars and birds. But his spree ended in the pleasure gardens, where he overdid things by swigging too much champagne while astride a roundabout horse.

Hylda, who plays Eli's sister Nellie, was not tempted by the high life. She strolled down to the sands, picked an amiable donkey called Satan and jogged peacefully up and down the beach. Then she and Jimmy got together to visit the Hall of Mirrors. "We only came here on reflection," said Hylda. After this they dropped in on a promenade photographer who specialised in saucy postcard cut-out poses, where you stick your head through a hole and look like a Donald McGill Fat Lady. Later on they were found trudging down a street full of the famous Blackpool boarding houses.

'Both knew the setting well, having played here many times over the past 20 years. "I always used to stay in theatrical digs," said Hylda, "and all that chat about dragon landladies is rubbish. We used to be treated like royalty, with breakfast in bed and all that. Better than a lot of hotels today. Just standing in a street like this takes you back 20 years, as this aspect of Blackpool hasn't changed."

'Despite the penny-in-the-slot gadgetry of 1969 Blackpool, there is still room for an old-fashioned works outing. The weather doesn't matter, you don't go there for the weather. The day *Nearest And Dearest* invaded town, the top of Blackpool Tower was shrouded in mist, the tide was out, and it was Monday, which is not the best day for fish and chips. But the workers from Eli Pledge's factory were happy, just as long as the candyfloss twirled, and the brown ale flowed, they were pickled pink.'

The next series was an even greater success, and the first episode was transmitted on 9 July, this one having been written by John Stevenson. The plot line was that Nellie had been brought home corsetless by two policemen from a shopping trip. She'd been caught in the supermarket with a week's supply of pickles down her drawers, and the police refused to believe her explanation that they were Pledge's pickles and she was actually taking them IN. How did they come to detect her in the first place? Well, the elastic in her knickers broke. The joy of the series was that it managed to outrageously colour reality, without losing all touch with it. It was pure, unadulterated Blackpool farce, with lines such as;

"I was just pickling up a jar of Piccalilli."

"And you pickled when you should have lillied."

And:

"I've got a conditional discharge."

"Well, let's go home and I'll put a poultice on it."

Once more Hylda got a glowing review and one can imagine that Jimmy Jewel wasn't best pleased with the comments about his character:

'Hylda Baker's performance really is worth staying indoors to see. It is full to overflowing with comic business, perfectly timed, but the best of it is that in this dumpy, beatle-browed, bustling, absurd figure there is a real character for a comedy script to explore, one of only four in 14 years of ITV; (The others I suggest were Bootsie and Snudge, and John Alderton's teacher in *Please Sir*). Jimmy Jewel's part was allowed to sag a bit. I hope this gets put right, as the format needs two real people.' (*Daily Mail*).

The third series was screened in October, and like the first two series it climbed into the top TV ratings. There was a wonderful article in the *Sunday Mirror* on 19 October, written by Gordon McGill, which is worth reproducing here, as it is so descriptive of not only the programme, but also of Hylda herself, and shows yet another person's reaction to her on first meeting:

'You don't giggle or titter at Hylda Baker. You groan and wheeze at the puns, the bent vowels, the battered grammar, and when the laughs come, they are brought up in blasts from the belly. Hers is an old humour, dredged out of the damp, dirty gutters of her native Lancashire. The humour of ordinary people, sharpened and tested over the years in the music halls to become Blackpool farce and seaside postcards. Hers is the humour of knickers and lavvy seats, making mock of the middle classes, capitalising on pompous landladies and gormless mill workers. It should be old fashioned, now we are supposed to be semi-detached, educated and flying off to Spain for our holidays. But somehow it survives and flourishes.

'*Nearest and Dearest* is now in its third run. The woman Hylda plays is

Lancashire, rough and vulgar, ill-educated but with a heart of gold, working class but aspiring unsuccessfully towards gentility. "These people still exist in the minds of our senior citizens," said a production man on the series, "but the Nellie Pledges are a dying race." The same could be said of Hylda Baker. She is the real pro, the old trouper, a walking show biz cliché. Even those who say that she can sometimes be difficult to work with admire her ability and professionalism. A tiny, nervous woman, who bounces rather than walks, she now lives alone in an expensive flat in London's West End.

'She will tell you that she is nothing like Nellie Pledge, for Nellie has lived a narrow life. Hylda has done too much, been to too many places, but as she talks she slips easily into the role. The mouth turns down, the hands flutter and she rolls her eyes like a gormless Al Jolson. The background is smoke and terraced houses. The people are hotpot eaters who, if they ever leave their towns, go only as far as Blackpool. The people who put on fancy accents to talk about the doctor. When Hylda reads a script she thinks of the Castleford landlady who roared at her husband in the outside toilet, "Come off, the lady wants on," then whispering confidentially, "He's not doing anything really. He's only reading." Or being told at a funeral, "If you go and look at the body, they'll give you a cake and some wine." Or the woman in the surgery complaining that there were now three doctors in the practice, and she wanted the one she had been under for years.

'As she spoke she played with a champagne glass and her white fox fur. Lancashire seemed far away, but she has something to remember it by. It's the tubes, the bronchitis, the curse of those who know too well the damp and dirt of the industrial north. Last week, when she went north she tried something new. She took a seventh-floor room in the Piccadilly Hotel, Manchester, to see if the air is better. And underneath, the Nellie Pledges coughed in the remaining terrace streets of old Lancashire.'

In November the *TV Times* wrote:

'What there is of Hylda Baker, and she tells me her 4ft 11ins has now been shrunken by work and worry to 4ft 10ins, is rather more formidable than the statistics. She has all the compensatory built-in factors given to people born to be small but who possess a nagging, driving ambition to walk tall. She has a fighting spirit, a dogged determination to go it alone, the nerve to take a gamble, and an almost sublime belief in her own self-confidence. A product of music hall, who saw those rumbustious variety palaces shut down like Beeching-axed railway halts, Hylda Baker is a living transcriber to the show-must-go-on tradition. To ask her why, would be tantamount to blasphemy.

'As she patted the cushions of the sofa in her London flat she confided, "Always I had forced myself to go on with the show. In one called *Strike It Lucky* I collapsed, in another, *Lucky In Love*, I had to have an operation. Luck and me just don't seem to go together. I've not been lucky in love either. I married, and didn't divorce for a long time, although the marriage itself was short enough." She looked down at her size-2 shoes and said, "No, I wasn't much good at falling in love. I can't show affection readily for fear of being repulsed. I have to be sure it is wanted of me. In the same way I can't fawn around people to get something out of them, or creep. I'm my own woman."'

This was to be the beginning of a sort of 'new Hylda' who would let down her guard on many occasions, particularly to the press. It begs the question: after all she had been through, was she really beginning to experience extreme loneliness and was she aware, not only of the cause, but also the effect it was beginning to have upon her and that her life would no doubt continue in this vein? From now on she seemed to use the interviews she gave as a sort of cleansing, almost like being on a psychiatrist's couch, for they would listen to her where others would not.

CHAPTER NINE

Down the One-Way Street

IN the spring of 1970 they were making the fourth series of *Nearest And Dearest*, the first episode being screened on 14 May. Later that month the TV series was to be made into a stage play for a summer season in Blackpool — that town's very own Queen was to reign there once more. However, the new series was not so well received by the critics, with comments such as:

'A funny woman is hard to find, and Hylda is one of TV's greatest stand-bys. She has a natural, aggressive humour which is quite infectious. It's a pity that ITV does not seem able to match her talents.'

It was not altogether a fair comment, though, because the public seemed to be pleased enough, and often the 'critics' take that word too literally. How often have we seen a play on stage pulled apart in the newspapers, only to find that the box office returns are very healthy? The main criticism was aimed at the scripts but the proof of the pudding is that, at the time of writing, the series is enjoying a revival on satellite TV and is still as hysterically funny as it was nearly 30 years ago, and is now being appreciated by a new generation.

While filming the new series Hylda stayed at the Piccadilly Hotel in Manchester, and not her old favourite which was the Midland Hotel. Her description of the latter was that it was 'so lovely, old and smoochy', but she had been ill again with bronchitis and was having difficulty in breathing, so she decided that she should get a room on the 14th floor, and they didn't go that high at the Midland. She said, "I can get a good supply of ozone, here I'm above the smoke and the petrol fumes." The hotel used to arrange for her to have a hot water bottle regularly, and looked after her 'famously'. She said, "It's like that wherever I go, anyone will do anything for me, they see I'm not too uppity. But at one time chambermaids used to wash out your bits and pieces — they did things chambermaids are supposed to do. You put your bag down and they unpacked your clothes and hung them up. They don't come anywhere near you now. Not that I've got anything against chambermaids, it's just the way things have changed. In the old days it was all, 'Can I do this for you? Can I do that?' But not any more."

The first holiday she'd ever had was during the Second World War when she booked in for ten days at the Regent Palace Hotel in London, "I went up the road from my flat in a taxi with all my baggage, just so I could be waited on hand and foot. There were doodlebugs everywhere, and I never even thought of going to Blackpool. I have to stay in the best hotels now because I pay a lot of income tax and I can claim for it. Do you know I pay 18s 6d in the pound? I have also to live up to my position. Whether I like it or not, I have to live up to my status."

The Piccadilly Hotel was extremely luxurious, and in fact was the first five-star hotel to be built outside London. The head chef at the time became very friendly with Hylda and looked after her exceptionally well. She was even invited to the staff Christmas party and was a guest on the chef's table. She would telephone him in his palatial office, often just as he was getting ready to go home late at night, and say, "Brian, can I come down?" and he would always give her his time. The head chef in a hotel like this really is like God, but he would give Hylda very special treatment. She would even have a meal in his office, her favourites being smoked salmon and scrambled eggs, or a sirloin steak which had to be 'pink'.

These moments were obviously very special to both of them, as Hylda was indeed very lonely, which she admitted to him, and she seemed to indicate that she was an orphan, for she never talked of her father. However, Brian says she was always so very amusing, and a wonderful character. During those chats the barriers would come down and she would be herself, for she knew she could laugh with him. In fact he said she would have him in stitches more often than not. What is so very sad is that he had been orphaned at the age of six, and had a very hard time. In fact he, too, had lost his childhood and one gets the feeling that in him Hylda had found a kindred spirit. It worked both ways, though, and he says that she was 'different' and she reminded him of himself. Here was someone she learned to trust, someone who admitted that he was so frightened to say he had been orphaned, that even when he was 16 he would write letters to his dead parents and show them to the other apprentices at The Savoy where he learned his trade. Hylda really could make him laugh, and what a compliment to her, that all these years later, he still laughs at the memory of those times.

She would also, on occasion, take her chauffeur-driven Rover down to the UCP restaurant for tripe and onions and mashed potato, such was her longing for these. It is also said that she kept eggs in her room and would boil them in the kettle, her explanation of this when asked was, "Well, have they never toured?" She would spend the majority of the time when she wasn't in the studio relaxing and watching TV in her room, and did admit once that the last thing she would do would be to stay in an hotel if she was not well known there. This does seem a strange thing to say because she absolutely adored to be recognised and feted wherever she went, but one does get the feeling that she was at a bit of a low ebb at this time in her life. Perhaps it had something to do with the fact that she had lost her companion, her dog Cha Cha who had died so tragically the year before. She was alone again, and not only that but working with Jimmy Jewel was a cause of great stress to her. Indeed, it was an insurmountable problem, and so exhausted were her nerves that a favourite saying at the time was, "I must go and rest my body."

There is a lovely incident, recalled by Frank Windsor, of those days when she was staying at the Piccadilly Hotel, which, if Hylda had known about it, would certainly have pleased her. Frank had just recorded one of the *Call My Bluff* programmes and was sitting in a restaurant with Robert Robinson, when he spotted Hylda going by, so he went over to say hello as they knew each other from having worked together. Apparently Robert Robinson was extremely annoyed with Frank for not bringing her over to meet him, as he was a great fan of hers!

She continued to try to cope with the stress of the series, and although she had been dogged by her old problem with bronchitis, she would never contemplate giving up her career. What else did she have? Certainly not a home life because she was always working. She said, "I will carry on until I can't work any more, age has no bearing on anything. The only criterion should be whether or not you can do your job, and my job is my life to me. I always wanted to get to the top of the tree in my profession. I've been up here for quite a while now and I accept what it means. Relationships haven't worked out, but men are funny about women who have a greater earning potential. I get lonely, often, but I'm lucky for the public likes me and that's tremendously rewarding. You see, I'm nothing like the people I portray on stage, but if I'm playing a part then I become that person. Projecting another personality can be very strenuous. I put everything into it and it makes me very tense and highly strung. I am never in one place long enough to make real friends. The few I have are scattered all over the country. At one time in showbusiness everyone was so friendly, now many of my friends have left or retired. Things are not what they used to be. But still, Hylda Baker is my own creation — and I like living with her even if I am alone."

This outpouring of feelings, and to the press too, shows just what was happening to her, not necessarily in her private life, but in her work. She was well aware of the problems she faced every day, not just with working with her co-star, but the fact that deep down she knew she was having difficulty with learning her lines and this was having a great effect on her. But she would not ask for help or make excuses for it, she was far too proud. The final sentence of the above quote of hers is quite amazing as it really seems to say that she had manufactured herself into someone called Hylda Baker, someone who wasn't the real HER, and underneath was someone completely different. She is only living WITH this person, not BEING her.

It is sad to note that the headlines in the newspapers picked out the fact that Hylda was lonely — she obviously oozed this when being interviewed — with headlines such as, 'My Lonely Life At The Top,' and 'The Loneliness Of Hylda Baker,' and the tragedy of it was that at this time she appeared to have got what she had fought so hard for all her life.

The Blackpool summer season of 1970 was eventful to say the least. Vince Powell and Harry Driver were approached to write the stage play, as they owned the rights, and they agreed. They rehearsed in a synagogue in London's Dean Street and they tried it out in Bristol for a week before opening in Blackpool. Norman Robbins, a young member of the stage management team, was asked by the director, Dennis Spencer, if he would mind going back to Hylda's flat after rehearsals to go through lines with her, as she badly needed help. Apparently it turned out to be a nerve-wracking experience, and somewhat like living on a knife edge. Some nights she didn't want to go through lines at all, but just wanted, and obviously needed, to talk. Sometimes she would talk about the show, but more often than not it would be about her past, and having made sure she had given him a hot meal, afterwards she would always send him home in a taxi. It appears that during one conversation she was very concerned that others wanted to stick a knife in her back, and Norman found it was extremely hard to convince her that so many people admired her art, it would never cross their minds. She often used to talk about the artists she herself admired, and on several occasions sang the praises of Margaret Rutherford and Joyce Grenfell.

The day before the opening night, Vince Powell drove down to Bristol. It was Sunday and he went straight to the Hippodrome stage door to see how things were progressing. He was somewhat surprised to find Hylda outside the stage door on the pavement, standing precariously on a chair with a tape measure, appearing to be measuring the 'H' of her name against the 'J' of Jimmy Jewel. He asked her what on earth she was doing, whereupon she replied, "I'm making sure my billing's right!" She was serious, though, even if it appeared to be a joke, for this is what had become of the fight between the two stars. It even extended to the cars they chose because her brand new Rover was exactly same model as Jimmy's! This is somewhat surprising as you would think that she would have tried to 'go one better', but perhaps she reckoned that if she bought an identical car it might annoy him more.

They opened on the Monday night and all the press were there plus the lord mayor. Rehearsals during the day had been something of a nightmare and they staggered through it, due to the fact that Hylda really was having great difficulty with her lines and Jimmy was getting angry about it. After they had finished the dress rehearsal, Dennis Spencer reminded Vince that they had to arrange what was to happen about the speech at the end of the show — the 'curtain speech'. He asked Vince who was going to do it and he replied that Jimmy should start it and Hylda would finish it. Dennis said, "Will you come in the dressing room with me while I tell her?" They went in, and one gets the strong feeling that Hylda knew what was coming as she was rather 'huddled up' over the dressing table. Dennis said, "Now, about the curtain speech." "Yes?" said Hylda. "Well, we thought that Jimmy should start it..." Before he could finish the sentence she retorted, "This is not a blooming double act! I do the curtain speech. I am the star of the show!" The two of them bowed out ...backwards!

Now, Jimmy's dressing room was right next door to Hylda's and as the walls were somewhat thin, he had heard every word. They had no sooner opened the door than Jimmy retorted, "If she does the curtain speech, I'm on the next train back to London!" Apparently they both backed out of there as well. At this point it is important to stress that it was the opening night, and what on earth were they going to do? They decided to 'leave them to it' and see what would happen.

Hylda was very nervous, but the show went brilliantly, even when Hylda forgot her lines. Jimmy — no doubt wishing to be unkind — said, "She's forgotten her bloody lines again!" and the audience roared with laughter because they thought it was all part of the play. Underneath, however, Hylda's confidence was taking a real battering. It turned out to be a really great theatrical evening, but when the final curtain fell, and opened again with the line up of the cast, Vince and Dennis were at the back of the stalls asking themselves, "Now what's going to happen." It seemed like hours to them, so highly-charged was the atmosphere, but it was in fact only seconds. Suddenly, Hylda dug Jimmy in the ribs and said, "Go on then!"

He came forward, said a few words, talked about Hylda, then she came down to the front and did her little bit. The crisis was over and what a relief all round, but one has to point out that even after the way he had treated her on stage, in the end it was her professionalism that came to the fore.

After the show things seemed to be much better and surprisingly Jimmy said to her, "Look Hylda, we've got 26 weeks ahead of us at Blackpool, we should try to be friends. We're working twice nightly." She, equally surprisingly, replied, "Oh well, I'm willing if you are. Would you like to come and have supper with me tonight at my hotel. In fact everybody is invited." This was absolutely incredible as they'd never even had so much as a coffee or a drink together since the series started in 1968 — two years earlier! It had also been inevitable that the cast had often taken sides during the series and now the situation had got so bad that they were somewhat concerned, and as they were all in the stage show it was going to be marvellous that they would all sit down together that night and be sociable.

The company consisted of Joe Gladwin, Dierdre Costello, Madge Hindle, Barry Howard (he replaced Edward Malin who wasn't available for the summer season) and Roger Avon (playing her 'fiasco'!), who on that first night had constantly helped her when she forgot her lines, and indeed continued to do so throughout the run of the play. Unfortunately, Hylda forgot to invite Roger, nobody thought to tell him, and many weeks later, well on into the run at Blackpool, Hylda suddenly turned to him and said, "Why ever didn't you come to my party in Bristol?" It was the first reference that anyone had made to it, and when he told her that he hadn't been invited, she just said, "Good heavens!" The cast, minus poor Roger, had all gone off to the Hilton Hotel where Hylda was staying, and there were high hopes for the future of the show.

Sitting around the dinner table, all was going well until Hylda's agent, Bill Roberton, said, "Do you know, Hylda, this play is going to be a very big hit." She then replied, rather tactlessly, "Yes, well it's all due to me re-writing most of it isn't it?" Once again all hell broke loose, and one feels that maybe Jimmy got the wrong end of the stick, but he was a great champion of Harry Driver who was crippled with polio and in a wheelchair. Jimmy leaned over to Hylda and snarled, "You wicked *****!" Hylda threw a bread roll at him, he got up saying, "I am not staying in the company of this woman," and promptly walked out with Hylda firing bread rolls after him. That was very definitely the end of the attempt between them to call a truce. An even greater war had now been set in motion.

They all met the next day to talk over the result of the first night's performance, and to discuss any possible cuts. Hylda and Jimmy were stony-faced and wouldn't even look at each other. The upshot of it all was that the writers and director had to rehearse them separately, but eventually the director said, "Look, come on, we've got to do this," and so they did. However, when they met on the stage during performance, they still wouldn't look at each other even then! This may seem like a very amusing story but it must have been dreadful for the rest of the cast as you could cut the atmosphere with a knife. Hylda was once again to show her true professionalism, though, as during one rehearsal with the director, and out of Jimmy's earshot, there was a scene where once again she felt the line would be funnier if Jimmy said it; so she gave the line to him. Another time, there was a moment on stage where Jimmy had nothing to do, the director asked Hylda to 'flick a line across to him' and she replied, "Why should I do that?" The director swore strongly at her and there was a deathly silence before he said, "Right, let's carry on." She didn't say a word and on they went.

The second performance at Bristol was even more eventful and, as all actors know, second nights are renowned for being very difficult, mainly because if the first night has been highly charged with all the nerves and excitement, the second one can be extremely flat as you cannot recreate the adrenalin that flowed the night before. The first scene began, once again Hylda forgot her lines, and once again Jimmy said out front, "She's forgotten her lines again, she can't remember anything this woman." It was said rather nastily this time and she just glowered at him. A little later, she was doing a speech describing a dress or something — "You see it was all flowing like this, with fancy 'epilettes' on the shoulder" — and unseen by her, Jimmy started to 'upstage' behind her, doing funny business with a cigarette, a bit like Freddie Frinton and Jimmy James used to do. She noticed that one or two people were laughing, saw they weren't looking at her and turned around, saw what he was up to and promptly hit him with her handbag. The audience thought it was all part of the play, and after that, whatever Hylda and Jimmy did to each other, the audience just roared with laughter.

They got through the play that night, once more they had a tremendous reception and then it came to the curtain speech. They were all lined up and before anyone else could say anything, Jimmy pushed Hylda to one side and said, "Ladies and gentlemen, I do hope you liked the show. If you did – tell your friends; if you didn't – keep your mouth shut!" Hylda came forward, dragged him back, stepped out and started to speak, "And watch what you do when you get home ..." He then pulled her back and stepped forward once more. "And just be careful how you go ..." It went on like that, back and forth, back and forth, neither letting the other finish speaking, but it was still hysterically funny! In the end they'd gone so far forward they both had their feet on the footlights, and if they hadn't stopped they would have been up the centre aisle in the auditorium. In the end it was sorted out by Vince and Dennis, on a 'you do this and you do that' basis.

With this atmosphere raging, off they went to Blackpool, to the Grand Theatre, and from then on the play changed every night as Hylda kept putting funny lines and business in, but Jimmy was doing the same. He wouldn't tell her what he was going to do, and neither would she tell him. One night she actually spat at him and another night she kicked him on the leg, under the table so it was unseen by the audience, because he had suddenly put in some other funny business. Hylda would never normally have behaved like this, and there are so many other examples of her true professionalism that she must be defended strongly here because there certainly was a great deal of provocation. Not only that, but it really was a first-class example of an extreme personality clash.

Roger Avon said later that Hylda really was still very nervous of the show, which is perfectly understandable, but that it was alright eventually because she gradually got used to it. He did try to help her out on many occasions when she dried, and in fact she was very kind to his wife and family when they came for a visit, always getting them free seats for the show, and buying them presents like huge bath towels. He, in turn, befriended her and helped her a great deal, particularly giving her confidence in their scenes together. Often he would drive down to her rented house in Squires Gate and take her into Blackpool for afternoon tea, where he remembers that the tea had to be really hot and if it wasn't she would have it sent back. It is so sad to note that he observed that people who took against her did so without analysing the reasons. Roger, though, took the trouble to try to work out what was causing her to have what he shrewdly saw as being a major inferiority complex. Others just didn't bother to try.

Hylda had been so very independent all her life that she had never really been treated like a lady — no one thought to even try — but Roger took pains to ensure that she was. He opened doors for her, took her coat, pushed her chair in when she sat down in restaurants, and made sure that he saw her into the car before getting in himself. He put her on a pedestal which nobody in her whole life had ever done since her father. She knew she could rely on Roger and consequently she responded very much to him for he was a true 'gentleman'. He gave her a touch of life she hadn't experienced very much, perhaps because, generally speaking, she had been in the world of variety where, particularly in the old days, it was all 'cut and thrust' and often very self-centred. Needless to say there was a good deal of talk about their friendship, but that is most definitely just what it was, as Hylda had her moral standards and would never pursue someone in that way as soon as she learned they were married.

Roger was a tremendous help to her during that season. He gave her the courage which deep down she lacked, and often had to tell her that it was because others were envious of her talent that they behaved in the way they did towards her. Without him she would have been fighting a battle against people trying to find fault, only too ready to pull her down, laughing unkindly at her and sending her up, because she constantly felt she had to be funny, and had to MAKE them laugh. He said, "I brought her out of herself. I gave her a lot of courage and she was grateful. I could tell when she was on a 'down' or an 'up'. She didn't have to say. She was always ready to unbend and tell me things that perhaps she wouldn't have told other people, especially when I went to her house after the show. She was awfully good with the pressure cooker, serving up a huge meal in about five minutes! She couldn't have been more helpful to me, but her very demeanour made it clear she was lonely. There was one scene in the play, I was her fiancé and we were going to be married, she appeared at the top of the stairs with a special lighting effect, standing there in a white wedding dress, she looked gorgeous. I remember every night when the spot came up, there was tremendous applause. She loved it. A very pleasant woman, clearly very lonely, a very nervous woman. She loved company and was unhappy when she didn't have it. How sad, how sad, for she had achieved so much."

One day poor Joe Gladwin was taken ill with pleurisy, so the young actor on stage management, Norman Robbins, the same one who had helped Hylda with her lines during rehearsals, was thrust on stage to play the part. He ended up doing 27 performances in total, and there was yet another incident of the great tension during the show, when Hylda was supposed to say to one of the other characters, "Now, shall I write it down for you?" She totally forgot what to say, and despite several prompts from cast members and the stage manager in the wings, she still couldn't remember. After a few pretty desperate minutes, she managed to say it. They were about to carry on when Jimmy said, "I think we ought to write it down for you." The audience loved it but Hylda let fly on stage and all hell broke loose. Another time she was very upset with Norman because he had ruined one of her best gags by falling over a chair, and when he apologised by telling her that, without his glasses, he was practically blind, and that someone had moved the chair to a different position, she curtly said he should get some contact lenses. He explained that on his salary he really couldn't afford them, and was very surprised the following morning when Hylda rang him and told him to go to a certain optician in Blackpool, as she'd made an appointment for him to be fitted with contact lenses. He protested once again that he couldn't afford this luxury, whereupon she said, "I've paid for them," and put down the telephone.

She was, indeed, very generous in other ways, too, and there are many people who have said this. At Blackpool she would be very lavish with her tips to the stage crews every week. At first they resented her attitude when she got upset if things weren't right, but it wasn't very long before they appreciated that, forgetful though she may be, she really did strive for perfection on stage. Bearing this in mind, it makes it doubly tragic that she had such memory problems because this would be bound to frustrate her and make her angry with herself, coupled with the deep-rooted fear that she was going mad.

At this time, she also showed her concern about her father, but in true Hylda tradition it ended on a comedic note. Apparently one night she was leaning over the pier just looking down at the sea, thinking about him. She said, "I was feeling very miserable, I was in my own little world, just thinking, when suddenly I felt a cold hand on my shoulder. It was a shock. I just froze and slowly turned round and standing there was this policeman who said, 'Don't do it Hylda!'"

Throughout her life she had always told people that her father was dead, when in fact he didn't die until 1966, and was in the hospital all that time. She hardly ever visited him because she didn't want people to know the sort of establishment he was in because she felt it could damage her career as there had always been a stigma attached to those places; but all her life she carried the guilt of having denied his existence.

This is yet another example of why she dwelt on the subject of the mind so much in her act, with lines like, "It's her brain you know. She hasn't been the same since she fell, off that donkey on Blackpool beach. She landed on an ice cream cornet and it pierced her brain," and, "She knows about her brain you know, the pieciatrist spoke to her just as if she was human." Also Hylda was constantly telling the audience that Cynthia had had some terrible accident, usually a blow to the head.

During the run of the play, things were not getting any better, so Vince Powell decided to lighten the situation and have a bit of a joke with Hylda and Jimmy. He got one of those newspapers where you can get any headline you want printed on a real paper. Blackpool was a place where all these things were readily available. His mock-up read, 'Jimmy Jewel Elopes With Hylda Baker To Gretna Green!' He gave them a copy each but sad, to say, they were not very amused.

The reviews of the play at Blackpool were wonderful and *The Stage* wrote the following:

'When the history of Blackpool's showbusiness comes to be written, it will contain much that is interesting, a great deal that is scandalous, and certainly not a little that is truly remarkable — but it is doubtful if it will carry anything more notable than the record of the stupendous success of one of the 1970 season shows, in a period when the empty seats for many a show have yawned like the open mouth of a toothless octogenarian, those at the Grand Theatre have been filled with solid, fee-paying patrons — twice every night. And the bookings are solid right to the end of the run in mid-October. The cashiers' hands are rubbed raw counting up the lovely lolly.

'Who is responsible for this flood of cash into the Grand's coffers? Jimmy Jewel and the 59 inches of Hylda Baker, stars of *Nearest And Dearest*, the television series which is riveting viewers in front of their screens and, translated to the stage, having Grand patrons in danger of fatal convulsions.

'Hylda's is no instant success, but she has known showbusiness from the pit up. Her style is quite inimitable, and, in the great tradition of comedy. She can convey her character by the twist of a foot, or the twitch of a shoulder, and she can throw away a punch line with more effect than many a thespian can get after months of mouthing effort. Hylda was inventing 'malapropisms' years before she was even sure where the word came from, but had Richard Brindsley Butler Sheridan been alive today, instead of inconsiderately dying 164 years ago, he would undoubtedly have acknowledged his master.

'So successful was the play in which Mrs Malaprop first appeared that Sheridan became part of the Drury Lane Theatre establishment, eventually to graduate to be the sole proprietor of the place. It is not yet suggested that Miss Baker buys up the Grand at Blackpool, but she should surely be entitled to a solid gold plaque from the proprietors commemorating a season of unparalleled success. As she herself might say, "The whole thing's been a righteous excess!"'

A wonderful description of Hylda at this time, queening it in Blackpool with her magnificent gowns, coats, huge cars and everything, was that Vince Powell described her as a 'northern Gloria Swanson sweeping down the promenade'.

There is a memory of Hylda's great superstition regarding the colour green, though, as Rene Hardman, who had worked with Hylda a great deal and who was the wardrobe mistress at the theatre recalls. "She was very superstitious. She was giving a party after the show and, silly me, I bought a new dress. it was green. I got changed during the finale and went round to collect the costumes. When I got to Hylda's room she said, 'What the hell have you got on? It's green!' I said I thought it was a pretty green, but she said, 'It's not a pretty flamin' green. Get it off!' One of the cast suggested that I take it off and go in my underwear, but I had to go home and change or she wouldn't let me go to the party! I never wore it again. Almost at the end of the season — there was only a couple of weeks to go — Hylda suddenly burst into the stage manager's room, in quite a state, and said, 'You've got a green carpet, there's a green carpet on the set!' The only retort she got from him was, 'It took you a long time to find out!' She had been playing on it for the whole season and hadn't noticed.

Rene was also asked to go to London as Hylda needed a new checked suit for her variety act. The original had been made for her by her mother, but it was getting very threadbare, so Rene went to London to stay with Hylda while she made it, but then found, as everyone else did, that she was being told what to do — "Rene, there's some things to go in the washer," and so on — whereas she was supposed to be sewing. It was a very complicated outfit to make, being pleated and cut on a flare, and it had to be an authentic replica. Hylda's forgetfulness was always there; she'd put things down and forget where they were. She was also a great hoarder, and never got rid of anything. There was a cupboard right up to the ceiling in the kitchen and the top shelves were jammed full with packets of tea she'd bought during the war, and often they just fall out. "I can't get them up there, it's too high, so I just shake the cupboard door," she'd say.

Eventually Rene finished the stage costume and all she had to do was to sew on the buttons. She was relieved because she had been away from home for quite a while and was desperate to get back. She wanted to collect the buttons herself and had been waiting for them for a week, but Hylda insisted that she would do it on her way home from rehearsals. It was 8pm before she got back, and of course she'd forgotten to pick them up. Rene said that she'd had enough and was going home, to which Hylda retorted, "If you don't do this, I'm not paying you!" "I'm not bothered," replied Rene. She packed her bags and left, but true to her threat, Hylda never paid her, all she gave her was her train fare. Rene's theory was that she was cantankerous, but it was because her broken marriage had helped to make her bitter, and she never got over the fact that she felt her life had been wasted

On her 66th birthday in February 1971, after making yet another series of *Nearest And Dearest*, Hylda was once more getting aggressive about being asked her age. "Age is unimportant, and nobody's business but your own!" she snapped at an *Evening News* reporter, but the very next minute, as was her wont, it was past and forgotten and she was discussing her planned trip to South Africa, which was not just a holiday because she was on the lookout for possible theatre dates over there. Her energy was certainly boundless. Even though she was plagued by the terrible problem with her inability to remember her lines, she was by this time even more successful than she had ever been and was right at the top of the tree where she had always longed to be. She was featured in the *Sunday Times* in May 1971, in very glowing terms. Once again it is important to quote the article:

'Of all the entertainers offered to us 'low brows', Hylda Baker, uncrowned Queen of Blackpool, is the most about my mark. Each time her series has been on television I've religiously stayed in to watch. As Nellie Pledge she's all the aunties I've ever loved and laughed at. She is bitchy and bossy and mispronounces everything with more than three syllables. She is short and dumpy and dresses at the Co-op. Her hair is frizzly, punch drunk from over perming. She is nervous of drink, and egg-nog goes straight to her knees. It has continually topped the ratings, and there are a lot of us looking in.

'Meeting Miss Baker, it is difficult to separate her from her creation. Hard to remember that the person you are talking to is an immensely clever creative comedienne, who for years has written her own material. She fits all the showbusiness cliches of a music hall saga, many brothers and sisters, a broken unspoken-of marriage, and years of hard slogging, to become the star she is today. She represents the vulnerability and loneliness of someone at the top with a great deal of money and only herself to spend it on. At times between talking she seems afraid and uncertain, tense and very touching. Seconds later she is the life and soul again. The strains of having dedicated her considerable energy for so long to stardom are all too apparent, but then so are the compensations.

'She's an easily recognisable little lady, and appealing as she does to the masses and millions, she's felt by them to be one of them. Her time, her private life, belongs to everybody. Eating out or walking along she is engulfed in waves of love, friendly stares, whistles and cheers. And she loves it. This summer in Blackpool she'll be Queening it again from 18 June. Last year it was a smash hit, this year the thousands of people she delights will see to it that she does it again!'

It is so sad to read the sections that show so well how lonely and insecure she had become. Barry Howard, who was in that first summer season of the play, said that her lines were written on the back of the scenery, so at least she'd get her entrances right. At one point she had to come in carrying a TV set and say, "Oooh, I think me horizontal hold's gone," but for the life of her she couldn't remember it and was always getting it wrong. It really is so unusual that a comic will forget a gag line. Barry was very nice to her because he knew she was lonely, but did make it clear that he wasn't actually 'interested' in her in that way. She invited him back to supper at the Queen's Hotel after the show one night, and when he left she insisted on walking to the door with him and held his hand all the way to the huge revolving doors. As he went through and round inside the door, he turned to look back to her and smiled, and he was very moved to see that she had tears in her eyes. She was loved by the masses, but had no one to love.

Once, during that same season, she gave a big party, but somehow forgot to ask the stage management team. The next day she asked them why they hadn't come, and they said they didn't think they'd been invited, to which her reply was, "When I give a party — everybody comes." Often they would go for meals at the Lobster Pot restaurant, and she would telephone them beforehand to find out if Jimmy had been there and how much he had spent. When they told her, she would say, "Well, I want to spend £10 more!" It was constant one-upmanship.

For the summer of 1971 the show was back at the Grand Theatre and the title was changed to *Not On Your Nellie* as Jimmy Jewel did not do this stage version. This time it was written by Roy Bottomley and Tom Brennand, and Ken Platt was Hylda's co-star. Ironically, Jimmy was appearing not far away and one gets the feeling it was like a competition once more, only this time from a distance, so there was a split audience now, each one going to see their favourite. Although the play wasn't as successful as the year before, the atmosphere within the company was so much better. The reasons for the drop in takings on the year before can only be surmised, but it is probably true to say that some of it was due to the fact that Hylda and Jimmy were appearing at separate theatres.

Hylda was once more to be dogged by a good deal of bad luck during this season. In one incident, on Saturday, 20 June, she had a bad fall in the house that she had rented. A couple of nights after the show opened she got out of bed at 4am to get a drink of water, and fell headlong down the curved staircase. She hit a protruding wall which was decorated with flock wallpaper that had been painted over with emulsion, so the surface was rather like sandpaper, and unfortunately her face dragged along it, ripping open a patch of skin on her cheek; she also banged her left eye on the impact. She never missed a performance and although she was in some considerable discomfort, she insisted on appearing, against doctor's orders. Her face was still cut and her eye was very blackened, but she would spend all day in bed, then get up, go to the theatre and spend a long time painting, patching, and covering the unsightly areas with make-up. At the same time she was robbed at home of £4,000 and her car was stolen. Well they do say things come in threes!

However, Hylda continued to make the audiences laugh, and she said at the time, "Nellie Pledge has changed her name to Nellie Plunkett for the play, and I deal in black puddings not TV pickles. In fact I'm labelled the best black-pudding maker in Lancashire. I suppose you could say I can fix a black eye pretty well too!"

Her missing car was found the following day, having been abandoned in Birmingham, but there was no sign of the money which she apparently had hidden in her wardrobe. It was later reported (in October of that year) that the driver she had at the time had been jailed for a year for the offence. What is so wonderful about her was that even though she had no idea how much was missing, at the end of the show she took everybody out to dinner. As Roy Bottomley said, "You can't knock that!"

Nothing was ever simple in Hylda's life, and so very often it would end with a tragic/comedy situation, for when her abandoned car was found in Birmingham, the police drove it back for her — but while doing so they wrapped it around a lamppost! She naturally began to get rather worried around this time, nursing dark and secret fears, and being very superstitious by nature she became convinced that some strange and evil power had her off-stage life in its grip, and she even went so far as to say that so much seemed to go wrong for her, that she began to think someone was sticking pins in an effigy of her.

In August 1971, she told the *News Of The World*, "I know it's a man, but I'm powerless while his influence is over me. It's not a joke! A woman can tell whether the influence is for good or for evil, and in my case it's evil. If you're aware that someone hates you and wishes you ill, it can become an obsession with you, and in turn this brings you bad luck. I took a cruise to relax and prepare for the new stage play in Blackpool, and one day I had a nasty accident in my cabin. I fell and strained my heart and the doctor said I must rest or I'd never work again. I'm certain that accident was wished on me by a man. I was so ill, I spent a fortnight in Las Palmas, alone and in terrible pain. I was worried that my career might be over."

She claimed to know the identity of this man who had her under his spell, and the reporter asked if he were alive or dead, to which she became very indignant. "It has nothing to do with ghosts, I'm talking about thought transference from someone who is alive today. Now that I have spoken perhaps that will exorcise his power. I hope I'll have altered the pattern of my life by the end of the year." In yet another interview on the same subject she said, "Honestly love, I've been through the lot. I've lost my memory, couldn't write a script because of it and I was once told that I'd never work again. But give up the business? Not on your life! Like my father, I'll carry on until I drop."

The *News Of The World* reporter had gone on to say that he would normally have dismissed all this as rather fanciful nonsense but he had known Hylda for several years, and she gave him evidence of other mishaps. He ventured to guess the identity of this mystery man and apparently got it right, but she swore him to secrecy. She ended the conversation by saying, "I admit I'm superstitious but I'd like to know the theatrical artist who's not. I've tried to lose my belief that green is unlucky but I can't, and I won't have anyone whistling in my dressing room."

Her fear related to the colour green was not as unreasonable as it might seem because she certainly seemed to have more than her fair share of problems when it was in the vicinity. "I won't wear anything green, and I don't like being with anybody who is, and I won't allow it to be seen on any of my shows. Even if I see a green cushion on the set I ask to have it changed. I tell myself it's foolish, but throughout my life green seems to have brought me bad luck. I remember being in a stage show called *Lucky In Love*, and I wore a beautiful pale pink dress. Under the strong spotlight it faded to a dirty looking white, so the wardrobe department dyed it green. The first night I wore it, I not only lost the baby I was carrying in the early stages of pregnancy, but nearly lost my life. At the time I didn't entirely blame it on the green, but later I wore a green coat — with exactly the same result. There have been many, many other instances that make me think it's something much more than coincidence. No, green means trouble for me."

At the very first read through of the original series of *Nearest And Dearest* she had looked around and said, "Well, I can't work in here for a start." The walls were painted green, and even though it was her very first day with a new company she insisted that they move to another room, and they did! Later, it really is true that she would get upset if there was anything green on the set. She also, apparently, said, "Oh no, he's not is he?" and went a paler shade of green when she was told that Edward Malin (Walter) was quite a leading light in the Green Room Club!

The reactions to and problems with her attitude to Jimmy, and her consequent comments to the press regarding an evil influence, almost certainly indicates the state of mind she was experiencing at the time, for it is highly unlikely that the person she was so obviously referring to would go that far. She was so very unhappy, worried and frightened that it coloured everything for her, and two weeks after this interview the *Sunday Express* reported that Hylda had suggested to Granada TV that Jimmy Jewel should be replaced in the series by Ken Platt, who was with her in the summer show. Her attitude to Jimmy is constantly tinged with frostbite:

'Miss Baker is not well disposed towards Mr Jewel in real life. From Blackpool she says, "In my opinion Jimmy Jewel never co-starred with me in the series. He has been second feature always. I would not like to say whether I would do another series with him or not. I am the star. I was asked if I would accept him as Eli two and a half years ago. I have been approached about another series and I have suggested Mr Platt, but there has not been an aye or nay yet. Ken Platt is in the stage show with me at the moment because I refused to play with Mr Jewel. I was unhappy, and I just want to be happy in my work. Mr Platt is very good in the part and I would be happy to make a series with him."

'The trouble is that Jimmy Jewel would also like to make another series and Granada's boss, Lord Bernstein, at present on holiday, is thought to want the original team kept together. Says Jimmy of Hylda, "I got on well with her."' It is interesting to note that this time, for some reason he didn't feel the need to join in this particular game of backstabbing.

During this period, Hylda talked once again about her dream to make a film, saying that she would dearly love to do an Alfred Hitchcock, and play a killer. The *Daily Mail* said, 'Remembering her much-publicised tiffs with co-star Jimmy Jewel, Miss Baker might well have a victim in mind too!' She also made more remarks about her stature, and it really does begin to show how much she was trying to justify everything that was happening to her. She said, "My career and private life are geared towards being a small woman in a tall world. How could I play Nellie if I were taller? It just wouldn't suit her. Tall women don't look half as funny as us shorties. If I'd been taller I might have been a straight actress or an opera singer. I'm always on the lookout to see if people take advantage of me because of my smallness. They did when I was younger you know. Men don't like you to be independent — they prefer you to be the little woman, but my work is the most important thing in my life. It has to be — I've nothing else. I've got no one to go home to at night and if I'm unhappy in my work it upsets my whole life. I'm not still single because men have let me down, it's always been me I suppose." The main problem with this, of course, was that she had shown by her very attitude throughout her life that she had, in truth, found it very difficult to accept being the 'little woman', for in everything but her stature, she was actually a very big woman.

By January 1972, though, carrying many scars from this battle, a sort of truce was called and it was announced that the duo would come together again in February to do another series. They had apparently patched up their behind-the-scenes differences, but it was also reported that Granada TV had insisted that Jimmy stayed. The ball had never really been in Hylda's court, and she had obviously realised that, like it or not, she would have to accept the situation.

On to the scene at this time came yet another Cynthia, for Hylda was still doing her other bookings and therefore keeping the character very much alive; it was what many of Hylda's fans wanted. This new one was a young actor called Tom Hardy, 28 years old and 6ft 4ins tall, who at first said, "I went into the role with great trepidation. Hylda has this reputation for being tough — and she is tough — but when you get to know her she is also very kind. I like to think of her now as a friend." Theirs turned out to be an association which, at times, is a very moving story because she admitted many things to him that she would never have said to others. In Tom Hardy she had found a confidante, and she trusted him.

He had first met her when she was doing the summer season of *Not On Your Nellie* with Ken Platt in 1971. Apparently the current Cynthia had been a bit of a health fanatic, getting up at the crack of dawn and pounding up and down the sea front. Consequently he was somewhat tired when it came to the two shows and was known to have fallen asleep in the dressing room on more than one occasion, evidently missing several entrances. This naturally infuriated Hylda, which is probably a bit of an understatement, when one considers that she did experience something rather disconcerting. Imagine, she's given Cynthia the build-up, turns around, saying to the audience, "She's here now," — and 'she' wasn't! Cynthia was in the dressing room 'getting corns on his behind' as Hylda would say. She ended up going through the act without her stooge, telling the audience what she was like, giving a full description of what she was wearing, and saying it was such a pity the audience couldn't meet her. "I wouldn't like to go through THAT again," she is quoted as saying, which for her was quite restrained. She demanded that a replacement be sent for, so Tom was quickly summoned to Blackpool to audition.

Although Hylda complained that she considered him to be too young, she decided to give him a try, and off they went to the shops to get him an outfit. Wide-fitting ladies' shoes size 11 turned out to be not easy to find, particularly the old fashioned wide-fitting variety that the character wore, but eventually they had some sent up from London.

Tom recalls a memorable occasion, and a rare one as we know that Hylda considered it to be a cardinal sin to laugh on stage. No one can remember just how it started, but the entire cast, one by one, became infected by helpless laughter, even Hylda eventually, and all this was just before Cynthia's entrance. Finally Hylda managed to gasp out Tom's cue and he went slowly on, as required. The whole point about Cynthia is that she must never ever smile or even twitch the corner of her mouth, for therein lies the comedy situation, because otherwise it would kill the act stone dead. Hylda looked up at Tom's deadpan face, got no words out as she cracked up with laughter, literally howling, and finally was doubled up in a shaking heap. The audience by this time were in hysterics, too, but Tom somehow or other managed to keep a straight face. It went on for what seemed like for ever, until finally his face cracked with a little smile, the audience were off again, only louder, and inevitably he ended up joining in with the hilarity. It is so very difficult to describe in written form, but even the people backstage had joined in. It was literally mass hysteria, but eventually, with a couple more little hiccups, they struggled through

Hylda went to his dressing room that night after the show and said sternly that Cynthia must NEVER, EVER laugh again, but once more immediately began to laugh herself and said, "By god, it was funny though wasn't it love?" It is so obvious from this incident, that the atmosphere during this season was far removed from the one with Jimmy the year before, and perhaps this is why she was so keen to get Ken Platt for the new TV series. What a pity, though, that she still harboured all these other fears and experienced such bad luck at this time. In the autumn of that year she booked Tom to travel with her and appear in all her cabaret work, of which she had numerous dates lined up. I quote his own words here:

"I liked Hylda a lot. She was a brilliant comedienne, and to watch that tiny woman hold an audience in the palm of her hand was something to behold. Her comic timing was superb — of course I wanted to work with her again — and learn. She would snort when she read articles about so-and-so being the 'star' of a TV programme. "Them, a star," she'd say, "do you know what a star is Tom? When you stop someone in the street and say a name they immediately recognise, like Marilyn Monroe, THAT's a star, not some silly also-ran from some soap opera." Then she'd giggle and say, "I'm a star. Ask anybody."

Travelling to these cabaret dates they would amuse each other by making up silly stories and episodes in Cynthia's life, such as, "She's travelling by train to spend a day at the fun fair in Blackpool," to which Hylda would say, "Suddenly she wants to go to the loo, but forgets there isn't a corridor on the train ...and when her head hit that platform!" At times like this, Hylda really was very happy, and showed her true sense of humour, oblivious to the stares of her fellow passengers as both she and Tom were falling about with laughter.

They would always stay in the very best hotels, and although they often ate in the dining room, Hylda would like nothing better than to eat in their own rooms, which she always booked to be adjoining. They would shop locally and borrow plates and cutlery from the trolleys in the corridor, and when they had eaten they would wash them up in the bath and return them. Hylda's favourite 'take away' was fresh tripe sprinkled with vinegar. This period in her life really seems to have been much more relaxed and at last she was beginning to enjoy herself. It was not from being mean that she decided to eat these 'dormitory' meals, but a genuine sense of fun, and also she had someone who she liked and trusted. It was almost as if she was treating him like the son she never had, and was able to confide in him where she couldn't with others. She had learned to trust him.

They set off for a booking in Guernsey, knowing they were coming back to appear on *Saturday Night Variety* with Larry Grayson a week later. They travelled on a small twin-propeller plane, but as the engines started Hylda grabbed Tom's hand tightly and said, "I'm not letting go until we land, I hate flying." He tried to relax her by chattering on about this and that, but he could see that her fear was so great that nothing would work, so kept quiet. Suddenly they hit turbulence and she turned to him and said, "I don't want to die Tom, ever." He replied, "Billions of others feel the same way, but that's a battle we're all going to lose." He then saw in her eyes a look of such horror that a shiver went right through him when she said, "I'm so frightened of death, Tom. Oh god, I'm frightened, please don't ever mention the subject again." He certainly didn't but when he brought the episode to mind approximately 22 years later, he said he had gone 'goosey' just thinking about it.

The cabaret booking was for a few nights in a top hotel in Guernsey and the act went brilliantly as usual, but the night before they were due to leave, unusually for late autumn on that warm island, the snow came down and there was no way they could depart by air. What on earth were they going to do about the TV booking with Larry Grayson? They were snowed-in for over a week and were rescheduled to do the *Saturday Night Variety* show in the June of 1972. Hylda's nerves took a battering during that period, her old stomach problems (she'd suffered from a hiatus hernia during the summer of 1970) cropped up again, coupled with her anxiety at having missed a date.

Tom looked after her and sat with her a good deal, because she apparently became so frightened whenever she was ill, convincing herself she was going to die. He says that she looked so very frail propped up in bed, and not having any make-up on added to the appearance of a very lonely, frightened woman. She would insist that he went out to enjoy himself, but asked him to pop in on her before he went to bed 'just to say 'goodnight', and through this he became very close to her during that enforced stay in Guernsey. He is still exceptionally proud of the fact that she said he was a brilliant Cynthia!

One memorable thing that happened to Hylda in March 1972, and which would stay with her for ever and was to give her great pride, was that she was the subject of *This Is Your Life*. It was Roy Bottomley's idea that she would be a splendid subject and he was now working on the programme. In fact he had brought the show to ITV in 1968, when Thames TV was created. Hylda was rehearsing in Brixton for the new TV series of *Nearest And Dearest* and her agent, Bill Roberton, had been liaising with Thames, giving them as much detail as possible.

The day came and it was arranged that Bill would go over in the Thames TV limousine to Brixton and bring her back to Town as though they were going to a press call. They got in the car and off they went, Hylda totally unaware and chatting merrily away. All the time Bill could see the driver in his interior mirror. They exchanged glances as it was evident that they were making such good time they were going to be far too early, so instead of turning left towards Euston, he decided to go the long way round via Camden Town. This turned out to be a very big mistake because they got completely stuck in traffic. Quick as a flash the driver whizzed the car around and put his foot down in no uncertain terms. They had gone from a leisurely crawl to a sort of Keystone Cops chase, or in Hylda's terminology, he'd gone 'beresque'. She grabbed hold of Bill, terror-struck, and screamed, "We're being kidnapped! We're being kidnapped!" She really believed this to be the case. He tried to calm her with, "No it's alright dear, don't worry etc," but to no avail, until the car pulled up at the studios, whereupon she saw Eamonn Andrews 'lurking'. She realised what had been happening, and indeed what was about to happen, her composure returned immediately, she turned to Bill and said, "Oh, you sod!" and with that stepped out of the car, a lady once more. But for those few minutes she had been truly hysterical.

They gave her time to get herself tidied up, and when they brought her into the studio, the first thing she said was, "Oh dear, I have no idea what I'm doing here, I stepped out of the car, and there I was lying prostitute on the pavement." The audience roared. Her family were all there, and had been taken to the studios earlier in the day, but sadly her mother and her brother Harold had died by this time. Auntie Agnes was there, though, a real favourite of Hylda's, and one of the high spots of the show was that Hylda and her brother and sisters did the 'six Lancashire steps' with the clog dance. (Those very clogs, which were made specially for the programme, are now at a museum in Preston along with many of Hylda's memorable stage costumes and indeed the very birds of paradise she wore for the Diamond Lil sketch in *Frills With Thrills*. These, incidentally, are kept very much under wraps as they are a protected species.)

Charles Hawtrey and Ken Dodd came on, as did the cast of *Nearest And Dearest* — not surprisingly minus Jimmy Jewel — and many of Hylda's relatives from abroad. (Hylda got her own back on Jimmy when they did his life, though, for she wouldn't appear on his tribute. However, to be fair to Jimmy, he spoke very highly of her, saying, "She was one of the funniest comediennes I've ever known."). The final guest was her great friend Dorothy Squires, with whom she had a rather intense 'love hate' relationship over the years. Tom Hardy was very aware of the fact that Hylda appeared to be quite terrified throughout the recording. Perhaps she imagined every skeleton coming out of the dark recesses of the cupboard. The knowledge we now have about her father, and how he ended his days, was no doubt very much on her mind, coupled with the fact that she was determined to keep it a secret from the public. Luckily the researchers had been kind and she ended up enjoying every minute.

Everyone who visited Hylda's flat after that would comment that the *This Is Your Life* book was proudly displayed either on the piano or on the table, and when Tom Hardy visited it was always open at the page where they had been photographed together, as he too appeared on the programme (dressed as Cynthia!). She would say to him every time, "You had to get your name mentioned though didn't you?" And then she would smile and offer him a glass of wine. She still didn't want the identity of her stooge to be known, and in fact gave him, rather unfairly, a dressing down after *This Is Your Life* when his photograph appeared in *TV Times*.

Apparently when the researchers approached Tom, he said that he would appear as Cynthia, but his name must not be mentioned, and he refused to be photographed for *TV Times* because he knew it would upset Hylda. But he did agree to a telephone interview for a few comments to be quoted. One morning, Tom blearily left his flat to buy some milk, a photographer popped up from behind a hedge, snapped away and promptly jumped in his car and drove off, leaving his subject rather bemused. When the photograph appeared in *TV Times*, Hylda was apparently furious with him. Also, when Eamonn mentioned Tom's name on the programme, he was very aware of the repercussions when Hylda shot him a look that would have felled two giant oak trees.

However, she still remained friends with Tom and would regularly invite him round for dinner with his friend, Rob, and they would spend many an enjoyable evening with her as she was a superb cook. Once again here is a very telling quote from Tom: "I'm sure she was desperately lonely. Lord knows why, for she could be such wonderful company, extremely funny, but she had a wicked sting in her tail and could be quite malicious. I learnt to ignore it as she really didn't mean to hurt people — possibly she was so hurt inside herself that she had to vent her spleen on others."

The first week of June 1972 saw the live recording of the *Saturday Night Variety* show with Larry Grayson, and once again Hylda would experience a horrendous and frightening incident. She was on an icy slope and no amount of grit would help to stop her sliding even further down the hill.

CHAPTER TEN

Clinging to the Steering Wheel

THE *SATURDAY NIGHT VARIETY* show was wonderful, particularly because it was hosted by that great comedian Larry Grayson, whose famous catchphrase was, "Shut that door!" Hylda admired him very much and was obviously thrilled that after being unable to do the show the previous autumn, due to the adverse weather conditions in Guernsey, she was asked to appear in June 1972. Also on the bill were the Dallas Boys, who she also thought were very talented and professional. Hylda chose to revive an act that she had done many years before, with Hugh Paddick as her stooge, incorporating the song, *I Took My Harp To A Party*. She would play this huge harp, have some banter with Hugh, she would begin to play the harp again, but everything would go wrong and she would end up wrapped in the harp strings. It had been a very funny sketch in the past but, sad to say, it had lost its appeal for some reason. The show went out 'live' in front of a studio audience, which is a pretty terrifying experience even for the most experienced professional, and when this sketch 'died' and got very little response it knocked Hylda's confidence a great deal.

The whole show closed with the Cynthia act, which luckily was always a sure-fire hit. The start was wonderful, and she was getting the usual response once more, the audience were loving every minute. Suddenly she went blank and completely dried. Tom, who was still working with her, says that he will never

ever forget the look of absolute panic in her eyes. He did something which had never been contemplated by any of her Cynthias, because it had as yet never been necessary. He beckoned to her and whispered the next part of the act in her ear. She was back on course, managing to improvise to the audience by saying, "Do you know what she's just told me, etc," but eventually it happened again. She recovered once more, Cynthia exited, Hylda carried on with a couple of gags and came off to do her quick change before the final song she was to sing. As Tom went on to do his very 'slow' curtain call to cover her change, she whispered to him, "I wish YOU wouldn't tell ME my act!" He was astounded, but knowing what was going on in Hylda's mind at that time, and the way her pride outweighed reason on so many occasions, it is obvious that she felt she had to blame someone else. It just couldn't be all her fault, coupled with the fact that she was absolutely terrified.

By this time she had changed into her sophisticated stunning 'cabaret' dress, with the full glitter and the swansdown. On cue she entered as the orchestra played the introduction to *I Wish You Love*, which she knew it backwards because she had sung it so many times. She stopped dead and didn't sing the first line, the orchestra played it again, and she began to fiddle with her microphone, they kept playing, but she didn't sing. Hylda had forgotten the first line of one of the songs which was so deeply rooted in her memory as to be second nature; she should have been able to sing it in her sleep. This was a live television show, a Saturday night with millions watching. The whole company were staring in horror at the monitor, and there was pandemonium in the producer's box. Luckily, Tom was standing off-screen and did something on the spur of the moment. He knew she had a hand mike and there wasn't a microphone near him which would pick up his voice, although no doubt the studio audience heard him. He called out softly, "I wish you bluebirds in the spring." Luckily Hylda heard him first time, launched into the song and finished in her true style, but there were a lot of sweating palms in that studio as the credits rolled. As she came off and passed Tom, she mumbled to him, "Of course I knew the words, but I had a frog in my throat." It was so typical of her that she couldn't admit that she had a problem, but this really was the closest she could get to saying an outright 'thank you'.

Bearing in mind also that Tom had become so close to her, it does show that she still held something in reserve, however much she shared her private thoughts. She had shared some very happy moments, too, and not just with Tom, but with his friend Rob, for often she would invite him round for a meal on his own and he, too, remembers those days as being very special. She would cook wonderful meals for them, usually very simple 'old favourites' like her delicious sausages. She tried to 'convert' him to eating tripe and onions, but with no success.

Her big luxury flat was full of photographs of her monkeys and her dogs, and seemed to be furnished full of different tastes: those which she enjoyed coupled with what she thought other people would admire. In the sitting room there was a red carpet, with a red bar in the corner, over which was a black circular mirror with wrought-iron around it, and engraved on the mirror were the words, 'She Knows Y' Know!' There was a coffee table in front of the fire, sheepskin rugs everywhere, and pride of place was given to her small upright piano, which she regularly was given to playing when the mood took her, which was often. She also had a large old fashioned white telephone which, because she was so small, apparently looked very funny when she spoke on it as it was bigger than her head and the earpiece covered half her face.

She was very generous and when she took Rob shopping with her to buy things for herself, she would buy two of each and give him the other. Once they went to Heals where she bought two sheepskin rugs, one for him and one for her. He would try to decline politely, but she would insist. Sometimes she would ring up in the early hours of the morning and would admit that she was very lonely and frightened. She was a tortured soul, who tried to be so very strong, but now and then it would all get too much for her.

Often during those evenings with Rob and Tom, she would talk about anything and everything. They remember her as warm, kind and humorous, and as has been said many times before in this book, when you weren't a threat to her she would let her guard down. She put up many barriers, but if you broke down those barriers she was wonderful. In some ways she was bitter about certain things, but generous and very strong, and she would take you over if you let her. Her extreme forgetfulness was very evident, too, because after telling some wonderful stories on one occasion, she would repeat herself on the next visit. One thing she shared with them was the fact that her biggest regret was that around 1960 she had been very much in love, but had decided to go for her career instead. It appears she had never got over John, her ex-Guardsman.

Apparently Hylda had also become interested in talking about the 'after life' and had even been to spiritualists for readings, and when she spoke of her thoughts on this, she would kind of stare into the middle distance, which is quite disconcerting when one takes into account her fear of death. Maybe she was trying to find out about the 'other side' because of her fears. It wasn't all serious talk, though, as she would suddenly laugh and do the 'famous' Hylda, scratch her tummy and say, "Oh, I've got to get this flaming corset off!" You'd know when she was going to do this because she always scratched her tummy first. She also used to talk about how she never trusted banks, and dotted over the flat were at least four or five handbags all stuffed full of money. The one thing she never discussed, though, was this secret fear that she was going mad, even in those calls in the early hours of the morning. There were still some secrets she would not reveal because they were far too private for her to share with anyone.

The week that culminated in that almost catastrophic appearance on *Saturday Night Variety*, saw Hylda appearing on the screens three times in four days: the first episode of the new series of *Nearest And Dearest*, the variety show, and the very next day an appearance on *The Good Old Days*. She was given a standing ovation as soon as she walked on stage at this appearance. The City Varieties Theatre is very small and dressing room space is limited, so when Hylda refused to share a dressing room with any other artist, they gave her a broom cupboard — but they put a huge star on the door, and then she was happy!

There followed a rather sad end to her working relationship with Tom, who now says, "How I wish it hadn't happened and I hadn't been so hasty. Oh well, it did and I was!" After the variety show the 'money man' came up to Tom and said that his cheque was ready if he would like to come up and sign for it, but Tom said, "Oh no, Hylda pays me." He was then told that they had a contract in his name, so he said he had never signed one, and when they produced it, it was for considerably more than Hylda was going to pay him — and she had signed it. There was great embarrassment all round, and Tom refrained from saying that they had no right to let her sign on his behalf, but he made light of it and left.

Later, when he confronted Hylda, she said she must have signed it by accident, but he was so upset and angry that he shouted, "Come off it! I know you and contracts — you even read the page numbers! You don't need this money, but I do. That's it, I'll never work for you again." And he never did — he was too proud. Even when Hylda telephoned and offered him more work, he turned it down and she got yet another Cynthia. Tom regrets it to this day. The explanation for her behaviour could be more complex than at first appears, and it seems that somewhere deep down she had never got over the deals she used to strike in the old days, when everyone was on the make and she often came off worse. But how sad that having found a friend she trusted, she couldn't help herself where business deals were concerned.

A couple of years prior to this, she had shown enormous generosity to a member of Tom's family, someone she had never even met, when he explained that they needed a loan, just for ten days. He hated to ask her if she'd help, but without further question she went out of the room and came back with £1,500 in cash! All she said was, "Please pay me back in cash in exactly ten days. Now, who'd like a drink?" There was no IOU or anything. The family member turned up with the money on the appointed day, whereupon she took it, together with the flowers they had brought, said, "Thank you," and promptly served them a superb meal. Hylda had trusted they would be there and they did not betray her trust. She really seemed to be on top form that evening and she and her guests enjoyed themselves enormously, and the loan was never mentioned again. In her eyes this was private and not 'business', and this is the only way one can try to understand why she behaved in such a way over that contract.

The new series of *Nearest And Dearest* began on 1 June 1972 with a very funny episode where Nellie and Eli use a computer dating service in order to find partners, but they end up picking each other. Two weeks later, back in Manchester for filming, she was interviewed in her hotel and during the interview a barman managed to ignore her order, not once but twice, to which she said, apparently in very theatrical tones, "A large gin and tonic, please, ice and lemon and some civility!" The reporter said that it was beautifully delivered, but that it wasn't all that terrifying because it was followed by her infectious laugh. He also described her thus:

'She may be tiny, but like an atom, she is a force out of all proportion to her size. I got the feeling that if she leaned out of the window and bellowed, "Stop raining!" the raindrops would obey — even in Manchester. If she wanted, Hylda could fell any hairy, muscle-bound wrestler with one verbal blow. She has a tongue that is razor-edged and a wit that is even sharper. A formidable weapon, but blunted because she is rarely cruel and almost always charming, and she can make you laugh without really trying.'

In the same article, Hylda appears to be less concerned about her loneliness and this time defends herself and denies it is the case: "But I can't be lonely. How can I be? There are always so many people around. From the moment I walk out of my flat there are people who know me and want to know how Nellie is getting on. There is a street market I go to where I get told off if I'm not on TV enough. Once when a newspaper printed a story about how lonely I was, I had hundreds of letters from people asking me to go and have Sunday dinner with them and such like. They were all such nice letters. There must be some marvellous people around."

Perhaps she said all this because she didn't want to be inundated yet again with all those invitations, but it would more likely be that on that particular day she was feeling jollier and in a good frame of mind, for her reactions and her moods would change in an instant.

That first episode of the new series put *Nearest And Dearest* back in the Top Ten of the TV ratings that week with 7,200,000 viewers, the others being:

2. *Crime Of Passion*
3. *Coronation Street* (Wednesday)

4. *Des*
5. *The Hunters* and *News At Ten* equal (Tuesday)
7. *The Sky's The Limit*
8. *Doctor In Charge*
9. *Look – Mike Yarwood*
10. *Albert*

Nearest And Dearest was now so hugely popular that it was decided that it should be made into a film for the big screen, and filming began in July. It now had to be taken into consideration that Hylda had great difficulty in learning lines and therefore couldn't sustain a long scene, and Roy Bottomley and Tom Brennand had quite a difficult commission on their hands when they wrote the film script. They got around it by virtually writing a series of sketches, with the other actors carrying the story thread. They would say, "Oh I wonder what she's doing now? She'll be up to summat," then it would cut to the sketch. It worked very well and the film is still repeated to this day.

Apart from Hylda and Jimmy, the cast included Yootha Joyce, Nosher Powell and Norman Mitchell, it was produced by Michael Carreras and directed by John Robbins. Norman was cast as Hylda's lover, Vernon Smallpiece, and he remembers many an incident during the making of it. He had never worked with Hylda before but he had with Jimmy Jewel, and they had got on well together. He knew all about the situation between Jimmy and Hylda and was very much aware that he had to be diplomatic at all times. The first day he was taken to the location which was in the middle of a field, and the scene was a cod dance sequence with the two lovers coming together, Norman in a white suit as her 'knightly lover', and Hylda in a flowing floral robe.

As soon as he arrived he greeted her, "Hello Miss Baker, it's lovely to meet you."

Hylda eyed him carefully and said, "Have you met him yet?"

Norman asked, "Who?"

"Jimmy flaming Jewel!" she said.

"No," he said.

"Well, you've got a big treat coming," said Hylda. "He's mean that man — he earned a fiver in 1936 and he hasn't broken into it yet!"

Norman was desperate to laugh but felt that diplomacy must reign as he hadn't even shot one scene yet. He needed the job and they had six weeks to go!

She looked him up and down and said, "What are you going to do?"

Norman replied, "Miss Baker, you are the star, the people are paying to see you, what would you like me to do?"

With this she laughed and took his arm, telling him, "That's right Norman, I like you — we're going to get on well together."

They did the sequence, then she said, "Norman's coming with me," and she took him back to the studio in her car. During the trip back she said he must come and have dinner with her one night, and he said that he really would like to but was rather booked up that week. Hylda told him that they must do it another time. He really had made a hit with her.

That very afternoon Norman had a scene with Jimmy who asked, "Have you met her?"

"Yes," said Norman, "we did a scene together this morning."

Jimmy said, "Did she kill your laughs?"

Norman said, "No," to which Jimmy replied, "Well, she blooming well will do!"

Once again the 'idiot' boards were everywhere and whoever had a scene with Hylda had to be in a position where she could see to read the lines. At these times Jimmy would say very loudly to the director, "John, will you tell Miss ... Hylda Baker it's time she learnt her flaming lines!" to which the director would smile diplomatically and begin, "Miss Baker, Mr Jewel suggests perhaps..." but he didn't get any further for she would interrupt saying, "You tell Mr smart-arse Jimmy Jewel to get on with his own dialogue, and I'll get on with mine in my own way."

Everyone was treading on eggshells every day and this sort of exchange happened so many times that eventually Norman would stand up, which took a lot of bravery, and say, "When you've decided what we're doing, I'll be in dressing room 54," and he would go and lie down until they called him back on to the set!

The end of the first week of filming came and the producer threw a party for everyone with waiter service, and there was caviar, steak, champagne, the lot, and much jollity, but still Hylda and Jimmy were kept poles apart. The next day, Norman had to do a drinking scene, which was unfortunate as the alcohol was no doubt still in his system! The director asked him what was his favourite drink, to which he replied, "Guinness," and when the director asked him if he could knock a pint back in one, he said of course he could, but he wasn't going to do it until they were actually shooting the scene, for obvious reasons. When it came time to do it for real, Jimmy dried on the tag line nine times, each time after Norman had sunk his pint. He downed nine pints before 9am, poor thing. In the end he collapsed and spent the rest of the day in the dressing room, but it turned out there was no such scene in the film, and he had been set up by the director and Jimmy who had planned it all! It seems rather unfair, to say the least, but one imagines that the humour had turned that way with the kind of atmosphere that was created by the two stars, and they felt they had to get some kind of laughs for themselves out of the whole thing, however cruel.

There follows a quote from Norman:

"I was telephoned to be on *This Is Your Life* with Hylda, which I would have loved to have done, but I had to say, 'I'm sorry, I can't make it,' and the voice said, 'Please, please do come, you're the 35th person to turn it down!' I said, 'I'm not turning it down, I just can't be there because I'm working. Give her my love. I think she is a genius, an original one-off comic. A great performer. A great person. Lovely lady. Good to me.'"

About the same time that they were coming to the end of shooting the film, there appeared in the *News Of The World* an article, full of malapropisms, all about football and written by Hylda herself! At least it was a change from the articles about the strife between her and Jimmy. It is imagined that she needed to keep her publicity as varied as she could, but in the article it is indicative that she tries to show that she is definitely NOT Nellie Pledge, so perhaps this was really the reason, and that she needed to be Hylda again in the eyes of the public! Not only that, but by putting it in her own words she was proving her skill at writing, and showing her ability to make up her own malapropisms, as she was becoming more and more on the defensive about who was responsible for putting them in the series:

'Before I explain why I am entitled to talk about football I must establish that I don't own a pickle factory in Lancashire. Nor do I have a woman-chasing brother called Eli who wouldn't know what to do if he caught one. I want to deny, too, that I deflower the English language. Fancy accusing me of using the wrong words when the right ones are perfectly inadequate. And I do come from Farnworth, the Oxford of the North. No, Nellie Pledge, the extrovert yet innocent little woman who never knows where to put her gherkins in *Nearest And Dearest* on the telly, and I have nothing in common.

'For instance, Nellie has no interest in soccer. She has been protected from the dismissive society and so would not dream of going to a match. Men in shorts would terrify her. And she would be shocked by those obscene chants from the terraces once their meaning had been explained to her. But me, I am passionate about it. The game, not the chants. This is not surprising because I come from the same place as Alan Ball and most people are football fanatics in Farnworth. Like Bally, I have plenty to say about the game. For a start many clubs will be bankrupted soon unless they change their ways and allow women into their boardrooms.

'There are female film producers and directors, and women in politics. So why not in football? We would bring ideas and creativity, and we would be better in a crisis. I have no doubt, either, we would understand players' problems better than men. If I was in charge at Old Trafford and George Best said he would rather not play for a while as the elastic in his shorts was chafing his sunburn, I'd be sympathetic. Could you see Frank O'Farrell being so commiserate? I think we should do a lot for all players, not just the most expansive ones like Best. They could talk to us about their domestic worries knowing that we would make them a nice cup of tea and give sensible advice. There would be no sending them away with a bee in their ear.

'And don't think I'm not serious. Football can well do with a woman's touch. Look at the catering, on most grounds it's a disgrace. Tea in dirty cups, pork pies that have overstaged their welcome and crisps that once were, but are not any longer. Before Bolton or any other club have the pleasure of me, I would demand something was done about faculties for women. The last time I went to a match I asked where the nearest powder room was. The man on the turntable came out with a mouthful that would have brought the pickle factory out on strike. This bloke thought I was joking. He couldn't see that a refinery lady like me never call them loos or lavs. But once I found it, I wish I hadn't. No woman would allow such a mess. She would have too much pride. After all, what would the neighbours say?

'You know how we women love a gossip, and once it got round that ladies absolutions had been allowed to disintegrate, we would never have the front to step outside the ground again. Given half a chance I would smarten up grounds so much that women would be attracted to there just to use the powder rooms. And from what my football friends tell me, the game's so short of money, that anything that gets them inside the gates is helpful. Next I would sort out those players who have trouble keeping their age under control. But though I am the type who would deprecate their problems, they would soon realise I would not be trifled with.

'I would not tolerate bad manners and displays of temperance on the pitch. What gets my sheckles up, in particular, is when I see players lying prostitute pretending they are injured. That, to use a favourite football expression, is carbolic. They must be honest if they want my help. I would let them know who is boss, because from some of their behaviour, they don't know yer know!'

By the beginning of December, although the feelings between the two warriors began to flare up again, Granada announced that there was to be no further series of *Nearest And Dearest* and Jimmy was going to join Thames TV. The final series was released for a seven-week run from 21 December 1972, so by February 1973 there was to be no more battling either on screen or off, but not before Hylda had her final and, as it turned out, not so final, say on the subject! They were both quoted in the *Evening News* on 4 December 1972:

Hylda told the newspaper, "I have nothing to say about the series except I shall not be doing another one after this present lot is over." Jimmy said, "Nobody is indispensable and they could still continue the series without me if they wanted. After all they have Hylda Baker, and she's a funny woman …a very funny woman."

Hylda, that bitter-sweet woman, was also at pains to stress that there had never been a quarrel. "Jimmy and I have never had a row, we never had a quarrel because he just didn't speak to me! I did tell Granada that I didn't like rehearsing in Manchester and wanted to be in London. At first they said it was impossible so I said I could not do the show. Eventually they agreed to come to London. So you see the situation was not solely and wholly over Jimmy Jewel, although I did ask them to suggest that he was a bit more sociable with me."

Inevitably, a personality as huge as hers tended to upstage the people appearing with her. Was she aware of this and did she think it might be the reason for resentment? "I can't say, but in all honesty I would never deliberately try to steal a scene because I should hate someone to do it to me. You hear about these directors and writers putting shows to the top. Well, more often than not they will put a show right to the bottom if you don't watch them. On this show I do a lot of watching."

There was a rumour that the show was destined for the American market, and unfortunately this particular grape turned out to be pretty sour for her. "If they intend selling the idea to America I shall make it clear that they had better not copy my style, my character or any words written by me, because this is my material and my living. I put myself into the character of Nellie, I created her, I conceived her character. I put in my mis-wordings."

When asked, she denied that she thrived on all the dramas and excitement saying. "I have never had all these battles before and it has given me bronchial asthma. I didn't have it when I started working on the series, but now I have to take a pill daily to stay alive." Little incidents hurt her deeply. "I went to join everybody at a table in the canteen and they all moved away from me, I don't know why. So many people try to bring me down all the time, and do you know why? Because I can teach them their business and they don't like it. I'm not tough, I'm very sensitive, but I am a fighter. I have had to be a fighter …circumstances have made me one."

The article continued, 'Loneliness is a big problem for her. Suddenly she looked small and frail and those shrewd beady eyes had the trace of moisture. Suspicious, I looked to see if she had an onion up her sleeve, there wasn't, not even a pickled one. Hylda Baker is a fascinating character — an extremely hard nut with a soft centre.'

It is such a shame that with regard to the atmosphere at the studios it really was true that she was often avoided. One actor, James Beattie, who was in just for one episode, joined her, feeling sorry for her, and they ended up going out to dinner. He says she was the most wonderful company, they talked about star signs and had a very lighthearted evening. At one point she wanted to go to the loo, but they were hemmed in at their long table, so she slid down and crawled underneath to get out. He has never forgotten this sight!

Just a week after the announcement that the series was to end, she was defending herself once more, but this time there was an indication of the confusion which was in her mind.

"I'm a loner. I don't have any close friends in showbusiness. There isn't the same camaraderie among TV showbusiness people as there used to be in the variety halls. They don't speak the same language as I do and I've lost contact with people I knew so well, like Renee Houston and Beryl Reid. So now I sit by my own fireside when I'm not working. You have to cope with being on your own or you'd go under. When I'm finished at the studio I sit down and let myself unwind. Possibly, I'll go where the rest of the company are having a meal or a drink, but they all have their own lives to lead, so I go back to the hotel and have something to eat. Of course there are places where I'm made welcome after the stress and the strain, but I don't have any women friends. Women aren't the same as friends, are they?

"Sometimes I'll go abroad for a cruise, if I have two or three weeks to spare, but I always go alone because I've no one to go with. I don't lose out, though, because everybody aboard ship knows me. I didn't realise this at first. A true friend is someone who will listen to you and keep his or her mouth shut. Someone who helps when you're in need, with no strings attached. A true friend is someone you can 'phone and say, 'Please, I'm ill in bed and have nobody here,' and that friend will soon be at your side. I've always been a fighter, and now I'm fighting for my existence ... I don't give a damn, damn them all ... I'll win in the end."

Sadly, to be a friend to Hylda the individual had to contend with somone who was used to getting her own way, and one gets the feeling from the above that she would use any friend as no more than a sounding board, and probably wouldn't listen to good advice should the friend be able to get a word in and air their views. She had been on her own so long there was no changing her now.

It is such a pity that she couldn't say to some friends what she said sometimes in the newspapers, as in the following example, because she really does admit to certain failings, although she will once again immediately defend herself!

"They say there have been rows over the series, I have had no row with anyone. Sometimes I know people think I'm abrupt and aggressive. I'm not really, but I have to make myself do things that make me seem unpopular. I don't necessarily like doing these things but they are things I think are right for me and the character I'm playing. I like to be liked otherwise I am unhappy. We all like to get on in this world with other people or we become outcasts. I hope I have never been an outcast. I do know there are a lot of pitfalls such as jealousy.

"In any business though you never stop learning; as soon as you think you know it all you are in trouble. I think I know what is best for me. That doesn't mean I don't listen to other people's advice. You can work yourself into a real state churning over what people have said. If someone says something odd to me, I reply, 'What do you mean?' That's the best way to play it — straight. I have had some bad luck, but always come up smiling, and I've had to bounce back, particularly because of my parents. My mother died only two years ago and my father three years ago, so I had that responsibility until recently. I wanted my mother to come and live with me in London, she used to visit me, but would never stay long, she liked it best back in Farnworth.

"Do I get lonely? How can I? If I'm feeling a bit blue all I have to do is go out and someone will stop me and say, 'Hello Hylda. How are you? She knows y' know!' It gives a warm feeling inside that lasts. No I don't feel lonely. The only time it is bad is if I am ill and there is nobody around to look after me. That can be very depressing. I still wish I had had children. That I couldn't have them still makes me very sad. There are so many things I now want to do. Touch wood, my health is now good and I want to go on for ever."

Contained in the above quotes is the one big lie that Hylda carried with her all through her life: that of exactly how, when and where her father died, and even in this interview she gets it wrong. One gets the feeling that she's told so many contradictory stories that she can't keep up with herself.

What is clear, though, is that she was still very astute, and those who spread it around that she was an alcoholic were not correct in their assumption. Too many people, people who knew her well, have said this was most definitely not the case. They have all said that during the period right up to the mid-1970s she would like the odd glass of wine but that was all, and it was only much, much later in her life, when she was becoming very ill, that she would indulge herself in order to escape her problems. Her extreme forgetfulness was a disease, not self-inflicted. Likewise it is so important that the record is put straight about her relationships. Of course, she liked male company, but there is sufficient documentation from those who knew her personally, that much of it was a craving for affection, and she would never ever have anything to do with married men; she had very strict morals on that score.

The writing partnership of Roy Bottomley and Tom Brennand were commissioned to write another film for Hylda, due to the fact that the powers that be were very pleased with the *Nearest And Dearest* film. *The Godfather* with Marlon Brando had been a smash hit, so they wrote a sequel, a pastiche which was to be called 'The Godmother', and Hylda was to play the godmother. She said of the role, "It's about a kind of female Mafia leader, but comedic, so it won't be all blood and shooting. She will be surrounded by her henchwomen who set out to right the wrongdoings of others." It was a wonderful idea, and would certainly give her career yet another boost. However it was still being written, and the film of *Nearest And Dearest* had yet to be released, which happened in the spring of 1973.

At the same time it was finally announced in the newspapers that Jimmy Jewel had said his final goodbye to his nagging TV sister, and the series he was to now star in was called *Spring And Autumn* for Thames, and written by his old friends Vince Powell and Harry Driver. He said at the time, "If I wasn't a teetotaller I'd be knocking back the champagne now." It was official, and so finally ended a relationship which thrived as a big audience puller, lasting for five glorious years, but which caused so many who worked on the show to, metaphorically speaking, wince with pain. Hylda threw an end-of-series party at the Midland Hotel, but hardly anybody came, just the producer, Bill Podmore, the wardrobe lady and three or four others, that was all. It was the end of a not-so-beautiful friendship.

Roy Bottomley said of the whole affair, "I think there was a conspiracy of silence between the two of them, and that is the worst kind of row because it's on-going and they would explode in the privacy of their own dressing rooms. Hylda's comments about the producers, writers and directors, when she knocked them, was because she came from the music hall background and she couldn't quite get it into her head that a script had to be written for situation comedy. You can't just go out there and do your act because there had to be some sort of story thread and she found that very difficult to get around. Each week you were doing, in essence, a one-act play. If you diverted from the plot too much then you'd never get back, and this was always a problem. She would say, 'Why don't I just say I'm going to Blackpool?' 'Well, because in the next scene you're supposed to be round the corner.' She would find the disciplines of working within a dramatic formula difficult to contend with, therefore her outbursts of criticism towards writers etc, were because she felt everyone was against her, and all they were trying to do was to make her stick to the storyline.

"She would say things like that, but she didn't really mean them, it was just another expression of insecurity. She was actually very fond of Tom and myself, and Vince and Harry. We'd go to her flat to talk about a script, and once you were in there you couldn't get out, for she'd entertain you and pour lavish amounts of drink."

Roy was obviously very fond of her, too, and his reaction to the fact that she was so scathing about the writers shows why he is so successful in his job. He has a great insight into human nature, in particular that of Hylda, for often she tried to make out to the press that she had written the series and had to show them how to do it! She would make comments such as, "If you write *Nearest And Dearest* down it looks like a load of rubbish. I know what I want in a series and I tell them so." And, "I've had writers doing a show for me and felt I've practically had to teach them how to write. They were rarely grateful." It shows how much Hylda was liked and indeed understood by many who worked with her, for Roy was most generous bearing in mind the nature of her comments.

Around the same time, in April, Hylda was involved in trying to save jobs in a pickle factory, a real one this time, that was threatened with closure. The factory was in Nottingham, and the firm was Jubilee Pickles, who had apparently been forced to sack 18 women due to 'rising overheads and a world shortage of onions due to an onion famine'! Hylda wrote to the Minister of Agriculture to protest, and was quoted as saying to a reporter, "If it were not so tragic, this would make a first-class comedy script, but I do hope the government will act. It really is a tragic situation for real people." The managing director of the firm was quoted as saying, "It is nice to think that Miss Baker cares enough to write to the minister. I must say I am a fan of her series, although it is not a good advert for the modern pickler."

In the summer of 1973 Hylda was once again doing summer season, this time at the Windmill Theatre, Great Yarmouth, doing the play they had done in Blackpool in 1971, called *Not on Your Nellie*. Jack Haigh took the part which Ken Platt had played, and the cast also included Rose Power, Billy Tasker, Victor Woolf, Nicholas Brent and Norman Robbins. Bill Roberton, who was still Hylda's agent, had booked Jack to play opposite her specifically asking him to look after Hylda, to which he had readily agreed — but it all went wrong. They just didn't get on. Hylda's problem with lines was getting worse, and Jack used to stand at the mantelpiece, his pipe in his mouth, smiling away, but all the time muttering under his breath, "You don't know a blooming word you're saying, do you dear?" On another occasion he was supposed to be lying on the floor, either ill or listening for what was happening below, it's not clear which, when once more, Hylda got lost. He looked up at her and said, "I'm not saying anything until you give me my cue!" During that season he also did something rather cruel when he put an advertisement in *The Stage* newspaper, saying where he was appearing and with whom, and in very large letters he had printed 'HELP!' Bill Roberton did say this of her, though: through all his long association with her, although she was very hard work, first and foremost she was 'a pro'.

In that same show was Norman Robbins, who she had bought the contact lenses for two years before, and apparently he had to go on for Jack Haigh who eventually went sick. The show that night went better than ever and Hylda felt that Norman was no danger to her so she relaxed, and in fact when HE forgot a couple of his lines she helped him out! In turn, he gave her many of the lines she couldn't remember, and at the end of the show she did something very rare and that was to thank him for helping her. He says of his association with her:

"I saw little of her after that season, as my jobs took me all over the world, but despite everything that people say about her, I still think she was the funniest woman I've ever seen on stage. Her timing was immaculate, and I could still laugh at her minutes after getting a bawling out for Lord knows what reason. She was sometimes monstrous, but under that dragon-like exterior she was generous, too, and she knew her craft."

When *Nearest And Dearest* came to a close, Michael Grade was the programme controller at London Weekend Television, and he asked Roy and Tom if they had any ideas regarding a new series for Hylda. They went to the drawer where, all those years ago in 1968, they had put aside the idea of a series about a pub landlady, took it out and presented it to Michael Grade. This is how *Not On Your Nellie* was born. The idea was that she would be a pub landlady who had come to London because she had inherited this pub from her reprobate father, who had moved south many years earlier.

The irony of it all was that Nellie was a complete teetotaller and absolutely hated anyone who drank, which meant there was a great deal of comedy to extract from the situation. Famous lines from this were, "Hello, Brown Cow speaking," and "Hello Gilbert, and what are you today?" Her surname was changed from Pledge to Pickersgill, but she was still Nellie. It is interesting to note that in *Nearest And Dearest* the character of Walter never spoke, and in this new series there was the character called Gilbert who was also silent. Hylda's comment on this was, 'My representation of a mute in each series was a continuation of Cynthia. That's my own thing! The character is mine. I always have people who take after her and I write them in."

Norman Mitchell, who was with her in the *Nearest And Dearest* film, was also in the series playing the local sweep and coalman, and also, as in the film, he was her screen lover. A great deal of the time Nellie was trying to keep various ladies from getting romantically entangled with her father, and in one episode, he is in the sitting room with a lady. Hylda, in a white suit, is looking through the keyhole at them, the coalman surprises her from behind, grabbing her by the buttocks and leaving two great black hand prints. Hylda was to turn and say, "So you're the latest paraphernalia of her afflictions," but all she said was, "Who are you?" This was so typical of what was happening to her, that she had forgotten once again one of her own magic lines! She did, however, get it right on the next take.

The project was launched on her birthday, which she felt was a pretty good omen. She would turn up to rehearsals in her white mink coat, no doubt feeling happier than she had done for a long time, but she was still being questioned about her relationship with Jimmy and her reputation for being difficult, and it upset her that people were saying she could not get on with her co-stars:

"I know what I want in a series and I tell them so. I'm a perfectionist about comedy. I'm only difficult when my co-stars don't talk to me, which happened before. So far, in this series, they are all talking to me. I'm not an unhappy woman really. I just like getting things right."

The first episode was shown on 15 March 1974 and it was a great success. The day before this there appeared an amusing article in *TV Times*, about how the producer, Bryan Izzard, found the right setting for the series. He wanted an authentic pub to model it on, so decided to go on a bit of a 'reccy' to find the right one. He set off with his designer, and it turned into a pub crawl because they apparently visited 15 pubs, having a drink in each, until they found the right one. The next day neither of them could remember which one it was, so they had to do another tour until they found it — the Nell Gwynne in Chelsea. He said afterwards that Hylda was inclined to dry up at times and forget names, but that day it was his turn to have a bit of a memory problem. In the same article, it is recorded, 'Since a car accident a few years ago, Hylda has been losing her memory. Places and names worry her.' That car accident, the one in Charing Cross Road, was actually 13 years before, and it was possibly, but not necessarily, as a result of this that Hylda was having trouble with her memory.

She commented to a reporter in the same article that when people rushed up and wanted to shake her hand in the street she found it was, "Genuine affection. You would think they were my long-lost relatives. Come to think of it, they could be, these days I have an awful memory for names. I try to remember names by relating them to something. It's a good system. It gets me through. I do recall the sort of gags I used to crack. I'm staying at an hotel and I find a pair of men's pyjamas on my bed. I called the manager. I'm not having this. Take them away at once — and fill them!"

And once again, about the malapropisms, she said, "Fancy accusing me of using the wrong words when the right ones are perfectly extortionate. I know who I am in this series, the woman who says drink is the 'eve of all roots'. Nellie would never become an alcafrolic. I do regret sometimes that women aren't allowed more freedom. I remember when they couldn't go into bars alone. It's still not the thing to do. Why shouldn't we be able to go into a bar, buy a man a drink and talk business? I feel I would have got a lot further in life, a lot quicker, if women hadn't this sort of disadvantage. Now don't misunderstand me, I'm not for women throwing away their bras. I never heard a more ridiculous phrase. Bras are good for the figure, so is corseting. You wear something that holds you in. Can't have a scatstastrophe can we? Not on your Nellie."

Yes, there is really no doubt about it that Hylda was born ahead of her time, and her career was somewhat held up in the early days by the very fact she was a woman, but there is also no doubt about the fact that those experiences took away any innocence she might have had about the world of showbusiness, and trained her how to fight.

Later that year, with the series a sure-fire success, she treated herself to another car, and once again got the publicity she thrived on. It was a shiny smooth silver grey Fiat 130 with the number plate AHH 40. She admitted that her cars were always for status, and said that the reason she changed to this particular model was because the garage man brought it round for her to see and she thought it was rather nice. She did get one alteration, and that was to have a sun roof put in. The following newspaper article about it is sometimes rather tongue-in-cheek and one gets the feeling that the writer was somewhat sending her up at times:

'"My mum said I was a small girl with big ideas," said Hylda, teetering on high heels against the glittering bonnet. She got in, sank against the sheepskin covers, which protect the transparent plastic covers, which protect the grey fabric upholstery 'while revealing it's beauty'. "I'll lower this window," she said. It's all electric. She pressed a button and the windscreen wipers started. Later she pressed another and the window lowered. Yet another and the radio aerial slid up. "The sunshine roof isn't automatic," she confessed with regret.

'She had considered buying an enormous car in America and bringing it over. It was all press-button that one. The Fiat is for prestige, she looks SOMEONE struggling out of it. The first vehicle she had up north was an air-cooled Rover. The red hot cylinders cooled as you moved as you drove. Cost her £25. Had to swing the crank to start it. Yes, she could change a fan belt, and a wheel. Doesn't have to with this one, though. Has automatic wheel change. "It's all in the boot. A hydraulic jack ... Friends advised me about the engine," she said as long black lashes glued to green eyelids, fluttered dangerously.'

In November 1974 they were filming a new series of *Not On Your Nellie* and once again she was picked on for reputedly being difficult, to which she answered:

"I know some people are giving me the reputation of being a right b******, but I'm as soft as muck. Although I act tough when somebody's making things tough for me, I go away and cry in private afterwards. The trouble is that many male actors resent a woman being the star of a show and do their best to drag her down, so I have to stick up for myself. If I wasn't firm, I'd get trampled on. I'm not rude to people, but a spade is a spade. You can put a ruffle round it but you can't hide the facts. I've been in shows in the past where I was sorry for the actors I was working with, and even wrote in funny jokes for them because they weren't very funny by themselves. No word of thanks, only resentment.

"I'll tell you, it's because I'm a woman. The only thing for me to do is a show where I'm the sole star with just supporting actors. In this business it's eat or be eaten, especially where women stars are concerned. Actors can't stand a woman topping the bill. I've been friendly with a few of them, going out and having a drink together, but soon they weren't around any more because they were jealous of my success. Can you wonder that actors are not my favourite people?"

It is pretty obvious from what we know that her personality was beginning to become much more intolerant than she'd ever been and she no longer seemed to worry if the press printed this sort of story. In trying to defend herself she came across as being rather bitter, which it is fairly obvious she was. It is sad, for she was still at the top of the tree, but no doubt her secret fears were nagging once more as she knew her forgetfulness was getting very much worse, and maybe she had an inkling that she couldn't go on like this much longer. Seven years had flown by since it first began to manifest itself, during the tour of *A Taste Of Honey* in 1967, into something more than just a case of forgetting little things, or mislaying something, but now she couldn't give up, for what else did she have but her work?

January 1975 saw the new series of *Not On Your Nellie* on the screens, but she was obviously still fighting her loneliness, and also the fact that she had also just got over a bout of pneumonia and once again, a nervous complaint caused by overwork. No one knew, of course, that she was now 70 years old, and often it was reported that she was '60 this year', so it was understandable that nobody would make concessions for her age, and in fact they never did all her life for this very reason. But it was what she wanted. Many who got close to her were suspicious, though, for Tom Hardy said when he worked with her she claimed to be in her late 50s. Apparently she didn't look old, quite the opposite, but when she started to talk about her touring days, showing him the amazing photographs in her scrapbook, he was shrewd enough to realise that the dates simply didn't tally with her being in her late 50s. (She would in fact have been 67 when he worked with her).

She said when the new series started, "The landlady of the Brown Cow is such a down-to-earth character that people feel they can confide in me. I don't mind, it gives me a terrific warm feeling. When someone comes up and gives me a little bit of her life, it makes me happy because she must like me. She knows she is going to get an answer and not be flung to one side. One woman on a train confided that she was worried sick because her 16-year-old daughter was going out with a married man twice her age. Then there was the Cockney housewife who stopped me in a supermarket. I found myself hearing all about the old man's operation and daughter Betty's disastrous marriage.

"I have one simple method of dealing with disappointment, ill health and loneliness. You get yourself dressed, never mind if you can hardly walk. You get out and see people. You will see somebody on crutches or with a white stick and you can say to yourself, 'Thank goodness I can walk on my own two legs and see.' There is always somebody worse off than you, and in thinking of other people you forget your own troubles. That's how you fight and keep on top."

She was interviewed for an 'At Home' article in the *Sunday Times* in March 1975, and was obviously still somewhat disturbed and erratic, but still very, very funny. When she opened the door to the reporter she had just spilt some fat on the front of her dress and was in the process of trying to dab it off with some very expensive perfume.

"I can't get it out. Of course, in my young day they called this stuff toilet water, which is what it is, but now they call it perfume and it costs five times as much.. Come in dear, hang your coat up in this wardrobe, but mind you don't get your fingers squeezed in the door. You must excuse me if everything's a little confused, but you see I'm all on my lonesome, by myself, alone. Oh yes, I'm advertising like mad for a housekeeper and a maid, but they don't want to know do they? It's when you've been poorly, as I have lately, that you find out who your real friends are. You see I've had a bit of a spasm. I was up till four or five o'clock this morning. You're lucky if you've got one real friend. Which I thought I had ... Well this stain doesn't seem to be coming out, I'll cover it up with my Bolton Wanderers rosette."

During the whole interview it appeared that she was very nervy and constantly on the move. At one point she became rather fraught because she had lost a little hand-carved glass and thought it might have been 'purloined' by someone who came in, "To watch the 'what do you call it? You know, the thingummy. What IS it called, when all the government is on? Her, missus what's-her-name. That's it, the election! Never mind. An evening spent with Hannah in a big armchair, is like walking through Alaska in your underwear!"

Her forgetfulness was very evident, and in fact she did indeed find the glass a little later. It was on the floor behind the bar. She picked it up and immediately went into a dramatic pose and recited, "Under the starlight glitter, stands a little fragile girl. Heedless of the night winds bitter as they around about her whirl." She went on to say that she used to do all that 'rubbish' because she really wanted to be a dramatic actress, but that she loved cheerful music and promptly went to the piano and played two very sentimental songs, *A Good Man Is Hard To Find* and *I'm A Little On The Lonely Side*!

This was followed by a parody of the latter, and in fact she was very fond of this form of humour, just as her father had been before her, but she got totally lost in her own little world and wandered off after the first line, not really making any sense. "To the altar I had to falter and promised I would be his bride. He cut a dash with all my cash, as my sister used to say when I had that terrible time that lasted eight months, 'You're so cheerful nobody would know you had anything wrong with you.' I said, why should I depress other people? I know what would happen if I did. Sorry I can't say hello — and not half — because I'll be on my way, Lily."

Just reading the interview gives one a feeling of sadness because although some of it is very funny, there is such an air of desperation about her behaviour. She spent a good deal of time talking about the photographs around her, one of her with Lew Grade and Bernard Delfont, and also talked incessantly about the contents of her *This Is Your Life* book. She talked of doing the clog dance with her sisters, of Cynthia 'blabbing his mouth off to the press', Barney Colehan making her a star overnight, her Aunt Agnes, Dorothy Squires and a cousin of Hylda's they had flown over specially from America. Hylda had a funny story to tell on that subject:

"Eamonn Andrews flew her all the way over from America to tell the story about me and the fish knives. You see I was in this very expensive restaurant in America and I was so shocked they didn't have fish knives, I said it was like a fish and chip shop. She tried to tell the story but she got in such a muddle at the rehearsal that they cut it down to a few seconds and we said was it really worth flying her all that way?"

Hylda also spoke about her friendship with Dorothy Squires, saying that when she broke up with Roger Moore she was so upset that Hylda used to go and see her to try to make her laugh. "We're very close friends in trouble, not just when things are going well. I've known a lot of trouble myself, and that's when you need friends, and you find you've got nobody."

Then, off at a tangent once more, she said, "This sheet music on the piano is the theme song I wrote for *Not On Your Nellie*, but it's only handwritten so I don't think I can play it for you. I don't know where I put my spectacles to tell you the truth. I wanted them to bring it out as a single, with a nice honkytonk pub piano background. Well, it's taken them long enough, they've had it 12 months. They told me it would cost a thousand pounds to make and I said don't be so daft. Yes, written AND composed by Hylda Baker. I've written a lot of songs and never done anything about them. I wrote my own revues — no, not reviews! — or I'd have made myself a star 30 years earlier!"

The film of 'The Godmother', which never came off, was something else she became quite heated about, but blamed it on the fact they couldn't get, "That big Scotch fellow, I can't remember his name, but I'm not supposed to even know why it didn't come off." She may have been right, but no one really seems to know exactly what happened.

The very next minute she jumped up and read out a fan letter from a little girl of nine: 'This is just a letter to tell you that I think you are very good and very funny and my Mummy and Daddy think so too. I look forward to the Brown Cow every week. My Mummy says you have a go at anything, you are smashing.'

Said Hylda, "There! What can't speak can't lie! That proves I appeal to all ages. The first time I used 'rickidoodleous' there were these two little boys waiting for me outside the flat and they said, 'Miss — now what do they call me? — Nellie, do say rickidoodleous for us.' So I stood there like a mug and said, 'Don't be rickidoodlous!' Oh well, whether you like it or not, there's somebody that does. Or so it seems."

Jumping from subject to subject like a jack-in-the-box, she suddenly said out of the blue, "I've got to stay in London till Tuesday because I've got an appointment on Tuesday. Then I'm free. I think I'll take a holiday. I need one. I thought I was free today but they can't make up their minds about how much money I want for the next series. What they offered wasn't quite what I expected. So I kept quiet about it and told them what I did expect. They bought me a very nice lunch. But they needn't have bothered, really, because I'll get what I asked for in the end." At which point she burst straight into singing, "Roll me over, lay me down, and do it again!"

With the knowledge that we have of this complex and fascinating character, it is poignant to note her extreme forgetfulness, her desperation to be admired and respected, her boundless energy, but above all it shows that she is so desperate at times that it becomes almost manic. The end of the article, and the observations of the interviewer, are very telling:

'The hour I spent with Hylda Baker in her spotless home near the Tottenham Court Road had somehow reminded me of the last few minutes in a pub before closing time, when the atmosphere of jollity intensifies to an almost dangerous degree and everything seems to be hovering on the brink of getting out of control; drinks are spilled, saucy or sentimental tunes are sung over a piano that isn't quite in tune, and intimacies are struck up which are immediately forgotten.

'A star who will countenance no co-star — and who is even slightly suspicious of her supporting cast — she turns one into an admiring audience who is also, like Cynthia, a happily speechless stooge. What makes her comic timing so unique? Partly her voice, strangulated between robust North Country vulgarity and a peculiar camp refinement; partly her odd, fractured timing (which is much funnier than the verbal confusions that are her stock in trade); partly the vehement exaggeration of her gestures, which agitate every inch of her tiny body; and partly, beneath the lapses of memory and the near-hysterical vagueness, the suggestion of a shrewd, cynical appreciation of the human race.

'She may be the broadest of low comediennes, but one can be reminded of her on unexpected occasions. For example, in Benjamin Britten's opera based on Thomas Mann's *Death In Venice*, Peter Pears as the ageing Aschenbach, lusting after the Polish youth, reiterates a phrase from Myfanwy Piper's libretto: "He notices when he's noticed." Did anyone connected with this impeccably highbrow production realise that he was echoing the immortal words of Hylda Baker? "She knows you know!"'

Very soon after this interview, Hylda was to find that fighting to keep on top was a battle which she was yet again about to have to face. And, indeed, something catastrophic happened yet again which made her previous comment about being grateful that at least she was able to walk, rather ironic. Six months later she had an accident on the set in the TV studios, and she broke her ankle. Things were getting steadily worse and once more she was on rocky ground. It was almost as if she was going backwards towards the alley, and the back gate which she had fought to get through beckoned once more.

1960: With Albert Finney in *Saturday Night And Sunday Morning.*

As the tough little woman, Albert Finney's Aunt Ada, in *Saturday Night And Sunday Morning.*

Hylda's TV drama debut, playing the part of Aunt Beatie in *Where The Difference Begins*, 1961.

With Joe Gibbons in *She Knows You Know*, Hylda's second film, in 1961.

December 1961 and Hylda reads her 'get well' messages after the accident which put her in hospital for Christmas. "They've just dognosed my case and here I am laid lying down, all alone, by myself, with nobody with me."

With Jack Woolgar in *Our House*, the ABC television series, 1961.

Another television series, this time *The Best of Friends*, 1963.

Dress rehearsal for *Aladdin* at the Wimbledon Theatre in December 1963. Hylda was Widow Twankey, while Tommy Cooper played the part of Abanazar.

Christmas 1964 saw Hylda starring in pantomime at the New Theatre in Huddersfield, in *Babes In The Wood*. Here she is pictured with Nita Valerie.

April 1964 and Hylda leaves the High Court in London smiling after her successful battle for damages following the Christmas Eve accident nearly two and a half years earlier.

With her beloved pet Cha Cha, who died in the most unfortunate of circumstances.

A remarkable study of Hylda in the black comedy *Fill The Stage With Happy Hours* at the Vaudeville Theatre in London in 1967.

With Harry H. Corbett and Sheila Hancock in a scene from *Fill The Stage With Happy Hours.*

1968: With director Peter Collinson rehearsing for a scene in Paramount's *Up The Junction*.

An intense role: playing the abortionist, Winny, in *Up The Junction*.

1968: As Mrs Sowerberry in the film *Oliver!*

CHAPTER ELEVEN

Slipping Up And Back

ON 22 JUNE 1975 they were filming the third series of *Not On Your Nellie*. Everything had gone well until they were recording the second episode. They used real beer on the pub set, but had been doing so from the start, so everyone knew the danger of slipping on the wet floor. During one of the scenes Hylda slipped and fell, but immediately got up and carried on filming, being the trouper that she was: 'the show must go on, etc'. No one realised until later how badly hurt she was, and even the viewers watching the last few minutes of the episode, after the accident had happened, would never have guessed that anything had gone wrong.

She had sustained a broken ankle and there were also torn ligaments, and she had injured her ribs too, which was discovered when she was taken to hospital after the show. She came back to do episode three, which was rewritten for her so that she filmed in a wheelchair. She said later, "When I slipped there were only a few more minutes of filming to do, so I managed to get through it, but I was in dreadful pain. I had to bite my lip to stop myself from screaming. After the show I went for an X-ray. I fought to get back to work, but after I did the third episode I felt much worse, so I had to stop."

She was apparently suffering from shock and the following quote, with the little white lies about the cue cards, shows her determination to convince even herself that it was only this accident that had caused her immediate problem. She was very much aware that her memory was failing, but she was far too scared to admit that it wasn't something new. "I couldn't remember my lines, and for the first time ever I had to have them held up for me. I was a nervous wreck. I knew I couldn't go on." In fact she had to be written out of the fourth episode, the last three were cancelled, and it was announced that in further shows they hoped to introduce Jack Douglas as the new central character running the pub, as Nellie's cousin Stanley, and who was in the series already.

Two months later it was still not certain when she would be able to work again, as she was getting about with the help of a crutch but was still very far from well. She was very down and it had obviously taken a lot out of her, but she still said that she would very much like to do another series, as soon as she felt up to it. Of course she would, because this was all she had, it was her life, her only existence, and the only way she could feel loved and wanted. She seemed unusually full of defeat when she said at the time, "All my old sparkle has gone at the moment, and I've lost a lot of weight. The trouble is I've lost touch with the public since I gave up doing live tours. I'd love to hear from a few people to find out what they think of the show and if they want me to do any more. I'm worried that the troubles I had will show on the screen. I'm a perfectionist you see."

No doubt she hoped that if enough people wrote in, she could persuade the TV bosses to carry on with the series, but it wasn't to be; the next six or seven months were going to be a very hard and difficult time for her.

November 1975 saw her at the Palace Theatre, Manchester, in Gordon Pleasant's *The Lancashire Laugh In*, with Old Mother Riley, Jackie Carlton and Meg Johnson, but unfortunately the show lost money for Hylda was no longer the big draw she had been. She also still had her leg bandaged, and in fact would look down in performance and say, "Look, one brown leg, one white leg," which rather baffled the audience because many of them didn't know about the accident. Whatever fears were lurking beneath at this time, she had outwardly lost none of her bravado, for she said to Gordon Pleasant that on stage Cynthia should not be referred to at the curtain call. "I'm a solo act. Cynthia is a prop!"

The show ended with a big number which Gordon had written specially for the production and which featured two brass bands on stage. There was the walk down, then Hylda was announced by the off-stage microphone. Gordon stepped forward to do the 'thank yous', with Hylda muttering, "Don't you mention her," and he said wickedly, "Without two ladies it would not have been possible to do this show tonight (*pause*) Hylda Baker and — my mother." As she swept off the stage, Hylda turned to a member of the cast and said, "What did his mother do in the show?"

One of the members of the cast, Karen Lodge, remembers one very amusing incident when they had to find someone who lived locally to play Cynthia for the show, and having found someone who fitted the height requirements, he was engaged. However, after the show, he wouldn't take the costume off because, for reasons that we can only guess at, he obviously enjoyed wearing it. Apparently it was very funny as Hylda was chasing around after him trying to retrive it!

She always referred to Jackie Carlton, who was apparently a very good comic, as 'that alleged comedian' because she wasn't keen on him. The first-night party had been held in The Rembrandt, but it was a lesser place that was to be the venue for the last-night party, and Hylda's first comment was, "Will there be food?" She arrived late, the cabaret was going on, and Jackie went out to the lobby where the sandwiches were. He put some on a plate, unseen he curled the edges with his fingers, brought them over to Hylda and put them on a stool in front of her. She said, "What's that?" to which he replied, "A running buffet," and then he kicked the stool and the food to the other side of the room. She never said a word, just turned and spoke to someone else.

After this she starred in *Mother Goose* at the King's Theatre, Southsea, which was directed by Mimi Law, who obviously had some problems with Hylda because she said afterwards, "I directed Hylda and it almost gave me a breakdown, although I had great admiration for her as a performer."

The public still loved her, though, and on an LBC radio chat show late one Sunday night, Monty Modlyn invited listeners to ring up and ask her questions. One lady had the nerve to suggest a rather bizarre bit of comedy business with an apron, and told Hylda, somewhat disgruntled, that she had written once to her agent with this suggestion but had received no reply. Hylda politely said, "Pity I didn't know!" but one could sense her real thoughts.

There was also a call from a lady who claimed to be very shy, but who immediately launched into the fact that her sister-in-law was the double of Hylda and was always impersonating her. Hylda said, "Oh that's nice. I hope she doesn't use all my material though." The woman didn't listen and carried on with, "If she went out more, they'd take her for you," but Hylda's reply was wonderful: 'Oh really, well tell her not to overdo it!" It fell on deaf ears.

Monty also asked her if she felt she had a tough job being a comedienne, and her reply sums it all up: "What more joy is there in life than making people laugh. Tough job? I don't look upon it as being tough. It's my life, I like it. If they're enjoying it then we're both having a good time aren't we?"

In February 1976 she was interviewed for an article in *Woman's Realm* and seems to be getting back on form again, but of course she was in her favourite restaurant in Soho; she was known there and she also had someone to talk to. The article said:

'As she talks, her accent becomes French to middle-European, and her tiny jewelled hands twirl and loop and curl in gestures that could never be native to Farnworth, Lancashire, where she was born an unspecified number of years ago. "It's the atmosphere here, The minute I get into a foreign set-up like this, it goes to my head." Grasping the menu, she reads it as if she's never seen it before. It's all part of the enjoyable ritual. When she orders steak tartare the waiter congratulates her on her choice, and she beams as if she's just made a new discovery. The raw minced steak will do wonders for her stamina, she says, and since she's been so virtuous about the main course, well, we might look at the sweet trolley later.

'Queening it at her favourite table, nobody would guess at her four feet ten inches. But that's what she is. That, added to a quite remarkable vulnerability for someone so successful, made her more sensitive to personal and professional set-backs over the years. It has brought her out with fists flying from time to time, and has given her the reputation of a fighter.

She suddenly swoops to clear up any illusions about her wealth, "I'm not that well off you know. I couldn't be could I? Not with the kind of income tax I have to pay." The shrewd eyes spit fire, and every auburn curl takes on a new fire. As if to compensate for her harsh treatment at the hands of Inland Revenue, she summons the sweet trolley. Her choice is something extremely succulent and infinitely soothing. The waiter says there is no hurry and confides that he suffers from insomnia since becoming a widower. All Hylda's warmth rises to the surface. She's a great believer in love. Star or no star, the future holds as many doubts and fears for Hylda as for anyone else approaching a certain stage of life.

"I'm beginning to worry about providing for my old age," she says grimly. "Not to mention the after life about which I'm beginning to puzzle more and more." She glares into the middle distance as if daring it to come out and get her. She certainly knows all about loneliness. Even showbusiness, she says with an almost moist eye, isn't the close, matey community it used to be. Coffee is served with quiet dignity by the insomniac waiter. It's getting late, but Hylda is unwilling to sacrifice one minute of the slow-sipping ceremony. She's worked hard for it, and by gum she's going to enjoy it.'

Two months later, in April, she talked of the period she had just been through since the accident and how it had affected her:

"I was in constant pain, but the worst thing of all was my mental attitude. I had this terrible fear I'd be a cripple for life. I was incredibly depressed and all my old sparkle had gone. I couldn't concentrate you see. If I talked to someone it was like I'd hear their voice and then it would fade away. I longed to be alone, and sometimes I stayed in bed all day. What was there to get up for? I was lonely, damned lonely. You realise who your friends are and how few real ones you have when something like this happens. Truly I nearly went under. Thank God I didn't. One day I said to myself, 'C'mon Hylda stop feeling so bloody sorry for yourself,' and I started having these very hot Epsom Salts baths — marvellous for aches and pains — and made myself start working again.

"Today my ankle still hurts, but I can manage. I did *Mother Goose* over Christmas, and appeared recently in *The Good Old Days*. Now I've got a three-month tour in a comedy thriller which is the biggest thing since my accident. I start rehearsals tomorrow, and after the tour, please God, I'll be back in another telly series. Retire? You must be joking. I know I'm not exactly 21, but I'm not old. I don't feel it anyway. My biggest battle was with myself. It was a case of would the accident win — or would I. You have to work out your problems and settle them in your own way, and that doesn't only go for broken bones either. It goes for everything."

The Good Old Days performance turned out to be a difficult one for her, but just before it she was filled with her usual optimism. "It made me famous back in 1954, I'm hoping it will change my luck again." She couldn't even remember the most important date that had ever happened to her, for that special night was actually in 1955.

Matthew Kelly was working with her around this time. He was very fond of her, admired her enormously and saw through the façade of bravado. Before *The Good Old Days* performance, she was a bag of nerves, dripping with sweat, and during her act constantly drying and fluffing. In fact she once said the correct words 'elocution' lessons instead of 'execution' — and this was the act she'd been doing for 30 years! Nonetheless the audience as always loved her. Matthew got on with her very well and once when she was ill, he looked after her and was saddened when she turned to him one day and said, "I wonder if this is my Waterloo." This is even more poignant when we know that one of her nicknames was 'The Little Napoleon'.

The tour she mentioned in the *Woman's Realm* interview, was Jack Popplewell's comedy thriller, *Busy Body* and also starred Valentine Dyall ('The Man In Black'). But it was disastrous and she should never have done it because her memory was now so bad that she really seemed to be going downhill at a rate of knots. She was playing a part which has an incredible amount of lines to remember, a know-all cleaning lady who tells everyone everything. Hylda just couldn't learn it and as Valentine was playing a police inspector, he carried his notebook with him all the time on stage, with her lines written down inside it and he prompted her throughout the performance.

Once she just completely forgot everything, and ironically just as she had done in 1967 in *A Taste Of Honey*, she stepped forward and went into her act. There were four actors behind her not knowing what on earth to do, in a sitting room set, and when she was asked afterwards what she was doing she said, "Oh, I had to get it going love."

This tour was a disaster for her and had been marred on occasion by theatregoers actually demanding their money back. When asked if the laughing had stopped and her long TV career was finally over, she said defiantly, "No. I'm not a tired old woman. I still have promise." But the truth had to be faced and the future did not look too rosy. She had just spent six weeks in a Blackpool convalescent home after suffering a very bad nervous breakdown, and was about to go to a health farm to complete the treatment of rest which had been ordered by the doctors.

Maurice Leonard, the well-known producer, also met Hylda in the mid-1970s as Thames TV were doing Ivy Benson's *This Is Your Life* and Hylda was one of the guests. Maurice was asked to collect her as they knew she'd never get there on time, so up to her flat he rolled in a chauffeur-driven Daimler, to find her totally unprepared. Eventually, after much opening of wardrobes full to the brim with mink coats, and with shoes falling out everywhere, she decided on a very flashy pastel chiffon evening dress, Shirley Bassey style, donned one of the mink coats and off they went. She kept saying, "Go through my lines with me. What do I say?" They went through it at least 20 times and she only had a paragraph to do. Once more she was a bag of nerves.

The moment came, Eamonn Andrews announced her, she came on and her face went blank. She launched into, "Do you like this coat? Shot it myself you know. Look at the time..I must get a little hand put on this watch. I think I can say about Ivy Benson ...I'm filling up with emulsion, and I say that without fear of contraception." She had forgotten what she was supposed to be saying — but they all stood and cheered!

Maurice went to work for her because she needed a secretary, and he said she was so lonely and frightened. Her office was a mess and when he first went in he couldn't see the desk. There were dozens of cheques lying around that she'd forgotten to pay in, but eventually he sorted it out for her. She would insist on taking him to the Post Office Tower for a meal, and walking home would start to sing, getting him to join in: "Follow me ...Because God Made Thee Mine, etc." Then she'd turn to him and say, "Not like that. You've to sing it like you mean it!" And off they went back to her flat. She'd sit at the piano and sing her favourite songs like *A Good Man Is Hard To Find*, but once she'd got you there it was very hard to get away.

One evening she managed to persuade Maurice to stay a bit longer by insisting that he borrowed her car to get home, but five minutes after he left the flat the police flagged him down and arrested him, saying the car had been reported stolen. He rang her from the police station. Hylda was half asleep and had no recollection of lending him the car, but the police soon realised the mistake and Maurice was released. Her memory had got so bad that only minutes after he left, she had completely forgotten what she'd said.

She often took lodgers into her flat — there was a self-contained unit — and one day she asked Maurice to ask the lodger for his rent as he hadn't paid. The lodger insisted that he'd given her £15 the night before, saying, "I gave you a tenner and a fiver and you put it in your handbag." "Did I?" she said, and when she went to look they were there; she'd forgotten he'd given them to her.

Maurice adored her, though, and said of her, "She was so good she'd never ruin a scene, even if it was to her disadvantage. Hylda struggling to get on a bar stool is worth ten minutes of anybody's time! She had the most beautiful hands, they used to whizz up and down that keyboard doing the heartbreak songs, for that was what she wanted to do. She could change the mood in an instant and you'd be with her all the way. One minute you'd be falling about and she'd switch to the sentimental. A brilliant woman. With all her incredible success it was not a happy life. I don't think she had many truly happy moments ever. She never knew a life when she didn't have to fend off people, and be exploited, there was no one to turn to, no one to say, 'What shall we do now love?' She was on her guard throughout her whole career. This was her life, a pugnacious life, but she had a pugnacious spirit, which was why she survived."

In 1976 the television companies had no plans for her. LWT and Granada were not doing any more *Nellie* series and ATV did not want her on *Celebrity Squares*, but all she would say to this was, "I've not done too well in the last few years, but you have to accept what fate has in store. But I can't bear to think of retirement. It's a terrible thought. But there's plenty of life in me yet, don't you worry." She still refused to give in, and whatever happened she was going to go out with a fight.

And try to fight she did, but this time she tried to take on the might of the TV companies. Alas, to take on London Weekend TV was being just a bit too bold. She was advised against it but she was as determined as always. She sued them because she innocently thought that she would get enough money to live on out of it, and perhaps this would be the answer to her problems. LWT counter-sued, naturally with more lawyers and more power than Hylda could afford, but she still engaged a QC and spent a great deal of money.

This is really the main reason why they had decided not to do any more series. The writers had in fact been commissioned to do another 13 episodes, but when she announced she was going to sue them for negligence over her fall the year before, this was out of the question. She was claiming £12,400 damages, issued a writ in the High Court and alleged that the company were negligent by not keeping the floor free of anything which would cause anyone to slip. She claimed that she had lost £10,900 earnings over seven months, out of an average annual income of £18,172. In addition she asked the High Court to award her £360 medical expenses and £1,178 travelling and other costs connected with her medical treatment.

It really was a very big mistake to try to fight the strength of LWT's legal department and their lawyers said that there were no witnesses to the incident. Her argument was that it was being filmed in front of an audience of 300 and appealed to the public in the *Sun* newspaper: "I have got to find some members of that audience." What she had forgotten was that after the accident happened, it was stated in a newspaper that no one would have guessed anything was wrong. After the case first came to light in the press in November 1976, nothing more was heard of it because it never came to court. But Hylda still hoped it could be settled, as the following report in June 1978 shows. She had really well and truly cooked her goose with this one, for they would never employ her now.

'Hylda Baker is all set to make a TV comeback — in a 15-second TV commercial. Once Britain's best-loved comedienne, she hopes her fleeting appearance will jog the memories of producers who have left her out in the cold for so long. Hylda, the tiny 70-year-old, reckons she knows y' know why she hasn't been given any TV work for more than two years. "It is obvious that someone has put the block on me. I know I'm supposed to be too old, too difficult and too accident-prone, but it's a load of rubbish. I have been poorly but I'm fine now. And if being a perfectionist is being difficult to work with then I can be difficult, but there's nothing wrong with trying to get things right."

'Her career took a tumble three years ago when she slipped and broke her leg filming an episode of her series. She sued London Weekend, and the case still hasn't been settled. That commercial? Hylda reckons, "Well, it's not like topping the bill at the London Palladium but it's good money and it will mean getting my face on TV again."

It is so sad to read that one phrase which implies that her long career was finally over and she was no longer a best-loved comedienne. Also, although she was indirectly blaming the TV company, she couldn't see that, although she would always hang on to the fact that she was a perfectionist, the real reason was because she certainly could no longer sustain a role on stage, and it must have been very frustrating for the others who were on stage with her, particularly if they too were perfectionists! Not only that, but the cabaret bookings had dwindled too.

She was in a terrible state. The paperwork concerning her litigation was constantly arriving in the post and she would say, "Oh my head. My brain hurts!" She didn't know what to do. One particular booking at Lewisham was a disaster and she couldn't really do the job any more. In the end she had to settle for the costs of her QC and other things that LWT agreed to foot, provided she would drop the case entirely. She'd already incurred these expenses, so all she got was her money back.

Her private life was also extraordinary, for she took in a series of lodgers in her huge flat. With the knowledge that we have of her loneliness, it is fairly certain that she did this for that very reason, but often she would come unstuck and there was a court case in January 1977 where Hylda claimed she had been blackmailed. Apparently she had asked one of her lodgers to leave, whereupon, she alleged, he had said he would if she gave him some money. He said he had been unfairly evicted and took out an injunction to let him move back in, but he lost the case. It is very possible that, as with the previous lodger, a misunderstanding had occurred. Her forgetfulness was there all the time, and it would continue to cause her even more distress.

Then suddenly, in August 1978, it was announced that Arthur Mullard and Hylda were to do a record together, a zany send-up of *You're The One That I Want*, the number which was a chartbuster for John Travolta and Olivia Newton-John. It actually did rather well, getting to number 20 in the charts, because of the novelty value, although it is very painful to the ear. They also made a memorable appearance on *Top Of The Pops* with it. Hylda was all dressed up in tight black leather trousers, a crocheted black top, gold peep-toe very high-heeled shoes, and sporting a long curly blonde wig. Arthur tried his best to look trendy, too, with all-black T-shirt and jeans with white braces and shoes. A more unlikely pair of 'trendies' you never did see. Apart from the single, they also released an LP entitled *Band On The Trot*. It said on the cover: 'A must for parties. 16 hilarious tracks including *You're The One That I Want*. There are some frightening renditions of songs such as *The Rivers Of Babylon*, *Save Your Kisses For Me*, *Sweet Kind Of Guy* and *Sha La La La Lee*, all in the name of 'comedy'.

Hylda and Arthur went to the Reading studios to promote the record and there was a huge poster displayed in the foyer which had got Arthur's name in the top-billing slot. He said that she became very hysterical as soon as she saw it saying, "Take it down, take it down. no one gets their name in front of mine." The poster was removed. However, the front sleeve of the record gives Arthur the left-hand slot, their lettering is exactly the same size, and his photograph is higher than hers by at least one inch! On the hit single, however, it is interesting that her name comes before his. The chemistry between them was not good and later on, when they went to the London studios, where all the gold and silver discs were on display around the walls, Hylda looked around at them and said, "Eh, eh, look at that, they've been doing our songs." When he remembered it 15 years later, he would be falling about with laughter, but mainly because he was convinced that she was serious. However, Hylda's vast experience of the world of music would indicate that she was most definitely joking and the laugh was on him for believing it.

When they were sitting around waiting for publicity, recordings etc, she apparently talked non-stop about her father. Indeed, this is all he remembered of their conversations, for she was constantly saying to Arthur, "Oh he was a great man. He knew everything about the theatre. No one could tell him anything. We all listened to him." Arthur said that in his opinion nobody would ever live up to her father, and how she remembered him. Once again he said that he fell about laughing when he asked her how her father had died, because all she said, very abruptly, was "A sandbag fell on him." Without a full explanation it really would seem quite ludicrous, and Arthur would not have hidden his laughter, which would surely have upset Hylda.

On another occasion they were asked to make a promotional film for the record and were taken to a fairground. It was a dreadful day, the rain was pouring down and for one shot they were asked to go on this very tame roundabout, but for some reason Hylda was absolutely terrified of it and refused. "I can't go on it, I can't!" she screamed. Eventually she did end up doing the shot, but was hanging on for dear life, going round and round singing and crying at the same time, with her mascara pouring down her face from the tears and the rain. Later on they were asked to go on the 'caterpillar', but this was too much for her and she stayed in the caravan, still in tears, and they filmed Arthur by himself with a lot of solo shots which they were going to cut around later.

It really is a very surprising incident, for here was the woman who had ridden the Wall Of Death in her youth, driven fast cars all her life, and was well-known for her bravery in the face of most things. Perhaps she had had such bad luck with accidents, lost work and self-respect recently that she was going to take no chances any more — after all, she was 73. (One has to admit that she really gave no indication of her true age in her outfit for the send-up of the Travolta-Newton John song, even though it was far from glamorous.) Or perhaps it was the simple fact that her nerves had taken such a battering over the years that she could stand no more.

When Arthur returned to the caravan she was apparently fuming, pacing up and down, and as soon as he came in she said, "Where do you think you've been. I should have been there. I'm the star not you!" He found this, too, highly amusing, he said, mainly because it was by her own choice that she was in the caravan. Some friend of one of the crew then came to the caravan and asked for Arthur's autograph first, then passed the paper to Hylda, who became very annoyed and said, "I'm not signing that. I want my own piece of paper!" Not long after this, the William Hickey column in the *Daily Express* published an article about their being the oldest Top Ten pop act in history, and Hylda spent a long time in rather a dark mood, as they had printed her age, but she still insisted that they'd got it wrong by at least five years.

Making this record did mean that, as it was a relative success commercially, Hylda was able to get some cabaret bookings and her musical director from October 1978 to the following summer was Mark Cowling. She had been booked to appear at The Amsterdam in Huddersfield, and the Bar-Celona in Leeds, and Mark was asked by an agent if he would do the job as he lived locally. In her cabaret act Hylda would open with a song, *The More You Laugh*, and do her stand-up routine with Cynthia, then *A Little On The Lonely Side*, and she would close with her favourite, which incidentally was a Dorothy Squires number, *I Wish You Love*. As an encore she would mime to the single of *You're The One That I Want*, doing a pretty uncharitable impersonation of Arthur Mullard in the process!

It became increasingly more difficult for the Cynthia to keep a straight face as he never knew what dialogue was going to be thrown at him. The content of the act, presumably due to her fast-failing memory, would vary wildly, and if the audience response was good, she would begin to add lib and go off at a tangent. This meant that invariably she would lose her place, and would close a routine without any warning whatsoever, either with a complete non-sequiteur, or she would suddenly come out with a punchline without ever having done the lead up to it. In Mark's words, "This was somehow almost always as funny, if not funnier, than the original routine and while the audiences generally loved it, it meant that the band and I had to stay on our toes the entire time because she could be expected to go into the next song at the drop of a hat. On a couple of occasions we were doubled up ourselves, which resulted in missed cues and a certain amount of scrambling around on stage."

Because Hylda always chose these very sad or sentimental songs — they were always very downbeat and her final number was so very sad — it is an indication of her true character, for although she would usually try, and succeed, to be amusing when in company, she was really a person who was full of sadness who yearned to be loved but didn't know how to receive it. People will be bound to wonder why she had to carry on performing when she could have given it all up for a quiet life, but the yearning for someone to love is what drove her on. The only world she knew was in front of the footlights, where she could get this love from her audience, but it would never be enough. She had given her whole life to the art of performing, but from now on she couldn't give what was required. She just wasn't able because she was ill, and likewise it couldn't give her what she needed.

She continued to tour, though, to the rather low-key venues. It was all she could get, but the budget was tight and consequently Mark had to find a different bass player and drummer in each of the places that they played, so naturally this meant a great deal of rehearsal every time they got to a new town.

It was a traditional variety tour: Hylda topped the bill, with Keith O'Keefe as compere, Katy Budd as guest star and various other singing, dancing and speciality acts, and they played such places as Southport, Mersea and Blackburn. The musicians had to be rehearsed for absolutely all the material, and although she sang only those three short numbers, her rehearsal alone could take up to an hour, for as we know she was a complete perfectionist when it came to timing her introductions for a song. However, this would very often be made pretty worthless on the night, as she'd ad-lib the end of a routine and therefore not give the cue for the music. Mark's comment on this conjures up many a picture: "Sometimes one could double-guess her, but this can have its own dangers as I'm sure you are aware!"

He was very new to the business at this time, and by golly he had to learn the hard way, and fast, for he was to experience Hylda's ferocity when one day he went to her dressing room and whistled to her to illustrate a tune. He had not known about this superstition before, but was made to stand outside the door as she shouted instructions through it, as to what he had to do to exorcise the 'curse' before she would let him back in. Through all this, however, he says she was always very fair and very helpful to him, and since then he has worked with many people who have a huge amount of respect for Hylda Baker and cite her work as some of the very best done by any English comedienne of any era.

His final quote is rather moving: "I became aware of just how lonely she was when I went, on one occasion, to her flat off Tottenham Court Road. The sitting room was crowded with mementos and photographs, her *This Is Your Life* book taking pride of place on the upright piano. The room was dominated, however, by just one big armchair facing the TV with a little drinks/snacks table hooked over one arm. One got the feeling that in moving away from her roots, she had never really found a new home."

She did get invited out to neighbours for dinner, one in particular being Simon Quinn who had asked her over one evening. It was a short time after the record with Arthur Mullard had been getting a good deal of publicity, and Hylda brought a copy along with her. She asked Simon to play it, and in fact insisted that they play it constantly throughout the evening. Robin Mitchell, another one of the guests that evening, remembers the look of sheer delight on her face, and all the while she was beating time to it with her fists. This really does bear out the theory that at last she was in the public eye again, she was almost like a little child in her excitement about it, and perhaps felt that at last her career was on the up again.

Poor Hylda, she was always deluding herself. Robin also remembers the first time he met her, which was in the Marlborough Arms pub near her flat. She didn't go in there that often but she was always alone, always isolated. He had no idea who she was and didn't know she was famous, but she proceeded to tell him her life story and his quote about her was, "I got the impression that she knew life from the basement up, but it had been a tough trip!"

One particular evening must have also given her ego a boost again, when Simon took her to Jack's in Goodge Street, a small drinking club with strippers too. He took Hylda there because she told him she had never in her life been to a strip club (here was a woman who had toured her own 'girlie' revues!). The girls at Jack's recognised Hylda instantly. They loved her and she revelled in it. They all refused to work that night as it was such an occasion for them, so they had a party instead!

Simon was a very good friend to her at that time, and Hylda thoroughly enjoyed his company. However, he did not realise how bad her memory was because she always seemed very 'together' when she was out, always very smartly turned out too, and it seems that she would only venture forth at the times when she was feeling up to it. She was still endeavouring to keep up the façade of everything being alright and refusing to admit she was ill.

By the summer of 1979 Hylda seemed to be becoming almost resigned to her fate. Perhaps she was getting tired, for she said in an interview, "I think being alone is the worst thing in the world. In my work I'm an extrovert, but outside I'm shy. I'd like to go for a holiday abroad, because of the weather and you can really relax, which you can't do in England. But it's not where you are, it's who you're with."

Hylda had nobody, but that was because she had, at this time, begun to alienate anyone who tried to help her, and she had never been one to have much time for real family affection, apart from the fact that she would have been too proud to admit to them that she had a problem; so she just carried on her life in the only way she could. She tried to keep on working but she was nearly 75 years old, she wasn't mentally capable any more, and although she didn't know it, she had that illness which is now more commonly known as Alzheimer's Disease. There was no stopping it, and now there was only one path down which she could go because she could no longer control, as she had always done before, what was happening around her.

CHAPTER TWELVE

At the End of the Day

AUDIENCES are like medicine to an artist, for they desperately need the energy that is given back from a live performance, and to feel the warmth of the spotlight. In the past this was always what had helped Hylda to rise up and get back on her feet, but not this time. She was becoming very ill and life in her large mansion flat was not getting any easier. She tried to do a few cabaret engagements in 1980, but she often just didn't know what she was saying on stage; she was getting so much worse, and more often than not it would end in disaster. It really all seemed to happen very quickly — only two years earlier she was at least well enough to make a record.

On one final occasion, in 1980, Hylda was booked to appear for two nights at a night club in Manchester. The first performance was a disaster: they announced her, she came on in her fox fur and cocktail dress with all trimmings, but she suddenly stopped dead; once again she couldn't remember her act, the act she had been doing for donkeys years. She battled, on saying whatever came into her head, and eventually when the Cynthia came on he practically had to prompt her under his breath with every line. One of the reasons for this, though, was that once again her confidence had taken a huge knock because the club was supposed to have arranged a great deal of publicity with TV appearances etc, but there had been none, and consequently the audience was somewhat thin. The whole thing was a total disaster and she went back to her hotel that night and burst into tears.

The next day, determined as usual to put the past behind her, she went out shopping and had lunch in Manchester, but when she got back to her hotel later in the day, there was a message from the manager of the club to say that she would not be required that night.

"They don't want me? Over my dead body!" she said, grabbed the contract and, having got herself all dressed up, rushed out of her hotel room and fell from the top to the bottom of the stairs. She had tripped on a protruding stair rod, her leg was gashed and bleeding badly and she had banged her nose as well. She was taken to Manchester Royal Infirmary and, of course, the press got to hear about it and she was inundated with reporters. It turned out to be an 'ill wind' for her because she was able to say to them that due to her injuries she would not be appearing at the club that night, and she was able to 'save face' as it were. Poor Hylda, she just couldn't accept that her career was over. Yet it was all she had left to live for — work was the most important thing for her because she had nothing else. Back to London she went, and all that was left to her now was her lonely life in the flat.

Because she didn't have any close friends, the people around her tried to look after her and keep her company, particularly the head porter George and his wife Doll, who had in fact been Samaritans. They did as much as they could to help and often Hylda would ask them down to her flat and get George to play her piano, which cheered her up considerably. However, her memory was fast failing and once when she had asked them and some other people round for a drink, she was in bed, no doubt having forgotten that they were coming. She told them to go into the sitting room and help themselves, got dressed, came into the room, looked round and said, "What are you all doing standing there drinking my drink!" whereupon she ordered them out.

Another time when she was ill, Doll went to see her, and some other friends also popped in. She looked at them and asked, "What are you doing here?" but she perked up a bit and they sat round trying to cheer her up, which lifted her spirits. However, after a while she would suddenly say, "I've been stuck in bed, and all these people, they're taking over, they've commandeered my flat!" She had completely forgotten why they were there. It was so difficult for anyone to try to help her at that time, and she required a great deal of understanding.

Sometimes George and Doll would go out for a meal with her, purely because they felt sorry for her and wanted to help, and what is so touching is that they always paid their way, not like many others Hylda had experienced in her life. It is a shame to think that this couple were probably more good friends to her than even she realised. Certainly Doll would sit with Hylda and talk to her whenever she needed someone to talk to, but she was rarely grateful. She had experienced too many hangers-on in the past, people who weren't really being friendly for her sake but who just wanted to bask in her reflected glory.

When someone is as ill as Hylda was, they really do need a lot of care and support, but having such a fiery nature meant that she had to have somebody who would put up with a good deal. George and his wife would take her shopping with them and once, when they went to Romford market, Hylda wanted to get some meat, but the butcher's was just about to close. She looked through the window, saw the staff were still there and knocked on the door. They immediately recognised her and opened up again. The meat was rather expensive but she was happy enough, and even said, "Well, in some places they don't charge me at all!"

George and Doll took her with them to various places as they were desperately trying to help her, and once at a market nobody recognised her at all. This really upset her, so much so that she accusingly said they should have made a point of telling the stallholders who she was. They replied that they thought she would have liked to be anonymous, which is a very fair point, but her disappointment went deeper than that, for what she craved was the adulation, which was her way of getting affection. Alas, this adulation was becoming less and less because she had been out of the public eye for so long.

Not having worked since that fateful booking in Manchester, Hylda tried once more not to let the world of showbusiness pass her by. One particular day she contacted her neighbour, Simon Quinn, saying that she had a chance of a booking in Brighton but she wanted to try it out in the East End first, at a pub theatre, and she asked Simon if he would be her Cynthia! He was not in the entertainment profession, but she gave him a few rehearsals and off they went. Little did he know that he was going to save the day for her in the end. As soon as he walked on stage, not being the sort of chap who was used to wearing women's shoes, he caught his high heel on the step, it broke and he went flying! There was hysteria from the audience and they were a great success, so the fact that Hylda probably wouldn't have managed to get through her act once more was never discovered.

It shows how much she had changed because in the old days, if her Cynthia had made such a mistake, no doubt the sparks would have been flashing off the walls. This time she said nothing and on the way home in the car, she even said with excitement how much she was looking forward to the Brighton booking. Of course it never came to fruition. However, that night she appeared to be satisfied because she had tasted the laughter of an audience once more.

Life went on, George and Doll continued to try to help her and keep her company, and on one occasion they went to the Clink restaurant in Barking, where the food was usually wonderful. However, they chose salmon and it didn't have much taste, the manager was consulted and unfortunately made the mistake of failing to recognise Hylda. This upset her so much that they had to leave immediately without eating the meal, and went into a run-of-the-mill fish and chip restaurant nearby. She was recognised instantly in there, so with great inner sighs of relief they sat down at a yellow formica table, ordered fish and chips — and Hylda was in her element. From then on she thoroughly enjoyed herself that evening. All of this is pretty concrete proof, if proof were necessary, that she had to have attention in order to survive, but it was the affection of not just individuals, but the public in their masses that she lacked, for it was the only way of life she understood.

She once rather tactlessly said to George that they were lucky to have her and her company, to which Doll replied that they could reverse their luck if she'd prefer it! Her mind, though, was going fast and she was so ill that if she did behave badly, it wasn't the real her. George was very generous about her behaviour, saying that it seemed as if she was living another character, bossing people before they got the chance to boss her first. He saw that because her mind was going, she'd say anything, and he very kindly said that he couldn't hold that against her, particularly as very often she didn't know what she was doing.

It is interesting that George thought that he never once really got through to the other side of her, and yet she obviously trusted him because she told him all about her father's illness, her fear that she would go the same way; she talked of her childhood, her loneliness, her lost baby, in fact just about all the things that she would only discuss with the people she trusted, of which there were few. Both George and Doll felt very sorry for her and tried hard not to get too close to her because they were aware that this was something she wouldn't tolerate; on the other hand they made every effort to make it possible for her to get close to them if she needed to. They were very proud people, the salt of the earth, who were only there because of very unfortunate circumstances. George had been a professional person with his own business before taking the post. Then, three operations in two years had meant that in the end they lost everything, which is the only reason he took the job of head porter, so obviously they did not take it too kindly if Hylda treated them like servants, which indeed she very often did.

Such was Hylda's determined nature not to give in that she once more tried to start up the Cynthia act, but this time with George's son, John. She was still a performer and she just didn't want, or know how, to let go! She had got a booking for one night at the Floral Pavilion, New Brighton, Merseyside, for Saturday, 24

May 1980. She kept saying to John that they would rehearse, but every time they were going to work on the act she always put it off. She would say, "I'm going to do it in a minute," or, "We'll do it tomorrow."

The fact was that she really knew deep down that she wasn't well enough, and eventually, having not rehearsed at all, it came to the Friday night, the day before she was due to do the show. John went to her flat, wondering how on earth he could persuade her against it, but the matter was taken out of his hands when he found that she was distressed and upset. She had at last realised for herself that it was impossible. For the first time in her life she actually admitted defeat, saying to John, "I won't be able to do it," and asking him to ring the manager of the venue. He says it was very moving as she obviously realised that this was the moment of truth for her. However, the most important aspect of all this is that it wasn't somebody else who made the decision for her. This time she made the final break herself, and although this was the most devastating moment of her whole career, something she had vowed on so very many occasions she would never do, at least she must have felt in that brief moment that she was controlling her own destiny.

Eventually her illness became so acute that she began leaving the gas on when she was out and suchlike, which was a big worry to the other residents of the flats. It was eventually reported to the staff at the head office, who tried to contact someone about her. Her GP paid a visit and decided that it would be best to call in a consultant from the University College Hospital in St Pancras to see her at home. The consultant didn't really know how famous she was, although her name did ring a bell with him, and he recommended that she be admitted. She was described by him as being 'endearingly unco-operative' and he said she was, "A tiny bundle of energy with huge dark eyes, a very determined lady even in hospital, who was very keen to do her routine for the nurses at the drop of a hat." She was in and out of hospital a good deal, and on one occasion she was admitted to casualty, allegedly as a result of some disturbance at home with one of her lodgers. However, they still couldn't keep her in and back home she went.

Then on 29 December 1980, which ironically was her sister Mildred's birthday, Mildred's daughter Ann got a call from Ethel who said that one of the lodgers had called to say that he felt someone should come and see Hylda as he was most concerned about things that were going on. Ann went down and discovered that Hylda had gone down to about four stone in weight, and her eyes were nothing but dark circles. Social Services were contacted and regular visits were arranged. Then finally a place was found for her in the hospital and she was admitted. Reg Swinson, the executive administrator at Brinsworth House, the Entertainment Artists' Benevolent Home in Twickenham, was then contacted and he went to see Hylda in the hospital. After several visits he realised that she wasn't well enough to go home and look after herself, so he persuaded her to go to Brinsworth House, sort of 'on probation' to see if she would like it, but it was always made clear to her that she was only at the home to see if it suited her, and so at first she kept her flat on.

Hylda arrived at Brinsworth on 6 June 1981, and true to his promise, Reg helped her enormously, listening to all her problems, and she responded to him accordingly. Eventually, because it was obvious that she needed to be looked after, he managed to persuade her that Brinsworth would be safer for her as a permanent home, and she was finally persuaded to give up her flat. She trusted him, which is so wonderful to hear; after the years of never being able to allow herself this luxury, she poured out her worries, and they got on very well. The key he had found, which had unlocked all her defences, was that she desperately wanted affection and she certainly got it here.

The need for a home for retired members of the entertainment profession was initiated by Joe Elvin, who founded the fund in 1911. A committee was set up and they searched for a suitable establishment, and came across Brinsworth but didn't have enough money to buy it outright. The secretary of The Water Rats called upon members of the profession to contribute 50 shillings each, and in this way they raised £1,500 as 600 people contributed. As you go into the hall today, there is an oak tablet upon which are recorded those 600 names forming the 'Noble Order of Brinsworth House'. This house has been such a haven for the profession over the years, and in Hylda's case, very much so because she settled in very well, a prime example of this being the day of Prince Charles and Lady Diana's wedding, only a few weeks after Hylda had arrived.

There was a big party in the lounge, which had been cleared specially for the occasion, and afterwards Reg made a speech thanking everyone for helping and making it such a happy and momentous day. Hylda immediately took the stage and said, "We should all be thanking you. It's been a lovely day and this is such a lovely place!"

Brinsworth really is a remarkable place. It is alive and vibrant, and the residents take every day as it comes. They're on stage when they go out, they have the companionship and the fraternity of other pros, they are free to come and go as they please and they love it because it is their home. It is marvellous that there is somewhere like this giving care when it is needed, for pros are a race apart, they need to be with 'their own kind', and in Hylda's case this was vital.

One particular friend she always used to sit with was Frank Cowley, who had a cross-patter act with his brother and they were known as Morris and Cowley. He and Hylda would sit on a two-seater sofa and reminisce all day. The residents often used to go to the local pub, the Cherry Tree, but often the Brinsworth staff would worry when Hylda went out because, being so famous, she would get a great deal of attention from well-wishers who would latch on. Consequently they decided that it would be wise to look after her cheque book for her, and because Hylda had learned to trust Reg she was perfectly happy about this. He became her 'bank' and often she would knock on the door at 6pm saying, "Is the bank open?" and on many occasions would say, "This is the best bank I've ever belonged to!" She was perfectly happy for someone else to be in charge, which had never been the case throughout her life, but one gets the feeling that it was a relief to her for someone else to 'take the reins'.

Needless to say, she did still have an enormous amount of pride, so much so that when friends would visit her she wouldn't admit that she was there to stay, and would say, "I'm only here while my flat's being decorated you know," or "I only popped in here to see somebody." At times she could also be very demanding, but she did appear to have undergone something of a character change because when one particular theatre manager with whom Hylda had crossed swords in the past, asked them how she was settling in, he was amazed to hear that she was happy and contented. Apparently he had always lived in fear of her when she worked for him, and could only ever last about ten seconds in her company. It is so clear that all she needed was to be cared for with love, but of course those who worked with her rarely saw this side of her because her defences were always up.

At that time Brinsworth did not have any facilities for nursing, although they do now, so if there was any need of that kind the guests had to be treated elsewhere. The local hospital, Horton, which was a phsyciatric/geriatric establishment in Epsom, was called upon to assess any residents who were having problems, and they would go there for a brief visit before returning to Brinsworth with the reports. Because Hylda was obviously having difficulty, she went there for a short time at the end of 1982, but just before she was due to leave, the press got to hear of it and it was headline news:

'Hospital anguish for tragic star Hylda.'

'She Knows You Know star in mental hospital.'

'Secret illness of TV's Hylda Baker.'

'Sadness behind the laughter.'

'Whatever happened to? . . .'

'Hylda, a little on the lonely side.'

They reported at length that she was in a mental hospital and would never work again, and dwelt much on the 'private agony behind the public smile'. The *Daily Star* said, 'Hylda Baker has sometimes been called a difficult woman. And she certainly had her tantrums. But it was all part of a nervy, insecure 4ft 10ins tall comic genius's battle to show up at her best. And Hylda at her best could leave your ribs hurting, your eyes smarting and your lungs coming up for a gulp of air. Now she's feeling a bit bothered and bewildered in a grim, grey 937-bed psychiatric hospital in Epsom, and she must resign herself to the harsh truth that never again will she step out under the stage lights or face the TV cameras. "My real worry," she confessed in her hospital room recently, "is keeping track of TIME. I don't know what day it is!" Hylda never willingly gave up showbusiness. But in the end, amid accidents and legal fights, showbusiness gave up Hylda. Her life can be summed up by two of her favourite songs, *A Good Man Is Hard To Find* and *A Little On The Lonely Side*.'

The *Sun* newspaper carried the same story and included quotes from two celebrities who knew her well. Singer Dorothy Squires said, "Hylda is a lovely person, but terribly insecure. She had an enormous talent and I think she should have been even more of a major star than she was, but she never realised her own star qualities. If she is a broken-hearted clown, by God she's made an awful lot of people laugh on the way there."

Actor Jack Douglas, who worked with her in *Not On Your Nellie*, said, "She was terribly hard to get to know. She was like an island surrounded by sharks — you could work with her but you'd never get near her. She was brilliant and a delight to work with, but she never got involved socially. Like a lot of comics she took her work seriously perhaps too seriously. It is a tragedy that things should turn out this way for Hylda."

It is to be fervently hoped that she was well enough to read one particular article in the *Daily Mail* of 26 January 1983 because it was so full of praise and very moving too. It was headed, 'Tragedy Of A Comic Genius.'

'Hylda Baker frequently alienated co-stars and drove supporting acts to venom and drink. She was prickly, obsessional, touchy, paranoiac, and a comic genius. Happiness eluded her, lovers deserted her, employees cheated her. But first house on a wet Monday night on the bare stage of a crumbling theatre, she could make us believe we were back in the great days of variety at its finest. Today, when she lies sick in hospital and we are told she will never fully recover, the time has surely come for a stranger to say 'thank you'. She could dominate a theatre without props, without a mike, without glamour or a song.

'She stumped in front of us with her stocky body, frizzy hair, beady little eyes and raucous voice that could drown an orchestra. I can see her now tossing that moth-eaten fur boa around her neck with all the courage, pathos and grandeur of every insecure one of us who ever tried to keep up front. On stage she was 'common as muck' as we used to say, but determined to appear refined. In her private world she always yearned for children and a husband, but she couldn't have lived her life any other way. Her ego, her talent and her need were so great, fulfilment could only come from under the spotlight, euphoria only briefly from the laughter of strangers. She could never have stayed at home to look after a child while an audience was waiting. Hylda's tragedy was that underneath that strutting outward megalomania was terror and a lonely soul who could never believe that she was as great as she undeniably was.'

Although the press were treating her as if she had already died, Hylda returned to the calm atmosphere of Brinsworth. She was aware of the kind of hospital she had been in, and no doubt she was well aware of the irony of the situation, bearing in mind her secret fears and the knowledge of what had happened to her father. It was as if all these hidden fears were coming true. The one thing she had always been terrified of was dying alone, and often in her nightmares she had dreamt that she was being buried alive. At least back at Brinsworth she was surrounded by caring people, and loneliness was no longer such a problem.

Perhaps her awareness of the kind of hospital she had been in, resulted in the change in her after this first visit, because she was rather down, her old sparkle had gone and her memory had become even worse. It was almost as if she had given up her fight altogether. In November 1983 she said to the press, "I'm very well thank you. We're nicely looked after here." Friends who visited her were often shocked at her appearance, for not only had she lost a great deal of weight but her hair was becoming very thin. She was almost unrecognisable, she deteriorated quite rapidly and it became that she just didn't know people when they came to see her.

Leslie Lightfoot, who the reader will remember had been manager of the South Pier theatre at Blackpool when Hylda first shot to fame in 1956, was asked along with his wife, Eva May Wong, to perform their act at Brinsworth in a special show for the residents. While his wife was making up, Leslie went around chatting to several of the pros who were living there, when down a passageway came Hylda. He instantly recognised her and said, "Hello, Hylda," whereupon she looked at him blankly and said, "I've got a pretty dress and I'm going to a party." He tried again. "Hylda, it's me, Leslie, don't you know me?" to which she replied, "Isn't it a pretty dress?" and just carried on down the corridor. This was such a shock for Leslie, who went back and told his wife, who had worked with Hylda many times and was very fond of her. Eva immediately went to look for her, and after a while she came back crying her eyes out saying, "Poor Hylda, how very sad." She had had the same response.

Leslie and Eva weren't the only people who experienced this, for the comment about the pretty dress was something she would often say to visitors. Rex Jameson (Mrs Shufflewick), had a similar experience when he went to see her, and was very saddened by the fact that she just said, "Look at this pretty dress, isn't it lovely?" when in fact it was just a rather tired looking housecoat.

The saddest thing of all, though, is that very many people who had known her didn't visit her there, the reason being that others had said to them, "Oh she won't know you. It's no use going, and anyway she doesn't want people to know she's there." They didn't go, and the result of this is that now they all sadly regret it, and in many interviews have said this vehemently. One very moving comment came from Tom Hardy, who had ended his association with her over that argument about the contract in 1972. He said, "I wanted to visit her, but a director friend of mine said he'd been and she didn't recognise him or seem to know what was happening. 'It'll only upset you Tom,' he said, 'don't go.' I didn't. I wish I had. One good thought though, is that Hylda was so scared of dying, that hopefully with her mind wandering she didn't know anything about it — I sincerely hope so, but how I wish we hadn't parted in such a manner."

It is pretty certain that the lack of visitors was because they accepted that Hylda wouldn't want them to see her there, but who knows? She had such strength of character, and such pride that it is perfectly understandable that people who knew her would react in this way.

But in September 1982, at a presentation for Danny La Rue, the majority of guests ignored her and walked straight past. The treatment she endured that day from members of the profession was very unfortunate!

One amusing incident did, however, happen in her very early days at Brinsworth. One particular person, quite a large gentleman, came to visit and took her out for the evening. On returning to the house, he, of course, was supposed to have been looking after her, but they had obviously had a very good time as he was rather worse for the drink. The tables were turned and when tiny Hylda came in through the door she was having to hold him up, desperately trying to support him. The first time in many a long year that, the star that she was, she had ever 'supported' anyone!

On 4 January 1984, Hylda was once more admitted to the hospital in Epsom, never to return to Brinsworth, for she had become so much worse. It was with great regret that Reg Swinson finally realised that they could no longer provide the medical care that she needed. They just couldn't keep her, for it was this kind of help that was required now. They had done all they could for her, but it was a losing battle. Reg said of her, "Hylda as an artiste and a person was unique. It was a wonderful experience to know her and a privilege to have helped her." In fact it really is marvellous, particularly today, as they do now have the facility to nurse people, that a place like Brinsworth exists to give the care to pros when they are in need, not just financially, but in every way.

The last chapter in Hylda's life was spent in this huge hospital, but it must be said that, although funding was a problem, they gave her the best that they could, and in fact, because she was very often so unaware of what was happening around her, she wasn't unhappy, or certainly didn't appear so. She became the 'Queen' of the ward, and indeed one of the nurses, Brenda Barber, remembers her with great affection and even used to play tapes of *Nearest And Dearest* to try to encourage her to remember, and sometimes Hylda would say vaguely, "That's me isn't it?" She was really suffering greatly from this awful disease, which of course was relatively unknown in those days, and was just called it senile dementia. At this point it is quite interesting to note research has now shown that some people who suffer from Alzheimer's have a tendency to be fascinated with spoonerisms, and words being twisted around, so perhaps this seed was always there in Hylda's brain, so intrigued was she with the malapropisms.

There were occasions when she could be very sharp while she was in the hospital, and one day Brenda happened to ask Hylda what had happened to her partner Cynthia. Very cuttingly Hylda replied, "He wasn't my partner, he was my ASSISTANT!" She would constantly talk about being a star, and was very often heard discussing her problems with Jimmy Jewel, which proves she did have quite lucid moments. She struck up a friendship — and this could only happen to Hylda — with a lady called Moira who had been a trapeze artist and also had an act with chimpanzees. Moira was always singing, going through any song that came into her head, even in the bath, but Hylda would only hum along with her. She would trot around the ward, very much the Hylda everyone remembers, her handbag was always with her, always in place. No matter how she was dressed, the bag was always over the arm, she was always on the defensive and anyone who tried to touch her belongings got the rough edge of the tongue. This, of course, was quite amusing to the nursing staff because she was so very tiny, but with all that bravado, confronting a situation head on. They respected her for it, they felt she had earned it.

Brenda Barber said of her, "Although she was a manic depressive, she was really, I think, a star until she died because she was very good at putting you in your place. She would say, 'Do this, do that,' and what was she, four foot nothing? She'd really tell you off. I used to call her 'bossy boots'. You had to treat her like a lady — she was a lady. She was a notch above the rest, and she made that quite clear. She commanded respect."

One observation, though, was that Hylda loved to talk about all her friends in showbusiness, all the famous people she knew, and would often produce her diary, which was always in her bag, with many very well-known names in it. She loved to talk about Dorothy Squires, Bernard Delfont and Val Parnell, but according to the staff not one theatrical person ever came to visit her. Brenda said, "It used to go through my mind, 'why has nobody picked up the 'phone?' because she was obviously friendly with a lot of people. But we never saw one person."

In defence of these friends, it is, of course, exactly what had happened in Brinsworth, and how would she have felt if they'd seen her in this place? They weren't to know that she was so unaware of what was going on that it would have mattered little. It is also more than probable that Hylda just liked to name drop; maybe she didn't really kept in touch with any of these people after all, and they hadn't heard from her for years?

It was apparently very difficult to tell how much Hylda was aware of her surroundings because her eyes always had a sort of faraway look in them, as if they weren't really focused on anything in particular. However, although there were so many things she couldn't recall, she did talk of her fears, particularly mentioning her father being in a mental institution, and one other thing she was always consistent about was that she had been mugged, hit on the head, and it was a story that she rigidly stuck to, it never varied.

She was in this hospital for two and a half years, and had visits from her family, in particular her niece Ann, and despite various attempts, she refused to go back north, because there were too many painful memories for her up there. One day when her sister Brenda visited her, she walked in and Hylda said, "Hello." Brenda asked how she was and she replied, "I feel quite well." After a little while she turned to Brenda and said, "Excuse me asking, but who are you?" It really was most upsetting for anyone, but particularly those who knew her as she had been before, an alert, fast-talking, witty, and intelligent woman.

Her niece Ann visited her every holiday and found a great change in her aunt who had always been frightened of family affection, so much so that Ann remembers when she was little that if she inadvertently started to sing one of Hylda's songs, she would be admonished in no uncertain terms with, "What are you singing for? Do you think you're a prima donna?" However, this time Ann would sit by her bed and sing to her and the reply would be, "Fancy you knowing those, fancy you singing my songs," and she would put her arms around her, becoming loving and caring. In Ann's words, "She couldn't show love all her life but she did so at the end. It was a privilege to share that time with her."

How comforting it is to hear that Hylda's character apparently changed in this way, almost as if this was the real Hylda and not the aggressive, dogmatic little fighter that she had manufactured herself to be. As was mentioned in a previous chapter, a favourite quote of hers was, "Hylda Baker is my own creation, and I like living with her even if I am alone!" But all the fight had gone out of her, she was just a very tired, very lonely old lady, and at last she had to give in, right at the end she was a different person; she hadn't got the energy or the inclination to keep up the façade any longer.

Eventually, towards the end of April 1986, Hylda just slipped into unconsciousness and stayed that way for two weeks. They didn't expect her to get through, so finally they sent for Ann. She cuddled her aunt and held her hand, saying, "Hang on darling." Then, while at the bedside, Ann began to write, 'I'm here somewhere towards the end of a life. A life that has had more than its fair share of happiness, perhaps, no, definitely unfulfilled. She has given so much happiness to so many people who didn't know her and yet she didn't know how to reach those who cared.' Ann held her hand and felt the life go out of her.

Ann was most concerned that Hylda would have somebody at her bedside, for she remembered very clearly the night Hylda's mother died. She was upstairs in the house that Hylda had bought for her back in Plodder Lane. She was very ill and near death, but Mildred had to go to work, so Ann said she would stay in the house. Deep down she was desperately hoping that somebody would say, "No, you can't stay, it would be wrong." But they didn't, and later on Syd came to the house and they were in the sitting room when she felt a shiver go through her. She asked him to go up and have a look, and he found that Margaret had just died. Apparently when they contacted Hylda, she was furious that her mother had been on her own. She was absolutely frantic that although there were people in the house, she didn't have somebody holding her hand.

Hylda did not die alone, Ann made sure of that, for she knew it was her one great fear. Nor did she go out fighting as many would have expected; she died gently and peacefully, going out like a lamb. The lights dimmed and her final curtain rang down on Thursday, 1 May 1986, between 9.30pm and 10pm. She officially died of bronchial pneumonia, which had been something which had plagued her all her life.

These are the words of Brenda, the nurse who laid her out: "She died beautifully, absolutely no problem. She was very peaceful looking. I put a corsage I'd made with some flowers on her nightie, up around the neck. She didn't know she was slipping away. I can see her now. I was fond of her, oh goodness me yes, everyone was. You get some old people who give up don't you, but she battled on, she was a battler. She had originally slipped into unconsciousness because she was very ill. She coughed a lot towards the end, but it wasn't a bad death, it was a good death really, it was peaceful. I was pleased I was there, it was a privilege really. Yes, we loved her, we all loved her. She had the best life we could give her, but in other circumstances she shouldn't have been here really because she was a star. You've got the shrug of the shoulders and the handbag always in position. Oh yes, she knew how to carry herself!"

She was cremated in Twickenham, and Roy Hudd says of that day: "As far as I can remember, there were only about seven of us at her funeral, which was so sad considering the great star she had been." The final journey was to be for her ashes to be taken back to Bolton to be sprinkled on her parents' grave. It is here that one final comedy incident occurred which would certainly have amused her, and as many who knew her would say, such was her life that it could only happen to Hylda! A family friend happened to be going to London, so he agreed to collect her ashes, and having done so he was on his way back to Euston station on the Underground, when a young boy sitting next to him looked at the package and asked what it was. "A dead body, Hylda Baker's," said the young man. The boy freaked out, which must have raised a few eyebrows in the normally uncommunicative tube carriage. It wasn't over yet, however, as the friend was running up the escalator at Euston, and being a bit late for his train, he had all his luggage with him, and the plastic bag containing the box of ashes caught on something and bounced all the way to the bottom, whereupon he rushed down the other stairs and retrieved it, luckily still in one piece! Had the ashes been scattered here, would British Rail have put up a plaque in her memory at the top of the escalator at Euston? It really is very amusing to think that this was Hylda's final walk-down staircase, after all the famous London theatres she had played, the Palladium and the Prince Of Wales to name but two.

It has been said that the very greatest and final challenge for any comedian is to be able to make people laugh at death, and could it be that Hylda was determined that she would do this even from beyond the grave? Often the very language that is used by people in the entertainment profession when they have a success, is riddled with references of violence and death: "We knocked them in the aisles," "I knocked them dead tonight," "I slaughtered them," etc, but it is all said in the glory of comedy and no blood has been spilt.

Sadly, there was very little press coverage on the announcement of Hylda's death, she really had been forgotten. *The People* carried just one small paragraph, the *Daily Mirror* a small article headed, 'Hylda the sad star,' 'the *Daily Telegraph*, too, had just a token article without even a photograph. A small article with, 'The tiny star is dead,' was the contribution in the *Daily Mail*, but the saddest of all was one tabloid that only saw fit to print the following, headed 'Hylda Dies':

'Comedienne Hylda Baker, who coined the catchphrase "She Knows You Know!" has died in a Surrey hospital, aged 78. Born at Farnworth, near Bolton, she was a stage performer by the age of ten.' Under this was the weather forecast which took up the same amount of space!

But for all that, she had the last laugh where her age was concerned because not one report got it right: some said 77, some 76, another said 79. She was in fact 81.

Hylda died on May Day, but it is a symbol of life not death, linking the reviving energy of the sky with the living matter of the growing earth beneath. The sun's energy, the growth of plants, means that the power is returned to the sky in a cyclic unending pattern. The eve of May Day is Walpugistnacht, a time when witches and fairies were said to be active, babies could be stolen, anything could happen and thus May eve is reputed to be a time of peculiar danger. On May Day, the May Queen would carry lilies and roses, the golden centre representing those who have awoken to a marvel that there is more to life than most people are able to see; it is a happy day. However, a final irony for Hylda is that it is the celebration of the colour green, and it was reputed that anyone found wearing this colour, for it was the colour of the fairies, risked being stolen away by them for they had such power.

'Never wear green. After green comes black,' was a particular superstition at Maytime, although here again is a most interesting link with Hylda's stage act, in that the original Maypole was not in fact what we sometimes see today on village greens, but it was human. It was represented by an unusually tall man! 'The Fool. Garlanded with greenery'! He was nicknamed Jack In The Green or Green George, and as part of the celebrations he 'died' to symbolise the death of winter, but he was the representative of life, green-faced and foliate-headed, he was a symbol of the land being covered in emerald and jade.

Some documented ritual chants of May Day are:

'You must wake and call me early, call me early mother dear
'Tomorrow'll be the happiest time of all the glad new year.
'Of all the glad new year, mother, the maddest merriest day,
'For I'm to be Queen of the May mother,
'I'm to be Queen of the May'

'Unite, unite let us all unite, for summer is a-come unto day.
'And whither we are going we will all unite
'In the merry morning of May.'

'March will search, April will try, May will tell if you live or die.'

The one thing any artist or comedian dreads is that they might be 'found out' by the audience, and that they might glimpse a crack in their armour. This, no doubt, was the cause of Hylda's extreme nerves which never once left her, but she had the indefinable quality, that real star quality, which made an audience laugh as soon as she appeared on stage, and from then on she had them eating out of the palm of her hand. She had an energy deep in her soul. If you're low, you don't show it, you smile through your tears — and she certainly did so with her public face. She lived in another world for most of her life, but as John Cleese said in John Fisher's *Heroes Of Comedy* television documentary on The Goons, "The greatest comedy writers create a world of their own." It was the only way she knew, but when her mental faculties were deteriorating, and then finally had gone, it was like no other disease. She just couldn't write her material or perform it because she could not remember anything, and this was to be much more distressing and debilitating for her because the memory is everything to a performer, it's their livelihood, their all.

Hylda Baker led a rich and full life. She experienced more than most, and achieved much that many would be proud of. Many people still imitate her, and her sayings are in constant use today, but if you ask them where they heard them, they don't know. Although she was rarely satisfied, seldom truly loved, much maligned and often ridiculed, there is no doubt whatsoever that her contribution to the world of comedy was great. She left behind a legacy which, hopefully, now will never be forgotten, and it is to be certain that although her life ended in sadness, the dream of stardom which she nurtured from childhood was something she certainly achieved. But the excitement it generated for her, was not in the finding, for it rarely is, but in that long, hard journey from Farnworth to fame!

AFTERWORD

The Grand Finale Cinderella Style

HERE I sit in the No.1 dressing room at Blackpool's Grand Theatre, Hylda's dressing room, and the theatre manager has just been in to see me. The reason? Last night was the first night of a three-night booking at Hylda's old stamping ground, the play was an enormous success, the audience laughed so much that we over-ran by ten minutes, and there was a standing ovation at the finale.

This engagement was one that I had fought to get for three long years, but it had finally happened, and now they were asking me if I would come back, regretting that they hadn't booked it for the week because the box office was getting calls from the public asking to reserve seats for the nights we weren't there! People who saw the show on the first night were booking to see it again, and the box office sent me a note to say that many people had been ringing up to leave messages of congratulation for me.

In an earlier chapter it was mentioned that TV had waved a magic wand for Hylda; could it be that this happy day for me is a result of my own fairy godmother waving hers? I'd very much like to think so, and there have been so many unexplained happenings over the years that makes me think there must be some greater force at work!

I also firmly believe that once you begin to delve into the private thoughts and feelings of a person, whether you are a believer in the supernatural or not, something is bound to happen. An associate once said of Hylda, "She had a great fierceness. The fierceness of this little woman." We can't see electricity, but it is a power, and my notion is that when you are dealing with a particularly strong and powerful personality such as Hylda, who must have created a sort of electricity around herself, then that unseen current can perhaps manifest itself, and 'latch on' to anything it should choose.

So many of the people who both worked with her, or became as close to her as she would allow, have said they hoped that this book will set the record straight as it were, with regard not only to her reputation of aggression, but also what really lurked beneath that tough exterior. As I have been at pains throughout to prove the reasons for this, and equally have shown many examples of her vulnerability and generosity, perhaps it is not unexpected that her energy source could become centred on my efforts in order to consolidate my findings? Suffice it to say that I have experienced too many so-called coincidences, with the result that I cannot ignore the fact that there might just be something else at work. The following catalogue of incidents might just prove that there is more to this than meets the eye, and not only that but perhaps we can pick up on vibrations too — and little Hylda certainly caused quite a few of these to fly around the atmosphere.

The night that I first spoke about my plans for writing the play was very dramatic to say the least. I went to dinner with John and Carol Gleeson (John being the writer I mentioned in the first chapter), and just as it was getting dark we began to talk about Hylda. I was full of enthusiasm, but didn't yet know how to go about getting it started. All the guests became caught up in the fact that here was something that could be very special. We were all talking at once, each one remembering the thing about her that had impressed them most, when quite suddenly there was an enormous flash of lightning followed by the loudest clap of thunder I've ever heard. It was right overhead and shook the house. That storm raged for at least two hours, it was actually pretty frightening, and the rain, too, was deafening as it was being thrown out of the sky with such force. In fact for some reason, Emily, the dog, decided to try going out of the back door, was only out for a couple of seconds, and shot back in again, her paws and legs were completely dry, there was just a great stripe of water down her back, and it hadn't even touched her sides, such was the force of that rain. I have never experienced a storm like it before or since, and we still talk about it today when we meet.

I mentioned earlier that when I first began the research all those years ago,

1968: With Alan Breeze at rehearsals for *Mr and Mrs*.

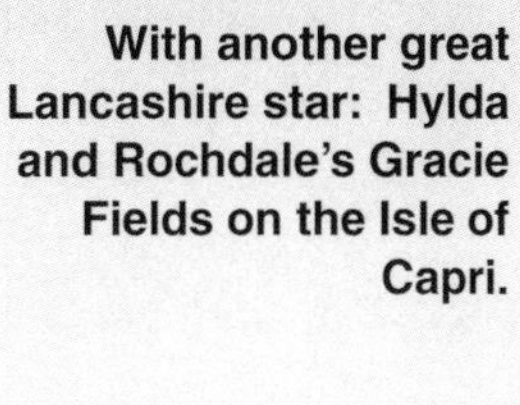

With another great Lancashire star: Hylda and Rochdale's Gracie Fields on the Isle of Capri.

"Who's been dallying with his afflictions?" The stars of *Nearest And Dearest*. Hylda with Jimmy Jewell, Edward Malin and Madge Hindle.

Too close for comfort. With Jimmy Jewell in *Nearest And Dearest*. "A laugh is worth a million tears."

"What are you trying to insert? Do I look like one of the Effluent Society?" Our Eli is after her cash, but Nellie keeps a firm grip.

On the way to church aboard Pledge's Purer Pickles cart, "When I get out I'd better not be lying prostitute on the pavement."

"Pickles, jar, vinegar, lid. Pickles, jar, vinegar, lid."

"Walter, have you been?"

"You could say I'm one of the Effluent Society now!" Another scene from *Not On Your Nellie*.

Hylda is all prepared in a scene from *Not On Your Nellie.*

1976, and her final stage tour: playing the know-all cleaning lady in *Busy Body*. It proved a disaster for Hylda, and it shows in her face.

Another scene from the stage tour of *Busy Body*, playing opposite Valentine Dyall.

1978: Doing a zany send up of *You're The One That I Want* with Arthur Mullard. It reached number 20 in the charts!

One of Hylda's final publicity photographs, taken in the 1970s.

Full circle: 1995 and Jean Fergusson, as Hylda Baker, meets the Queen at a charity event at the Grand Theatre, Blackpool. The Queen asked, "And who are you going to be?" And when told, "Hylda Baker, Your Majesty," she replied, "Mmm, I expect she was very big in Blackpool."

Hylda's agent had given me her niece's telephone number. The day I rang I was told she had moved a year earlier, but the new occupants had made a note of her new number, which they gave me; but had I rung the very next day, they, too, would have moved and would not have given it to the new owners. At this point I must mention that Hylda's family are very private people, and I doubt if they would have contacted me, even if I had made requests on the air and in the press.

When I rang her niece, Ann, explaining the reasons for my call, she was somewhat stunned, and she told me that she had buried her mother, Hylda's sister, only the day before. Since then I have become very friendly with her and she, too, is convinced that something is at work. I rang one day and asked her if there was a particular mannerism that Hylda had, as someone remembered her doing what they called 'thumb twiddling', but Ann said that she never remembered anything like that. The following Sunday afternoon she telephoned me to say that she had been sitting in church that morning, when she suddenly found herself flicking her third finger with her thumb. Immediately she thought, "That's it. That's what Hylda used to do," and found herself go quite 'goosey'.

When I was doing rewrites for the play, I desperately needed to know if Hylda had ever written down anything which showed her innermost feelings, and I also wanted the exact words of the 'diving board' joke as this was most important for one particular section. Ann said there was nothing that she had found regarding the former, but there might be the latter because she had all Hylda's jottings, notes, jokes and books with her material for the act; I was welcome to come and see if I could find anything. I was running a bit late when I got there and had only half an hour before I was due to leave for a charity show at the theatre, so when I was given this huge book containing all Hylda's material it was obvious that it would take much longer than the time available to find anything, if indeed there was anything to find.

At that moment a loose piece of paper fell out on to the floor — it was the diving board joke! Two minutes later, having pored through the gags in the book, the pages went blank, but on turning for some inexplicable reason to look at the end of the book, there were three pages of Hylda's very recognisable handwriting, Ann had never seen it before, but this time Hylda was being deadly serious and had obviously written it in great distress. This was what I had been desperate to find, but had held out little hope. Visibly shaken, and near to tears, Ann read out the following:

"All this is with no one to guide you. To me, as I have experienced, everyone needs someone who understands. People say of me, 'Oh you, you're afraid of nothing.' If they but knew. That agony of mind when I know I am not one hundred per cent. Something comes from somewhere for the time you are facing the public, and indeed, on occasions something takes over completely and you think you can go on like that, and then wham! That's you, you can't think what's happened. You're deserted, alone, irritable, useless. How you have changed. They don't realise you need help. Because apart from tending to your body you need understanding. Now I realise how people say, 'Oh she used to be such a nice woman — or man. She has changed.' But if you were nice for years and years you can't just become a horrible person without reason in a short time. The people not very close to you think you're impossible, but for the first time in your life you don't know what to do. You're ill. So you try to cover up your indecision by being more decisive in the wrong way. Frank Randle when he was ill, Jack Taylor said he'd lost something. Well, I know what that something is, because I lost it too. Because when the body is ill, then the mind is too. But that's just nature's way of easing the pain so you don't realise just how ill you are. Neither are you as capable of reacting to situations as you are when you are well. Your friends, they're not real friends any more, and indeed in some cases they are not. The world is against you because you've changed. You're not the nice person that you were. You are ...'

Sadly we were never to know what she wrote after that as she had ripped out the last page, obviously determined that no one would read further should they ever find this amazing revelation. It had taken just a few minutes to find what I was looking for, and the fascinating thing is that whenever this speech is performed on stage towards the end of the play, there is total silence, you can hear a pin drop.

I must also mention here that the charity show I was to attend that day when the speech was unearthed was at the Blackpool Grand Theatre in celebration of the centenary. I was actually on my way to perform Hylda's act, and the Queen was also to be there. Bearing in mind Peggy Mount's story in a previous chapter, it was ironic to say the least that I did indeed get to shake Her Majesty's hand, but there follows quite an amusing end to this. It was thrilling to have been chosen to be presented, but it was a scorching hot day and we were all in the final stages of heat exhaustion. I had spent an hour getting myself into the costume, wig and make-up, doing my best to recreate Hylda authentically. The false eyelashes were on the point of drooping, and the woollen costume together with the padding to make me look 'rounder' were acting like a sauna bath.

We had been standing on stage in the line-up for what seemed an eternity, then the doors opened into the stalls and the flashbulbs were popping nineteen to the dozen. How on earth do those photographers walk backwards all the time without falling over? I imagine they get quite disoriented when off duty and find they have to walk forwards — or maybe they don't, they just do everything in reverse.

When the Queen appeared it really was quite a moment. There was this tiny lady in powder blue, looking very cool and calm despite the intense heat. It seemed an age before she came up on to the stage, but when she began to walk down the line-up, she stopped when she got to me, looked me up and down and said, "Oh, and who are you going to be?" I said, "Hylda Baker Your Majesty," to which she replied, "Mmm, I expect she was very big in Blackpool." How are the mighty fallen! It wasn't clear whether she remembered her or not, although Hylda as we know had performed before her many times, and met her on at least two occasions. However, at least my hands weren't stuck behind my back.

Another time when visiting Ann, ostensibly to make sure that I'd got all my facts right, I was just leafing through all the material that I had been through before, certainly not expecting to come across anything new, when I suddenly found what appeared to be a synopsis of either a play or short story that Hylda had obviously had an idea for, and once again it was in her handwriting. Personally, I find it even more moving because it appears to be almost prophetic in that it is almost a summary of her own life:

'Maiden lady. Loves children and animals. Loves them to death and plays games with them on her own. She is mental. A kind old lady whose brain has gone. People make fun of her and she thinks it is funny and dances and sings. Nobody knows how mad she is until the disappearance of the child that she has killed with love, and has in her house. The search is on. They are looking for a man. She joins eventually. They come to her house. She says, "Be quiet there is somebody asleep." She is taken. All are against her, except the doctor who realises she is insane and takes her out after they have nearly killed her, to the asylum.'

There is a great deal of music in the show, and generally speaking, being 'oldies' they are all tunes that we hear very rarely nowadays particularly on Radio 2. The reason for mentioning this is that when rehearsing one version of the play, since when I have changed back to the original, I did feel that Hylda's character was becoming somewhat aggressive throughout, and for some inexplicable reason it made me feel very uncomfortable. I always work on instinct, and I had this niggling feeling that something was wrong.

Often in the morning while getting ready to go to the theatre, I would find myself going through a song from the show in my head, when it would suddenly start playing on the radio. Twice could be considered a coincidence, but this happened on four separate occasions. The songs were *Answer Me*, *You Always Hurt The One You Love*, *You're Nobody's Sweetheart Now*, and *Sentimental Journey*. I found myself wondering if the rest of the Radio 2 listeners were hearing them, too, or whether I was just imagining it. One night driving home, I was thinking about adding a little bit of the song *For All We Know We May Never*

Meet Again, to link with poor Eric Baker's death, when it too came over the air on the car radio, but the really weird incident was yet to come.

The song *I Dreamt I Dwelt In Marble Halls* is reputed to bring the worst bad luck for any show, and the superstition against it was very strong in the vaudeville days, so much so that when I mentioned to a member of Hylda's family that part of it was played during the show, they advised against it most strongly, saying, "You're not seriously going to do it? Oh no." Well, it is included in the show, and I was driving to the theatre for the opening night of the version I felt had lost its way, when I decided consciously to 'look for a sign' as it were. It takes about three quarters of an hour to do a 'speed' run of the Act One dialogue, so I said to myself that I would do that, then wait for exactly one minute before turning on the radio to see what was playing.

This I did, and I am sure the reader will have guessed what happened, although because it started with an instrumental introduction I wasn't immediately aware of what it was — yes ...it was *Marble Halls*! It's lucky I didn't go straight over the roundabout I was approaching. I quickly had to check my driving mirror to see if Hylda was in the back seat, but needless to say it was empty, and I know I didn't imagine it because Terry Wogan gave the title after the song ended.

Then there was the morning of my 50th birthday. I was in pantomime, and the night before I had been chatting in the dressing room, saying that so far Hylda had influenced things to quite an extent, and bearing in mind that she had just had her 50th birthday when she got overnight fame on T*he Good Old Days*, I was wondering in a jokey sort of way what my 50th year would bring. The next morning the very first telephone call I received was from the priest who had been with Hylda during her last years in Horton Hospital, Peter Naylor, who had heard about the play and had gone through many channels before finally managing to contact me.

I had left until the very last the visit to Horton Hospital which it was necessary for me to make during my research in those early days. I was pretty sure that it would be quite a depressing experience and I didn't want the play to be influenced by this. There was no reason why I chose to go on this particular day, but I did. It really was a very imposing building, with high concrete walls all around, and I couldn't help but think of the day that Hylda first went through that gate, relatively aware of what was happening to her. There is a description in a book by Ruth Valentine, tracing the history of Horton, entitled *Asylum, Hospital, Haven*, from which I quote:

'There is the familiar institutional gatehouse. The job of gate porter was sought after, well into the 1970s. It had not only prestige but power; to report who came in late, who lingered outside with a boyfriend. That shiver, the thought of being observed, can still come over the visitor.'

I have one vivid picture in my mind of that day. As we walked down the long tunnel-like corridors which looked like something from a film set, crouched against the wall was a lady who seemed totally unaware of her surroundings, just playing with spent matches and cigarette ends. The first ward we came to was the Eden Ward where Hylda was first, and then the Bevan Ward where she had died. They were both closed, no longer in use, but what struck me, and is with me to this day, is the remains of human habitation that was there. There was a record player in one corner, covered in dust with some very old records lying around, but there was also an old piano, and on it was a doll, which for some reason made me feel very sad. Who had left it there, and why? It had obviously meant something to someone, but they had just walked out of there and never come back. The staff who showed me round were very kind. They were genuinely caring but everyone knew that soon changes would have to be brought about because funding was grim, and in fact the Horton has now closed. However, the Riverside Mental Health Trust has taken on Horton's commitment to following up on former patients for the rest of their lives, and helping them to resettle in the community.

The reason that the day I chose to go there proved to be so important was because I was introduced to Brenda Barber, the nurse who looked after Hylda so well and even laid her out. She only worked part time, and it just so happened this was one of the few occasions she was there. Had I chosen another day, perhaps we would never have met, and it was Brenda who arranged for the administrators to lend me the authentic bedding, and also one of the beds from the closed wards for the hospital scene in the play. That bed has now travelled the country, appearing in so many of those theatres that Hylda herself played and not one member of the audience until now would be aware of the irony.

Getting the authentic costumes for the show was vital. Although there were enough photographs of her with Cynthia, I had not much idea of what she would wear both for a 'day' dress and for her finale, so it was left to instinct. What made me choose a white dress with little sparkly collar, and detail on the belt for day wear (being very specific as to what I wanted when it was being made) I will never know. However, when Matthew Kelly came to see one of the performances at the City Varieties Theatre in Leeds, where he had worked with her in 1976, not only was it quite spooky for that very reason, but afterwards he said to me, "How did you know about the dress? She had one exactly like it, right down to the detail on the belt!" The finale dress, I decided, must also be white with as many sequins as possible and a good deal of swansdown, a really showy item. Just recently I was asked if I had copied it from a TV spectacular that she did in the 1960s, because she wore an identical one for her walk down singing, as I do, her favourite song. I can honestly say that I have never seen that programme. In an earlier chapter, Gaye Brown talks of the dress, the song and the fur, but I spoke to her three years after the play's first performance. I rest my case.

Then there was the catalogue of events leading up to the show being presented in 1997, as a *Saturday Playhouse* on Radio 4. The night we did the charity performance at the Fortune Theatre in London, an actor called David Holt happened to pass the theatre that day, quite by chance as it was not on his normal route, and decided to come and see it. He wrote to me saying how much he had enjoyed it and if I would be interested, he would see if he could get a drama producer friend of his to see it somewhere. As it happened we were doing a week at Hornchurch, and that is where my association with the lovely Enyd Williams began.

From the day she saw it in August 1995 she was determined that she would produce it, and my dream finally came true in March 1997 when we recorded it in front of a live audience at the BBC Radio Theatre, with Michael Haslam as the musical director, the wonderful David Holt, who instigated it all, playing the stage manager, Cynthia, Hylda's father and all the other characters who had to be introduced for a radio version. Imagine the thrill when I was told that there wasn't a seat to be had and they were queuing outside right around Broadcasting House. And not only that — we got a standing ovation at the end of the performance!

I was beside myself. After those days of pushing the hospital bed down the lane, loading and unloading the scenery in the early hours of the morning when we were so tired we could barely stand, and struggling to get the show recognised, who in that audience could possibly have known how emotional it made me feel? At this point I would like to thank the apparently unprecedented number of people who telephoned and sent letters of congratulation to the BBC, two of which were printed in the letters page of the *Radio Times*, and who also sent letters to me after the play was transmitted on 31 May 1997. I hope the reader will forgive me, in my moment of triumph, for printing three of the reviews; after all, Hylda's have been mentioned throughout, although to be fair it is thanks to her that the play has been possible. But now it's my turn! As they are quite lengthy, I reproduce a precis of each.

Gillian Reynolds in the *Daily Telegraph*, 3 June 1997 wrote: 'There was a trailer for Saturday afternoon's Radio 4 play on Friday's *Today* programme. "Inimitable," John Humphreys said afterwards, chuckling. Perhaps he didn't realise that this was an imitation, so good was it... The play zipped up and down

Hylda's life, looking back from memory-failing age, over a career that stretched from desperate beginnings to successful middle age. It showed her scraping a life, building an act, becoming a star, insisting on star treatment. Fergusson was magnificent, a performance way beyond the merely mimic... It didn't take long before I realised that knowing the original was a plus but not an absolute necessity for appreciation. Fergusson had gone deep into the character to make this portrait and it shone for itself.'

Sue Arnold in *The Observer*, 1 June 1997: 'Ronald Pickup's "Prospero" was just pipped to the post for this week's 'tour de force' award by Jean Fergusson playing comic actress Hylda Baker in *She Knows You Know!* (Radio 4). If Tony Hancock had a female equivalent, it must have been Hylda Baker, a shining example to today's stand-up comediennes such as Jo Brand and Jenny Eclair. You don't have to be grubby to be funny. Impeccable timing and a good script will do very well, or am I just being old -fashioned to laugh at jokes about Greta Garbage and Rudolph Vaselino and relish lines such as, "No one has ever dallied with my afflictions and I say that without fear of contraception."? All right, it's the way she says it, and Jean Fergusson says it so brilliantly and so poignantly.'

Moira Petty in *The Stage*, 5 June 1997 wrote: 'This was more than potted biography and nothing as insipid as hagiography. Fergusson got at the character touching on somewhere deep down in her dark soul. There was Baker in a nursing home yet running through her act in an age-ripened quaver. There was Baker, queening it on stage in her prime, the mistress of the malapropism and the dirty double entendre. And there was the ego of a great performer ("modesty is for the imperfect") set against the uncertainty of a loveless life. To conjure up a world within a world is a great triumph. Fergusson achieved this.'

It is also possible that on two separate occasions Hylda sent one of her Cynthias to my aid when I, too, was experiencing a bit of a battle. It was decided that I should cut the finale number, which I definitely did not want to do, as it was the way she always ended her act. I was in deep discussion about this in the theatre bar, when a very tall gentleman came over to us and said, "Forgive me for interrupting but my name is Des Maidment. I've just seen the show. I was one of her Cynthias, and I do hope you won't mind my asking why you didn't end with her favourite song *I Wish You Love*. She always ended her act with that song?" From then on the finale number was back in the show.

The second occasion was when I was trying to trace the consultant at St Pancras Hospital who had first dealt with Hylda's case, before Ann was told that something was wrong and her aunt needed help. The deadline for this book was looming, and the very day that I was to go to the BBC Radio Theatre to record the play for Radio 4, I had tried telephoning the hospital who said it would be somewhat difficult, it could take some time, and they doubted that they would be of much help, but they would see what they could do.

That very night I got home to find a message from Des asking me to ring him. The next day I did so, and he said that he had been meaning to tell me for some time that on New Year's Eve he had been at a dinner party and the subject had got around to Hylda, whereupon one of the guests said he had been a consultant at St Pancras and had dealt with her case. Des had told him about me and managed to get his telephone number, but I would like to stress at this point that he had no idea that I was trying to find the gentleman. Explain it, I cannot, but it seems as if whenever I ask for something, it just happens.

The reader must forgive this catalogue of 'strange but true', but it is important to include them all. The Grand Theatre, Swansea, has always been one of my favourite places to tour to, and we went there with the variety show I mentioned in the first chapter. I had a bit of an accident that day, falling on my wrist, and had spent a few hours at the hospital where they insisted that they put me in plaster up to the elbow as it might be broken but it wasn't clear from the X-rays. I was met with surprise when I got to the stage door, as they had just been looking up the records to see if Hylda had ever appeared there, and found that she had indeed been booked but had cancelled due to a broken arm. That sort of coincidence I can do without.

Finally, Tom Hardy's friend, Rob, was someone that I really wanted to get hold of concerning the research for the book, for I knew (and was proven correct) that his memories of her would be most valuable, but no one knew where he was. One night during the run of the play I was in at the Whitehall Theatre, I was told that there was an actor in that night to see the show who knew someone who had been friendly with Hylda. He came backstage, and the reader will by now have guessed that his friend's name was Rob, and I was given his telephone number.

When I rang him, I asked if Hylda had been interested in the supernatural. He said she was and at that point, for some reason, he said that one evening they were sitting in front of the fire when she suddenly started to write a somewhat sentimental poem. I asked him to hold the line for a second, went to my files and came back with a poem which I read to him over the phone. He was astounded — it was the very one he had seen her write all those years ago in 1970. I had happened across it long before I started to write the book, when I was on one of my visits to Ann to do research for the play, and although it couldn't be included easily into a stage show, I decided that I would like to keep it, so copied it from the back of a small, very scruffy old envelope which was falling to pieces, and which once again I had found quite by accident. He then went quiet, for it turned out that she had indeed written it on the back of an old envelope, and how it had survived being thrown away after all those years we will never know. He had often thought of the poem, wishing he could remember it, and here I was reading it to him over 25 years later: There were a couple of alternative endings, which I also reproduce here:

'Without You'
I'm not foolish, I'm not wrong
When I say that all along
You're the best friend in the world to me
or (I have ever known/had.)
You know my feelings, know my sins
But you've stood by me through thick and thin.
(To me your friendship is a thing sublime.)
Don't let's quarrel, don't let's fuss
Don't let anything happen to us.
We've been friends for a long long time.
I was hasty, I was wrong
But I know that all along
Your friendship is to me a thing sublime
or (Sometimes foolish sometimes wrong,
But I know that all along,
Your friendship is to me a thing sublime)

Then there was my dream! I can't honestly say that I remember the content of it, but when writing the play I always used to keep a piece of paper and pen by my bed, just in case some inspiration came during the night (incidentally, I have since found out that Hylda did the same). One night I woke from a strange dream and thought I must write down a certain quote from it, which in my half-asleep state I did. The next morning I had forgotten the incident but very soon saw the piece of paper, and on it was written, 'If anybody does my life when I'm gone. Tell it like it is!' It is often quoted by people who have seen the play; they pick this line out from all the rest and once or twice the press have used, 'Jean tells it like it is!' as the headline to a review. History has in some ways repeated itself, as there are many links between my experiences and hers, what with being asked to do the variety tour, and just recently if I would be interested in me playing Hylda playing the dame in *Mother Goose*! They don't want to let her go even now. Also, as we know, Hylda organised everything herself when she toured her own shows, and this has happened to me, too, but I have to say that if I hadn't had my own struggles, I doubt if I would have appreciated hers quite so much, and my excitement at how things have turned out could not be as great as it undoubtedly is.

It is also very touching that on two occasions when Hylda's sister has been to see the show, she has telephoned to wish me luck, and arranged that her daughter, Meryl, came forward to the stage to present me with a bouquet at the finale, just as she used to do for Hylda. When she telephoned me in the dressing room, I suddenly looked up and saw myself, as Hylda, in the mirror and it felt very strange to say the least. Her family have all been so very kind to me, and I am so pleased to be able to say that they have become my friends.

Then there's the coincidence of birthdays. Although mine is five weeks before Hylda's, and I can't lay claim to being the same birth sign, her father's and Mildred's were the day before mine, and her brother Syd's is the day after. In fact last year he sent me a birthday card, having remembered the fact during one of our conversations from many months before. Needless to say, I was very touched.

The superstition of the colour green has crossed my path, too, for the only time I ever wore a green dress on stage was for a thriller where I had to be suffocated on stage, and one night the over-enthusiastic leading man forgot his own strength and nearly succeeded in finishing me off for real. I was terrified and struggling for breath, but he thought I was just acting. How strange, too, that my employer on that tour was none other than David Kirk, who had worked as Hylda's Cynthia in the 1950s. Another 'green' incident was when a designer decided to give me a dressing room set with green walls for the Hylda play, but needless to say I won my case after saying, "That'll be fine if you want me to play the whole show from the wings!"

My research has also shown me something that people are always asking me: did I ever see her live on stage? Until I began the book, I thought not, but when it came to light that she did *Cinderella* at the Dewsbury Empire in 1950, I realised that as a very small child I had been in that audience, as my parents always took us to that theatre for our Christmas treat when we were living near Wakefield. I do remember the show, which had a lasting impression on me. I remember the ponies and the finale and I can see now the girl in fishnet tights because I was very confused when they kept calling her a 'boy'!

I have also found myself working with people who knew her, particularly three members of the cast of *Nearest And Dearest*. I spent many a happy hour with Madge Hindle in a play at Birmingham Rep long before I began my research; we laughed a good deal and she often accused me of leading her astray when often it was the other way round! Kathy Staff, who played Beetroot Bertha in the Pledges Pickle factory, and has become a good friend through *Summer*

Wine, says of Hylda: "I thought she was so very funny. I did admire her comedy." And last but by no means least, there was the late Joe Gladwin, who used to sit and chat with me on the set of *Last Of The Summer Wine*, and with whom I would flirt outrageously. He was a treasure.

Of course, Dame Thora Hird, too, of whom we are all so very fond, has many memories of Hylda, and during breaks in filming she and I have often chatted together about her, even on a *Pebble Mill* programme dedicated to Thora's 85 years in the business. Incidentally, on a previous *Pebble Mill* programme, Alan Titchmarsh actually played my Cynthia, but as the height difference didn't match, I had to kneel down! When I recently asked Thora to give me a quote for this book, she happily obliged with the following:

"Hylda Baker. Well, you see there was a great comic because people walking about in the street were saying, 'She knows you know' and 'I must get a little hand put on this watch,' and it's only if people have impressed the public that they will use what they've said. There are a lot of comics where no one has used anything they've said. However, I must say at this point that in all honesty she didn't like me. I've never known why because we didn't know each other extremely well. It didn't upset me that she didn't, and neither would I be a stupid woman who thought she was jealous of me, because I don't think that at all.

"I remember playing a season at Blackpool, she was at the Winter Gardens and I was at the Grand Theatre. It was hard work, twice nightly let's face it. Somebody said to me, 'Do you know she's got some monkeys in that dressing room?' Now for the value of people who don't know, one of the rules of the theatre is no fish and chips in the dressing room, because of smelling the clothes, and no dogs, but I've never seen a dressing room that said, 'No monkeys,' so she wasn't really breaking any rules was she?

"I was once playing at Drury Lane and a couple of boy dancers in the show said they'd been to see a friend of hers who was a dancer at Blackpool. He said that they'd been going along the Promenade in her car, taking them back to her house, with 'She Knows You Know!' on a flag in the garden. I had no flag where I was staying, but she had you see. Well, she was driving a bit too quick, and a speed cop comes along on his bike and stops her. When he sees her he says, 'Oh, hello Thora, well, just you take it easy will you love?' He thought she was me! Now we didn't look like each other, we were both just trying to be funny, but she took great umbrage at this: 'Do I look like her? I hope I don't look like Thora Hird.' But that never stopped any of the admiration I had for her, and I think God would say to her, when she passed over 'Well, Hylda you've given a lot of pleasure.'"

Matthew Kelly, too, has become a friend through my research, and once when we were doing a charity show together, with me once more being asked to 'do'

Hylda, he was the compere during the second half, and therefore ironically was to introduce me. He even came to collect me from the dressing room to walk to the wings together as he always used to do with her. I was very moved, but it was also another spooky moment!

Victor Graham came to see a run-through during rehearsals, and even though I had no costume or make up for it, he was visibly moved at the memories it brought back, and later that evening he telephoned me having apparently surprised himself by saying as he picked up the phone, "I must ring Hylda and congratulate her." There have also been wonderful comments from audiences, like the lady who had just seen the play and was overheard saying to her friend, "By golly, she's looking well!" and twice it has been said to me that, "You're more like Hylda Baker than Hylda Baker herself." However, one of the comments that means the most to me was from Gordon Pleasant, the producer of the 1975 *Lancashire Laugh In*, which as we know was not a financial success for him due to Hylda's slide from popularity. He listened to the radio play, then rang me, sounding rather moved and said, "I never knew. Oh, it explains it all." My aim was to set the record straight, and perhaps this is proof enough it has been achieved.

Huddersfield plays such a big part in the lives of the cast of *Summer Wine*, our base hotel during filming is the Huddersfield Hotel, and Hylda walked back and forth to the Palace Theatre from the Southgate Hotel car park many times, with Mitzi the dachshund on the lead, on that very pavement outside the front door of our hotel. The site of the Southgate where she parked her caravan is on the other side of the main road and the Palace Theatre is just opposite the Huddersfield Hotel. Some time ago it was turned into a bingo hall, although it is now closed, and in fact Juliette Kaplan (Pearl) and Gordon Wharmby (Wesley) were often to be seen nipping over there for a game or two to pass the time! Shaw's Pickle factory is not so far away either and Hylda and I share the accolade of having been shown around for publicity purposes, she in September 1978 and me in September 1993, when we were planning the first performance of the play.

There are some who will say that I have over-glamourised and sentimentalised this book, but for every person who said Hylda was a monster there have been many, many more who adored her.

Not a bad average I think she would say. In a radio interview in 1976, she was asked if she minded that people hated her, but the interviewer changed it quickly to 'dislike.' She jumped in very quickly and said, "Oh, I hope they don't hate me. But you can't expect everyone to like you." Should she have got around to writing her own book, one wonders what it would have been like. Funny? Undoubtedly! Self pitying? Most definitely not! Well, perhaps it's better this way, as I am sure she would never have admitted her deep-rooted fears and insecurities to her public. As always, these would have been glossed over with a joke or an anecdote. I hope she approves.

How does one do justice with this sort of book? With a great deal of feeling, and the knowledge of not only her friends and acquaintances but of her critics and adversaries. It's a melting pot, you put it all together and see what comes out. You write what you see, hear and have observed. I think I know more about her now than anyone who worked with her or thought they knew her.

I also hope, if she is watching the reaction to her colourful life story, that she has learnt her lesson, for her friends at the end were few — that is the sadness. She needed but couldn't give, hence the small turnout at her funeral. This book has been a great responsibility and possibly there will be some who are not completely satisfied, for it would have been impossible to please everyone. The finished article can never be all things to all men, particularly in Hylda's case, for such was the diverse way that she touched people's lives either personally or with her public face. To the many who have read this book thinking it would be all comedy, I apologise if they are disappointed, but there is the tragedy for as Hylda knew to her cost, comedy was ever thus.

However, what is so joyful is the reaction to her comedy act today. Not many could boast that the act they were doing in 1955 could, in 1997, get the same laughs, not just with recognition, but from many youngsters who have never heard of her, falling about at her material and even taking the trouble to write to me to tell me. How many of our comics today will still be getting the same laughs in 40 years? Perhaps through this she really will be remembered by the masses instead of the few, and I will be eternally grateful to her for, through her, I too have learnt a good deal.

My particular Cinderella story is just beginning, for after all the hard work getting the play recognised, Stars And Angels, the management who came on board to help it progress, and with whom I am co-producer, are determined to further it. They booked two weeks of 'try outs' in July 1997 at the Bridewell Theatre in London, but the greatest news of all, which has happened in time to give this book a fairy tale ending, is that we are definitely going to the West End! We have been given an eight-week run, starting in the second week of October, at the Vaudeville Theatre, the one theatre that I have wished for. Why? Because although she appeared many times in variety shows and musicals in the West End, it was at the Vaudeville that Hylda got those marvellous reviews for her only straight acting role in a West End play, exactly 30 years ago, for *Fill The Stage With Happy Hours*. That stage will surely be filled with a very happy company in October 1997, my cup will have 'runneth over' and my dream come true. One very final irony is that her play was set, as mine is, backstage at a provincial theatre! Our tour has been a roaring success, and as I write this we are at the Civic Theatre, Darlington (once called the Hippodrome) where 48 years ago, in 1949, Hylda performed her own show *Bearskins And Blushes*. Tex was with her, he also trod the boards here, and no doubt left the odd tyre mark with his motorcycle. Last night was nearly a sell out, with yet again a standing ovation, and tonight is the same, 'House Full'!

The very final irony is that things have now really gone full circle, because it was at this very theatre, where I was playing pantomime seven years ago, that the chance remark that I resembled her was made, and my journey had begun. However, what I can't get rid of are the words that keep ringing in my ears, those of Brenda Barber, the nurse at Horton Hospital who laid her out. Her final words to me were, "You've got to get her story right, though. She'll have your guts if you don't!"

Index